Race and Culture Contacts
in the Modern World

E. FRANKLIN FRAZIER

RACE

AND

CULTURE CONTACTS

IN THE

MODERN WORLD

Copyright 1957 by E. Franklin Frazier. All rights reserved. No part
of this book may be reproduced in any form without permission in
writing from the publisher, except by a reviewer who may
quote brief passages in a review to be printed in a magazine or
newspaper. First published by the Free Press in 1957. This
arrangement with Alfred A. Knopf. The Beacon Press books are published under the auspices of the Unitarian Universalist Association.
Printed in the United States of America.

Second printing, September 1968

BEACON PRESS   *BOSTON*

CONTENTS

PART III *POLITICAL ORGANIZATION*

PART IV *SOCIAL ORGANIZATION*

CONCLUSION

Introduction

CHAPTER I

The Expansion of Europe and Racial Frontiers

INTRODUCTION

During the opening years of the present century, Lord Bryce stated in a lecture at Oxford University his belief that one of the most pressing problems of the modern world was the relation between the advanced and backward races of mankind.[1] According to Bryce, the close and widespread contact of the advanced and backward races was the completion of a world-process which marked a crisis in the history of the world. That Bryce was expressing the growing consciousness of the importance of the racial problem in the modern world was indicated by the fact that less than a decade after his address, The First Universal Races Congress met in London "to discuss, in the light of science and the modern conscience, the general relations subsisting between the peoples of the West and those of the East, between so-called white and so-called

[1] James Bryce, *The Relations of the Advanced and Backward Races of Mankind* (Oxford: Clarendon Press, 1902) , pp. 6–7.

coloured peoples, with a view to encouraging between them a fuller understanding, the most friendly feelings, and a heartier cooperation." [2]

World War I, which followed close on the holding of this conference, tended to increase the growing race consciousness among both the white and the colored peoples of the world. For example, Maurice Evans, who saw important similarities between the racial problem in South Africa and that in the southern states of the United States, wrote during the war:

For all the world over the coloured races are beginning to realize themselves and to press for answers to questions that have hitherto been evaded. The Japanese are knocking at the Western gates of the New World, and the leaders of the millions of India are asking for admittance to lands which have been so far closed to them. The development of the West African peoples goes on apace, and their increasing agricultural production is giving them a status in the modern world higher than that hitherto reached by any purely African people. And in South Africa there are uneasy movements betokening awakening consciousness. All these are but the beginnings of the stirrings of the peoples. [3]

Ten years later Sir Leo Chiozza Money pointed out that "The European stock cannot presume to hold magnificent areas indefinitely, even while it refuses to people them, and to deny their use and cultivation to races which sorely need them." [4] Another book which appeared at the same time and was concerned with the difficulties due to the association of white and colored races concluded that "If the racial segregation which the world has inherited from

    [2] G. Spiller (ed.), *Papers on Inter-racial Problems* (London: King & Son, 1911), p. v.
    [3] Maurice Evans, *Black and White in the Southern States: A Study of the Race Problems in the United States from a South African Point of View* (New York: Longmans, Green & Co., Inc., 1915), pp. 1–2. Reprinted by permission of the publisher.
    [4] *The Peril of the White* (London: W. Collins Sons and Co., 1925), pp. 159–60.

the past is confirmed instead of being broken down by the modern ease of transport, Europe, North America, and Australia would naturally be the chief homes of the white race." [5]

The appearance of these books between World War I and World War II was symptomatic of fundamental changes which were occurring in the relations of the "advanced" and the "backward" races of mankind. Economic changes, dramatized in the world economic crisis beginning in 1929, were upsetting the traditional relations of the European nations to the colonial and semicolonial countries. Then there were changes in the power relations among the European nations. Finally, the political domination of the European powers was being undermined by nationalistic movements in colonial areas. World War II accelerated the nationalistic movements among the colored races and brought an end to colonialism in Asia and aroused even the peoples of Africa to revolt against colonialism. The crisis in the relations of the advanced or European peoples and the backward races of mankind was accentuated by the world crisis created by the emergence of Russia and the United States as the two major powers contending for world dominance. Despite the attempt on the one side to redefine the racial problem in terms of class conflict, and on the other to minimize or banish the idea of race, the continuing importance of the racial factor is indicated by the calling of a Conference on Race Relations in World Perspective in Hawaii in 1954.[6] In fact, the world crisis arising out of the new relation of Europe to the colored or so-called backward races overshadows, in the thinking of one historian of human development, the clash between the two economic and social systems represented by

[5] J. W. Gregory, *The Menace of Color* (Philadelphia: J. B. Lippincott Co., 1925, pp. 241–2). The outstanding American contribution to this subject was by Lothrop Stoddard, *The Rising Tide of Color* (New York: Charles Scribner's Sons, 1920). This book presented in a more sensational form the change in the relations of the white and colored races.

[6] As the result of this Conference, the International Society for the Scientific Study of Race Relations was organized.

the United States and Russia. According to Toynbee, future historians will say that

The great event of the twentieth century was the impact of the Western civilization upon all the other living societies of the world of that day. They will say of this impact that it was so powerful and so pervasive that it turned the lives of all its victims upside down and inside out—affecting the behavior, outlook, feelings, and beliefs of individual men, women, and children in an intimate way, touching chords in human souls that are not touched by mere external material forces—however ponderous and terrifying.[7]

The world-process of which Bryce spoke and which Toynbee regards as the great event of the twentieth century had its origin in the economic expansion of Europe during the fifteenth and sixteenth centuries. This economic expansion coincided with the technical and intellectual revolution which enabled Europe to gradually establish its dominance over the rest of the world. During the period when European nations were establishing their dominance over non-European peoples, there arose the idea of the superiority of the white race. Although this idea could not be maintained on scientific or moral grounds, it nevertheless served as a means of separating the white and colored races and of justifying political and economic domination by the Europeans. The separation of the races was facilitated by differences in culture and standards of living which were employed in conjunction with the race concept to stamp non-European peoples as inferior races. Consequently, racial ideologies and race sentiment must be analyzed in relation to cultural differences in studying the problems which have resulted from the contacts between the white and colored peoples in the modern world.

    [7] Arnold J. Toynbee, *Civilization on Trial* (New York: Oxford University Press, Inc., 1948), p. 214. Reprinted by permission of the publisher.

THE EXPANSION OF EUROPE

The expansion of Europe began in what has come to be known as "the age of great discoveries" during the fifteenth and sixteenth centuries. In the thirteenth century Marco Polo's account of his travels in eastern Asia had awakened the imagination of Europeans and broadened their conception of the world. Following Marco Polo's account of what was considered a "New World," Christian missionaries were sent to China. In the fourteenth century Portuguese explorers made the Canary Islands familiar to Europe. Then under the guidance of Prince Henry the Navigator of Portugal, the exploration of Africa and the unknown world was systematically undertaken. The financial support provided by Prince Henry for the fitting out of ships and the encouragement as well as tangible assistance which he gave to the science of navigation enabled explorers and adventurers to chart the routes of future European expansion.

The first explorations were along the coast of Africa, a continent in which, it was said, was located a Christian state ruled by an Emperor-Priest, Prester John.[8] In 1486 Diaz sailed around the southern tip of Africa and advanced 500 miles toward India before he was compelled to return because of the fears of his sailors. Twelve years later Vasco da Gama sailed around the Cape of Good Hope and on to the coast of India. Cabral, while seeking a westward route to the Indies, touched upon Brazil. Portuguese explorers continued to explore the East Indies and built up an empire extending 15,000 miles along the coasts of Africa and India and in the islands of Sumatra, Java, and the Molucca. In 1492, Columbus discovered the West Indies and launched the Spanish upon their quest for em-

[8] Örjan Olsen, *La Conquète de la terre* (Paris: Payot, 1944), II, 109 ff.

pire. The islands of the West Indies were soon settled by the Spaniards. Under Cortez they conquered Mexico and under Pizarro they brought Peru into the empire of Spain. Balboa discovered the Pacific Ocean, and Spanish explorers marched through a large portion of what is now the southwestern part of the United States. Magellan, a Portuguese navigator, sailed under the Spanish flag when he started his famous voyage in 1519 which resulted in the first circumnavigation of the world.

It was not long before England, France, and Holland challenged the dominance of Portugal and Spain in the newly discovered areas of the world. Before the end of the sixteenth century, John Cabot had sailed 1,000 miles along the coasts of North America and established the claims of England to the North American continent, but only after 1600 did England and France found settlements in North America. The English settled at Jamestown in 1607 and at Plymouth in 1620, while the French established settlements in Canada and Nova Scotia. During this same period the Dutch established a foothold in New York and Delaware. All three of these nations, or at least the freebooters, buccaneers, and pirates who sailed under their flags, engaged in an attack on the Spanish Empire in the Gulf of Mexico and the West Indies. In the end Spain lost her control of the West Indies but was able to maintain her foothold on the mainland. At the same time England and Holland attacked the Portuguese Empire in the East. The Dutch gained control of the East Indies while the English gained a foothold in India. The French who had first settled in Madagascar moved on to India toward the end of the seventeenth century. By the beginning of the eighteenth century the Portuguese had lost most of their empire, while the Spaniards were confined chiefly to the mainland of America.

The defeat of the French by the English in India was a part of the struggle of these two nations, which lasted nearly a century, for supremacy in the colonial world. In North America, the colonies which the English planted on the eastern seaboard spread westward until they threatened the inland area stretching from Canada to the Gulf of Mexico to which France laid claim as the result of the exploration of Marquette and Joliet, Frontenac and La Salle, and the Jesuit missionaries. Despite the friendliness and support of the Indians, the French lost in the struggle to control this area. The English, who had come to settle the country in family groups, outnumbered the French more than thirty to one. Moreover, the English settlers had military and other types of support from the mother country, while France was indifferent to overseas colonies. By the treaty of Paris in 1763, England gained not only most of the French colonial empire but some of the remnants of the Spanish Empire as well, and thus she secured possession of the largest colonial empire in the modern world.

The most important factor in the expansion of Europe was economic. The Portuguese explorers and adventurers sought a route to the spices and wealth of the Orient which would be cheaper and safer than the overland route dominated by the Italian cities. In Venice, news of Vasco da Gama's successful voyage to India created a panic. The Spanish explorers and adventurers went in search of the precious metals of the new world. When precious metals were not found, the European explorers brought slaves from Africa to till the soil and wring the wealth from the earth. The Dutch drove the Spanish from the East Indies to secure the wealth that these islands offered. With the employment of slave labor, the French reaped a golden harvest in the West Indies. In order to secure a share in this golden harvest, the English attacked the French. Trade in slaves for use in the colonies became a rich source of profit for the traders of all the colonizing European powers. Although slavery did not take root as an institution in the northern colonies of North America, the manufacture and transportation of rum and the transportation of slaves became the chief sources of the prosperity of the colonists in the North.

The economic and political expansion of Europe did not result at first in the migration of large numbers of Europeans. Although the records of European migration are scanty and unreliable before the nineteenth century, there are some indications that, with the exception of England and Germany, overseas migration was on a small scale up to that time.[9] During the seventeenth century, probably 250,000 people left the British Isles, and during the eighteenth century, perhaps 1,500,000. It appears that before 1800, 200,000 Germans left for America. These figures may be compared with the total of 55,000 persons in New France in 1754, the majority of whom were the result of natural increase. Records indicate that during a period of nearly twenty-five years, beginning in 1509, only 150,000 Spaniards left the authorized port of embarkation, Seville, although there are reasons to believe that more Spaniards than that migrated to the New World. At any rate European overseas migration before the nineteenth century was on a relatively small scale as compared with what came later.

During the nineteenth century, over 50,000,000 Europeans migrated overseas. This increase in overseas migration was the result of the increase in population pressure created by economic crisis and crop failures. About 38,000,-000 of these Europeans went to the United States.[10] Large numbers of Europeans also went to Canada, Australia, and New Zealand, three countries where predominantly white communities were created. In Central and South America

[9] A. M. Carr-Saunders, *World Population* (Oxford: At the Clarendon Press, 1936) , pp. 47 ff.

[10] H. A. Citroen, *European Emigration Overseas Past and Future* (The Hague: Martinus Nijhoff, 1951) , pp. 4–5.

and South Africa, the Europeans constituted a minority of the population.

FRONTIERS OF RACE AND CULTURE CONTACTS

The expansion of European peoples and their culture resulted, all over the world, in frontiers of race and culture contacts. In some cases, the race and culture frontiers were created by the importation of Negroes into the Western world or the importation of Chinese and East Indians along Europe's advancing frontier.[11] These racial frontiers may be classified according to the character of race and culture contacts which has been determined by the extent to which Europeans were able to establish large and permanent settlements. At the same time the extent to which Europeans were able to establish such settlements has been limited by such factors as climate and the stage of development of the native peoples whom they encountered. On the basis of these factors, it is possible to define three main types of frontiers of race and culture contacts: European settlements with racial fronticrs; tropical dependencies; and the older civilizations of Asia.[12]

European Settlements with Racial Frontiers

According to our classification, there are six areas in which race and culture contacts have been created as a result of the development of European settlements. These were located in the United States; Latin America, includ-

---

[11] See Robert E. Park, "The Nature of Race Relations," in Edgar T. Thompson (ed.) , *Race Relations and the Race Problem* (Durham: Duke University Press, 1939) , pp. 27–30.

[12] Since this study is concerned with *race* and culture contacts, we shall not include an analysis of the phenomenon of culture contacts between ethnic groups as, for example, the contacts between Italians and French in France or the relations between the various ethnic groups in the United States. This study is concerned with contacts between European and non-European groups, though relations between ethnic groups of European origin may exhibit similar characteristics.

ing Mexico, Central America, and South America; the West Indies and the Guianas; South Africa; and Australia and New Zealand.

THE UNITED STATES: The expansion of European civilization created two racial frontiers in that part of North America which became the United States. There was first the frontier growing out of the contact of the white man and the Indian. When the Europeans began to settle in the early years of the seventeenth century in what was to become the United States, there were approximately 1,000,000 Indians organized in 600 societies.[13] Although these Indian societies had constantly engaged in war, the advent of the white man intensified the war-like activities of the Indians. At first the Indians and the whites lived on friendly terms, but as the colonists advanced into the interior, wars developed between the two races. During the latter part of the seventeenth century the whole frontier was ablaze with interracial warfare. Then in the eighteenth century, the Indian was drawn into the struggle of the French and British empires. After the Revolutionary War, the whites in their westward march, with the aid of the army, swept the Indians before them. Later the Indian became a ward of the American nation and a systematic policy developed according to which the Indian social organization was destroyed and the Indian was restricted to reservations. This policy was maintained until the second decade of the twentieth century when Indians became American citizens. Even then the problem of the relation of the Indians to American society was not solved, and it required another decade for the inauguration of anything approaching a humane and realistic policy for dealing with the Indian. In spite of this new orientation, the contacts of whites and Indians, who

[13] John Collier, *Indians of the Americas* (New York: The New American Library, 1951) .

number about 350,000, provide one of the frontiers of race and culture contacts in the modern world.

The second racial frontier to be established in what is now the United States was created by the importation of Negro slaves from Africa. Originally these slaves were imported to provide labor for the tobacco and rice plantations in the southern colonies.[14] The Negro population increased slowly in the seventeenth century, but during the eighteenth century the importation increased rapidly as the plantations spread southwest. At the time of the American Revolution it appeared that slavery might die out slowly, but the invention of the cotton gin and new developments in the textile industry, especially in England, brought an increased demand for slaves on the southern plantations.

As the result of the Civil War and emancipation, the American nation was faced with the problem of the future status of the Negro. For a brief period an attempt was made to establish a democratic society without racial distinctions in the southern states. Then there followed a period of race conflict complicated by a latent class conflict among the whites. Out of this conflict came an attempt to establish a legalized caste system based upon racial descent. Two world wars, which greatly altered the American economy and resulted in the urbanization of the Negro population on a large scale, changed the character of the race problem. The proportion of Negroes in the population of the United States has declined from one in five when the first federal census was made in 1790 to about one in ten in 1950. In the meantime, the rural areas of Negro concentration in the South have become smaller as Negroes have migrated, principally to northern cities. More than a dozen cities, both northern and southern, now have Negro

---

[14] E. Franklin Frazier, *The Negro in the United States* (New York: The Macmillan Co., 1949).

communities of more than 100,000 inhabitants. During recent years the principle of color-caste has tended to break down, and the Negro is being integrated into American life at a faster rate than at any previous time in the history of the United States.

LATIN AMERICA: MEXICO AND CENTRAL AMERICA: The race and culture frontiers which have grown up in Latin America may be divided, geographically, into two groups: Mexico and Central America,[15] and South America. Neither of these two geographic divisions is a homogeneous area from the standpoint of geography or culture. Mexico and Central America are characterized by a great variety of climatic conditions which are related to the proximity of the sea, the mountainous terrain, and the natural vegetation.[16] Originally the area was densely settled by an Indian population which numbered approximately 6,000,000. Here the Mayan Empires flourished and the Aztecs set up a predatory military organization. The wealth accumulated by this feudal organization attracted the Spanish explorers who were seeking precious metals. The Spanish conquest resulted in a great reduction in the native population because of the spread of European diseases. Not many Spanish people, perhaps not more than 300,000 settled in Mexico and Central America, and those who settled in these areas intermarried with the Indians.

In Mexico, racial mixture was so common that more than 90 per cent of the 25,000,000 present inhabitants are of Spanish-Indian ancestry. Moreover, the 30,000 Negroes who were imported during the colonial period have been largely absorbed in the Mexican population. On the other hand, in Guatemala about two thirds of the popu-

[15] This area, which extends from the southern border of the United States to South America, includes Guatemala, British Honduras, El Salvador, Honduras, Nicaragua, Costa Rica, and Panama, in addition to Mexico.

[16] Preston James, *Latin America* (rev. ed.; New York: The Odyssey Press, 1950), pp. 529 ff.

lation is of unmixed Indian ancestry and about 30 per cent of Spanish-Indian ancestry. In the other Central American countries there is a similar racial pattern: a small, so-called white upper layer and a great mass of Indians and people of mixed ancestry who form the majority of the population. The racial pattern becomes more complex in the other countries because of the presence of large numbers of Negroes, imported from the West Indies.

LATIN AMERICA: SOUTH AMERICA: In considering the continent of South America, with its great physical, political, and cultural diversity, as a racial frontier, one must first take account of the Spanish and Portuguese divisions of the continent. This division of the continent was the result of the Treaty of Tordesillas in 1494 between Portugal and Spain whereby the Portuguese secured title to all lands which might be discovered east of a line running north and south 370 leagues west of the Cape Verde Islands.[17] Thus the Portuguese came to colonize and develop what is now Brazil. From the beginning the Portuguese began to interbreed with the Indians and when they began importing Negro slaves for the sugar plantations in northeastern Brazil the same process of race intermixture continued. As the result of this racial mixture, the mulatto played an important role in the development of Brazil as an independent nation in the nineteenth century. During the twentieth century the racial composition has changed as the result of the immigration of Italians, Germans, and a smaller number of Japanese. Moreover, the growth of modern cities and the emergence of a large middle class have changed the nature of race and culture contacts.

The Spanish explorers expanded their conquests from Central America into South America. They conquered the densely settled Indian populations of what became Colombia. Under Pizarro a small band of Spaniards conquered

[17] Olsen, *op. cit.*, II, 257.

Peru and later entered Ecuador. By the middle of the sixteenth century the Spaniards had founded cities in Chile
and established themselves in what became Bolivia. The
settlements which were founded in Venezuela during the
early years of the sixteenth century soon spread into the
interior of the country. Paraguay was explored to establish
a short route to Peru. The fertile plains of the Argentine
at first held little attraction for the Spanish explorers in
search of precious metals, but they later attracted Spanish
settlers from the other settlements in South America. Uruguay, after being neglected by the Spanish for nearly two
centuries, finally emerged as an independent country as the
result of rivalry between Argentina and Brazil.

The frontiers of race and culture contacts which have
grown out of the Spanish conquests present a wide variety
of patterns. In Argentina about 90 per cent of the population is considered to be of unmixed European ancestry
with the remainder of Indian-Spanish ancestry, while the
Negro element has been almost completely absorbed in the
general population. A similar racial composition exists in
Uruguay. On the other hand, the majority of the Para-
guayan population is of mixed origin. In Colombia, probably a fifth of the population is of unmixed European
ancestry while three fifths are of mixed Spanish-Indian origin and a tenth of Negro ancestry. Fewer than a tenth of
the inhabitants of Ecuador are unmixed Europeans, three
fifths are Indians, a third are of Spanish-Indian ancestry,
and there is a sprinkling of Negroes. Indians form half of
the Peruvian population; mixed bloods of Spanish-Indian
ancestry more than a third; and unmixed Europeans about
a seventh. In Bolivia a similar situation exists. Although
about a fourth of the people of Chile are of unmixed European ancestry, all of the remainder, with the exception
of 9 per cent who are pure blooded Indians, are of Spanish-
Indian origin. Negro and European elements each constitute about 10 per cent of the population of Venezuela,

while the remainder of the population is of Spanish-Indian mixture.

THE WEST INDIES AND THE GUIANAS: The West Indies comprise a chain of islands varying greatly in size and extending "from Cuba and the Bahamas in the North to Trinidad and Aruba in the South." [18] Although these islands lie within tropical seas, they have a temperate climate. As we have seen, it was on one of these islands that Columbus landed. Here also the first European settlement in the New World was established. Hispaniola, on the present site of Haiti and the Dominican Republic, became the center from which the Spanish conquest spread. In less than fifty years, as the result of European diseases and cruelty, the native Indian population of Hispaniola, numbering about 1,000,000, had almost completely disappeared. Similar annihilation occurred in Cuba, Jamaica, and Puerto Rico. Then came the demand for Negro slaves to work the plantations which developed when sugar cane was introduced. In the struggle of the Spanish, French, English, and Dutch for empire, the West Indies was one of the richest prizes. This area, which was regarded as the "sugar bowl" of the world, was one of the main sources for the accumulation of European capital.

The fate of European settlements which grew up in the West Indies and the type of race and culture frontiers which they created depended upon a number of factors: ecological, economic, and political. On the island of Cuba, the Spanish mixed freely with the Negro and as a result it has a predominantly mixed population. On the Spanish part of the island of Hispaniola, the Dominican Republic has a similar racial composition. On the other hand, on the French side of the island the population is predominantly Negro; the few mulattoes are the inheritors of the culture of their French masters who were driven from the island. Jamaica is also predominantly Negro with a small mulatto

[18] James, *op. cit.*, p. 674.

element and an even smaller remnant of the former English ruling class. In the French islands, Guadaloupe and Martinique, the predominantly Negro population is regarded as completely assimilàted French citizens. In this area there are other variations in race and culture contacts which will be considered in detail in the course of this study.

AUSTRALIA AND NEW ZEALAND: Having remained unknown for over a hundred years after Dutch explorers had first glimpsed its shores, Australia was discovered by Captain Cook in 1770.[19] Then it was ignored until the British government decided to found a convict colony there. Gradually the island continent was colonized by convicts and free settlers. The natural pastures and favorable climate encouraged the development of the wool-growing industry. By midnineteenth century there were 8,000,000 sheep, and by the end of the century 70,000,000. Since nearly half of the area of Australia lies within the tropics and the central area is unsuitable for agriculture or settlement, Europeans settled in the southern portion of the continent. Today two thirds of the slightly more than 7,000,000 Europeans live in the modern cities which have grown up. When the Europeans arrived in Australia, the land was occupied by wandering tribes of dark brown peoples numbering 300,000. These natives were exterminated or driven from their hunting grounds, until now there are not more than 50,000. It appears that there is no future for the natives on this continent with its official policy of "white Australia," which means the exclusion of Asians and all colored peoples. However, there is a small group of mixed bloods who are increasing in number and causing difficulties for the policy of "racial purity." The natives of Australia have been spared so far the fate of the

19 Geoffrey Rawson, *Australia* (London: Chatto and Windus, 1948), p. 11.

natives on the island of Tasmania to the south, where the last native died in 1867.

New Zealand was also discovered by Dutch explorers, but it remained for Captain Cook to chart the islands.[20] At the time the islands—two large and one small—were inhabited by the Maori, a Polynesian race. Although the islands were visited by other Europeans, much of the early exploration was done by missionaries. Sheep raising and wool production found a congenial soil in New Zealand, as in Australia, but from the beginning New Zealand was an area of small farms and mixed farming has flourished there. Moreover, industry was introduced by the artisans who were selected to settle in the islands. In their relations with the Maori, the Europeans in New Zealand did not undertake a policy of extermination. There were bloody conflicts, but in time the Europeans came to respect the Maori. The Maori population, which had decreased to 40,000 by the opening of the twentieth century, has increased since to over 100,000. About one half of the Maoris are of mixed ancestry. Although they are not evenly distributed, these 100,000 colored people live in an area inhabited by approximately 1,500,000 Europeans.

SOUTH AFRICA: The race and culture frontiers which have grown up in the Union of South Africa are the most complex in the modern world. The Cape was first settled by the Dutch in the middle of the seventeenth century. They came into conflict with the Bushmen and the Hottentots. The British came at the end of the eighteenth century and took possession of the colony in 1814, upon the abdication of Napoleon. During the early years of the nineteenth century the expanding colony came into conflict with the Bantu, with their complex tribal system, who

---

[20] J. C. Beaglehole, "Discovery and Exploration," in Horace Belshaw (ed.), *New Zealand* (Los Angeles: University of California Press, 1947), pp. 3–19.

were driving southward before them various defeated tribes. Then ensued the Kaffir wars which lasted a third of a century. The Dutch or Boers, dissatisfied with the British policy in regard to the native and colored peoples and seeking cheap labor and free lands, began their famous Great Trek northward in 1834. The racial complexity of the colony was being increased by the emergence of the Cape Coloured through the mixture of Europeans and natives, and it was further increased by the importation of Indian indentured laborers in 1860 into Natal to work on the sugar plantations.

Thus there are in South Africa the following racial and cultural groups: Bushmen, Hottentots, Cape Coloured, Bantu, Indian, Boer, and English. During recent years the German settlers have added to the heterogeneity of the European population. The Boer War, at the end of the nineteenth century, did not resolve the conflict between Boer and English. At present the Boers constitute 57 per cent while those of British ancestry form only 34 per cent of the European population, which numbers about 2,300,-000. The non-European peoples include nearly 8,000,000 natives, the majority of whom are Bantu; nearly 300,000 Asians, the majority being Indians though including Chinese; and nearly 1,000,000 Cape Coloured. Because of their numerical superiority among the Europeans, the Boers have achieved political ascendency and are attempting to impose their notions concerning race relations on all the non-European peoples.

Tropical Dependencies

The second main type of frontiers of race and culture contacts consists of those areas, most of which are in the tropics, where Europeans have not been able to establish large settlements. There are three major areas of this type: Africa south of the Sahara (excluding the Union of South Africa) , Southeast Asia, and the Pacific Islands.

AFRICA SOUTH OF THE SAHARA: Although since the time of the Roman conquests North Africa has been an important area of race and culture contacts,[21] we are interested here primarily in Black Africa or, more specifically, that part of Africa south of the equator and north of the Union of South Africa. This area of Africa extends for 4,500 miles from Dakar, French West Africa, on the west, to Guardafui, Abyssinia, on the east, and for about 2,200 miles south of the Sahara. In this great tropical region, with a few areas of high altitudes and temperate climate, the native population is sparsely settled as compared with India, China, and the industrialized areas of Europe.[22] Three principal stocks are generally recognized among the natives in this area: the Bushmen, the Negro, and the Hamitic.[23] The Bushmen, who are regarded as most primitive and who are probably related to the pygmies in Central Africa, number fewer than 8,000 and are confined to the Kalahari Desert and Southwest Africa. Within this area the Hamitic stock is represented by the Fulani and such mixed groups as the Massai and Nilotes. The Negro stock is concentrated in the coastal regions of West Africa where the rich soils and heavy rainfalls can support a denser population than most parts of tropical Africa. The Bantu-speaking people, who are supposed to be a mixture of the Negro and Hamitic stock, spread southward from the Uganda and the French Congo to South Africa.

The peoples inhabiting Africa south of the Sahara represent varying stages of social development. Many of the Bantu-speaking people dwell in villages with a loose political organization. The same situation may be found, for example, among Negro tribes like the Ibo, where 2,000,000

21 See Ch.-André Julien, *Histoire de l'Afrique du Nord* (Paris: Payot, 1931).
22 Lord Malcolm Hailey, *An African Survey* (London: Oxford University Press, 1938), p. 2.
23 *Ibid.*, pp. 18 ff.

people are divided into 2,000 units. On the other hand, some Negro tribes as, for example, the Ashanti on the Gold Coast and the Songai in French West Africa, had achieved a high degree of political organization before the coming of the European.

This part of Africa is under the authority of four colonial powers: Great Britain, France, Belgium, and Portugal. Although Great Britain administers a smaller area than the French, it exercises control over a greater number of native Africans. Within the British colonies there are over 40,000,000 native Africans as compared with slightly fewer than half that number under the French administration. Living among the 40,000,000 native Africans under the British there are about 110,000 Europeans, a half of whom are in southern Rhodesia. Among the approximately 19,000,000 native Africans under French control there are fewer than 100,000 Europeans.[24] In the Belgian Congo there are about 11,000,000 natives and in Ruanda-Urundi over 3,000,000, with fewer than 70,000 Europeans among them. The Portuguese administer nearly 3,000,000 natives in Angola, where there are 30,000 Europeans, and over 4,000,000 in Mozambique with a European population of 10,000.

SOUTHEAST ASIA: The second area lying on the whole within the tropics, is what is known as "Southeast Asia." "Southeast Asia and its off-lying islands sprawl asymmetrically across the Equator and cover a zone not far short of 1,500 miles in radius from a point off the mouth of the Mekong, an area comparable to all Europe and its seas north of the African coasts." [25] Included in this area are Burma, Indo-China, Siam, Federation of Malaya, Sumatra, Java, Borneo, Celebes, and the Philippine Islands. This region is characterized by a uniformity in

[24] Jean de la Roche et Jean Gottmann, *La Fédération Française* (Montreal: Éditions de L'Arbre, 1945) , pp. 10–11.

[25] E. H. G. Dobby, *Southeast Asia* (London: University of London Press, Ltd., 1950) , p. 17.

temperature and a high humidity throughout the year. Variations in climate and in vegetation are the result of the differences in rainfall. There is an abundant and varied vegetation, including dense tropical forests. Malaysia, or that part of Southeast Asia exclusive of the adjacent mainland (Burma, Siam, and Indo-China), has long been inhabited by peoples exhibiting certain common culture traits which have been described as Malayo-Polynesian. At the same time, this area, like the adjacent mainland, has been influenced by contacts for nearly 2,000 years with India and for shorter periods with the Chinese and the Arabs.[26]

The system of "shifting" agriculture associated with rice, sugar, tea, coffee, cotton, and rubber was brought from the mainland to this area where agriculture originally centered about the root crops—sweet potatoes or yams.[27] Southeast Asia has become an area of commercial agriculture, rice being the chief product, and of mining interests under the control mainly of Europeans. Differences in the development of parts of southeast Asia have been related to the fact that this area has been divided among the European powers. With the exception of Java, relatively very few Europeans have settled in Southeast Asia, which has a population today of nearly 145,000,000. Up to 1870 only a small group of Dutch officials were settled in Java, but after that date the Dutch population increased to about 200,000. Intermarriage between Dutch and Javanese has created a large population of mixed bloods who furnish most of the nationalist leaders. As a result of the Japanese invasion during World War II and the subsequent revolt on the part of the Javanese, the Dutch population has been almost eliminated. Changes in the racial and cultural frontiers in Southeast Asia are

[26] Fay-Cooper Cole, *The Peoples of Malaysia* (New York: D. Van Nostrand Co., 1945), pp. 17 ff.
[27] Dobby, *op. cit.*, p. 347.

being brought about by the general rise of nationalism in Asia.

PACIFIC ISLANDS: The third area within the tropics includes most of the far-flung islands of the Pacific, known as Micronesia, Melanesia, and Polynesia (excluding New Zealand for our purposes). During the four centuries between the discovery of the Pacific Ocean by Magellan and the opening of World War II, these islands underwent many changes as the result of the invasions and conquests by yellow men as well as white men.[28] Although Micronesia includes hundreds of islands, the largest and most southern of which is Guam, its surface measures only 1,200 square miles. The numerous islands forming Melanesia vary in size from New Guinea to tiny islets built upon reefs. These islands, afflicted by all the violent manifestations of nature and all manner of plagues and diseases, are the dwelling place of the Oceanic Negroids.[29] The Polynesian group of islands includes among numerous small islands, Samoa, Tonga, Easter, Cook, Society, Marquesas, and Hawaii. The handsome brown-skinned inhabitants of these islands belong to the Polynesian group, who spread over the empty islands of the Pacific sometime after the beginning of the Christian era.

These islands were discovered during the sixteenth, seventeenth, and eighteenth centuries by the Portuguese, Spanish, Dutch, and English explorers. Then came the period of the whalers, traders, and missionaries, with the English playing a leading role in each of these activities. And later, Americans began to show interest in the Pacific.[30] From the middle of the nineteenth century, European planters began to exploit the islands of the Pacific. During this period, the "blackbirders," as they were called, engaged in a system of slave trading or of supplying natives

[28] Douglas L. Oliver, *The Pacific Islands* (Cambridge: Harvard University Press, 1951), p. 113.

[29] *Ibid.*, p. 30.

[30] *Ibid.*, pp. 73 ff.

to the plantations of South America and Mexico as well as to the islands of the Pacific. The merchant who supplied goods to traders and planters also made his appearance during this period. World War I brought a definite change in the history of these islands, with Japan assuming sovereignty over many of the islands and with Australia and New Zealand linking some to their economies. The great powers which divided the islands among themselves began to exploit the mineral resources of these areas. Then as the result of World War II the United States supplanted Japan and became the dominant power in this area. The era of an enlightened attitude toward the natives in these islands has been associated with a need for man power to exploit the resources.

From the standpoint of race and culture contacts, Hawaii has been an area of great importance because it has become, so to speak, a laboratory where Europeans, Asians, especially the Japanese, and Polynesians have intermarried and created a new community, largely European in culture, which has sought admission as a state to the United States. In the area as a whole the native population has declined since the coming of the European from 3,500,000 to 2,000,000, settled among whom are approximately 140,000 Europeans and 540,000 Asians.[31]

Older Civilizations of Asia

The third frontier of race and culture contacts is unique in that the older civilizations of Asia were relatively unaffected until recently by their contacts with Europe. The small European settlements, composed of traders and officials, have existed on the fringes of these vast native cultural groups which through several thousand years of history have scarcely altered their ways of life. Even India, although incorporated into the British

[31] *Ibid.*, pp. 254-5.

Empire, was unaffected on the whole by Western civilization. In the nineteenth century the influence of European
civilization became greater as the result of improvement in
communication, increase in trade, and the spread of
Western technology. In spite of these changes the older
civilizations never became areas of widespread contacts
between Asiatic and European peoples and they have
never lost the basic elements of their culture. As they have
taken over elements of European culture they have adapted
them to their own cultural heritage.

CHINA: Chinese culture had its roots in a peasant-
village culture of great antiquity, probably going back to
3,000 B.C.[32] Upon this basic peasant-village culture rose
the urban cultures in the second millennium B.C. During
the Chan dynasty which lasted nearly a thousand years and
ended in the third century B.C. the basic pattern of Chinese
life was established. It was during this period that a patriarchal government was established with the Emperor, with
his monopoly of arms, as the "Son of Heaven." It was also
during this period that the Chinese written language took
form and the four Chinese philosophers, Lao-Tzu, Con-
fuscius, Mencius, and Mo Tzu, who molded succeeding
generations, flourished.[33] A period of internal strife was
ended by establishment of the Han dynasty, which lasted
400 years and consolidated the empire. As the Han dynasty
declined, China became divided for awhile, but strong
rulers arose, established new dynasties, restored the unity
of China, and extended its culture into Central Asia and
Mongolia. The Mongols invaded and established themselves in China in the thirteenth century, extended the
rule of China into Korea and Indo-China, and attacked
Japan. The Mongols were driven out by the Ming dynasty
which lasted from the fourteenth to the seventeenth cen-

[32] Ralph Turner, *The Great Cultural Traditions* (New York: Mc-
Graw-Hill Book Co., 1941) , I, 407 ff.
[33] Kenneth S. Latourette, *The Development of China* (Boston:
Houghton Mifflin Co., 1937) , pp. 20 ff.

tury. In the sixteenth century, the Jesuits came to China. This marked the beginning of the contact of China with the West. The Manchus supplanted the Ming dynasty and established a rule in China which lasted until the revolution of 1911.

After 1800, the pressure of Europe on China constantly increased. The first great shock of this impact came as the result of the wars with the British, who forced China to open its doors to the opium traffic. Trade with the West grew and China was constantly forced to surrender her sovereignty over certain areas, especially ports, where the system of extraterritoriality was established. The defeat by Japan in 1894 was the signal for European powers to extend their authority over China. Antiforeign feeling came to a head in 1899 in an uprising known as the "Boxer Rebellion," which meant only another defeat for China. As the effects of contacts with the West through trade and missionary influence came to fruition, a revolutionary movement was gathering force which finally overthrew the weak Manchu dynasty. The republic which was set up could not deal, however, with the economic and social problems which beset the new state. Warlordism flourished and challenged the central authority. Foreign powers continued to take advantage of China's weakness. But the spirit of nationalism continued to spread and the foreign powers were forced to surrender some of their economic and political power. World War II marked the beginning of a new crisis for China involving a struggle with the Japanese. When Chiang Kai-shek and the Kuomintang party failed to solve the land problem, the small group of Communists gradually won the peasants and defeated the armies of Chiang Kai-shek and drove them from the mainland. As a result of the success of this revolutionary movement, direct foreign influence was swept from China.

INDIA: India seems to have been a country of mixed races even before the appearance of the Aryan tribes in the Indus Valley around 2000 B.C., and the racial diversity of the country has continued to the present day.[34] The Aryan tribes mixed with the indigenous Dravidian peoples, and out of the mingling of the cultural traditions of these two peoples came the basic culture of India. The caste system, with the ascendancy of the Aryan priestly class or the Brahmans, was the outstanding feature of this basic culture. The central idea of this culture has been that of dharma, which is a part of Rita, the fundamental law governing the universe.[35] Indian culture, like Chinese culture, has maintained its continuity from these early beginnings, in part by a rich literature—the Upanishads, and the great epics, Ramayana and Mahabharata.

The rise of Buddhism in the sixth century before the Christian Era was an important factor in the formation of the Indian heritage. Buddhism developed as a popular movement. Its spread coincided with the fusion of peoples and principalities which was to bring into existence the Indian State after the death of Alexander the Great. The great Emperor, converted to Buddhism, completed the unification of India. India experienced "many ups and downs" during the first thousand years of the Christian Era.[36] It was broken up into a number of states; and during this period the Arabs and Mohammedanism began to influence Indian culture. Then followed the centuries during which a common culture was developing despite internal struggles between different elements in Indian society.

In the eighteenth century India was a prize in the struggle of England and France for empire in the East. England won in the struggle and consolidated its rule over India, but not without violent resistance on the part of the Indians. Under the impact of a dynamic Western so-

[34] Turner, *op. cit.*, p. 371.

[35] Jawaharlal Nehru, *The Discovery of India* (New York: The John Day Co., 1946), p. 64.

[36] *Ibid.*, pp. 184 ff.

ciety, India was transformed. The organization of the Indian National Congress in 1885 marked the beginning of a new era in the political development of India. World War I increased the tempo of the movement for self-government. As the result of long negotiations with the British government, a veritable revolution started in 1930 with the inauguration of a second civil disobedience movement. A second world war weakened further the control of the British over India, and finally India became a republic within the British Commonwealth. However, India did not emerge from the struggle as a unified state. As the result of the British policy of encouraging separation on the part of the Moslem communities, Pakistan, the two sections of which are a thousand miles apart, became an independent state within the commonwealth.

JAPAN: Unlike the great Asian cultures, China and India, which resisted European influences, if only passively, Japan "after long hesitation voluntarily and of set purpose decided to meet Europe halfway and to remodel her national life upon Occidental lines." [37] This decision, as it were, on the part of Japan came after long experience with Europeans which revealed her powerlessness to resist the West. In its early history Japan had derived her system of government, her social philosophy, and Buddhism from the Chinese.[38] Thus the Japanese—the independent feudal lords—were disposed to accept foreign traders and missionaries who came in the sixteenth century. For sixty years the Jesuits labored in Japan, establishing missions and converting large numbers of Japanese. Then came a period of persecution of the Christians and the development of antiforeign feelings as the Spanish, Portuguese, Dutch, and English intensified the struggle for economic control in Japan. During the ensuing period of seclusion, the Sho-

[37] G. B. Sansom, *The Western World and Japan* (New York: Alfred A. Knopf, Inc., 1950), p. vi.
[38] *Ibid.*, pp. 106 ff.

gunate, which superseded the authority of the Emperor, established a military dictatorship based upon a military caste. It was thus that feudalism was gradually suppressed and a centralized state came into existence.

When Perry forced a treaty on Japan in 1854, there had already been internal movements against the seclusion of Japan. Nevertheless, the fall of the Shogunate and the restoration in 1868 of the Emperor marked a new era in the history of the nation. From this period onward, Japan rapidly began to industrialize and to take over and adapt to her needs the culture of the West. The defeat of the Chinese in 1894 and of the Russians in 1904 caused the Western world to recognize Japan as a modern nation. Partly as the result of economic development and partly as the result of outside political pressures, Japan launched upon an imperialistic career similar to that of Western nations. By a fortunate alliance in World War I, she was able to increase her political and economic positions in the East. But her conflicting interests with the American Empire which was spreading into Asia and her alignment with the Fascist and Nazi powers caused Japan to be defeated in World War II. The success of the revolution in China and the alignment of China with Russia have caused Japan once more to be lined up with the West.

It will not be possible, of course, to study in detail the character of race and culture contacts throughout the areas which have been defined and briefly described in this section. The available data on this problem within these areas will be drawn upon to provide materials for a sociological analysis which, it is hoped, will provide a basis for generalizations concerning race and culture contacts.

RACE AND CULTURE CONTACTS:
A SOCIOLOGICAL PROBLEM

The problem of race and culture contacts in the modern world is essentially a sociological problem because it involves the relations of peoples, not merely as individuals in their interpersonal relations, but people as members of groups, which are differentiated because of both physical characteristics and cultural differences. These cultural differences include differences in technology, customs, habits, values, and the resulting personality organization of the members of the various racial and cultural groups. The sociological approach to the study of race and culture contacts requires, therefore, a selection of data which are relevant to this particular phase of human relations. However, the analysis of this phase of human relations should not be restricted by the narrow point of view of what is generally called "intergroup relations" or the relation of small groups to each other.

The sociological analysis of race and cultural contacts must include the study of the influence of the geographic environment and the technological development of peoples as well as the effect of economic and political institutions upon the relations of men of different races and cultures. Therefore, it is necessary to draw upon the findings of all the social sciences: human geography, anthropology, economics, and political science. It is not difficult to show that the character of race and culture contacts is determined, partly, by the spatial distribution of people, their method of gaining a livelihood, and the distribution of economic power. Moreover, the traditions and culture of peoples with different racial backgrounds shape their attitudes toward each other. Finally, the existing political structures, the distribution of political power, and the laws regulating the relations of peoples with divergent racial and cultural backgrounds are all determinants of the kinds of group contacts and interpersonal relations which exist at any moment in history. Therefore, the organization of the materials which form the subject of this study is based upon the broad sociological frame of reference which is indicated here.[39]

As sociologists we are interested in the relations of men and in the structures of social relations which develop out of the contacts of peoples with different racial and cultural backgrounds. But we are not simply concerned with the static or formal structures which develop and determine the attitudes of men toward one another. We are interested in the social processes which bring these social structures into existence. Therefore, we shall study race and cultural contacts as a dynamic process, taking into account the character of social relations in each stage or phase of this process.[40]

The first phase of race and culture contacts is characterized by contacts that are not truly social, in the sense that persons with different racial and cultural backgrounds who are brought together are not members of the same moral order. Although they look upon each other with a certain fascination, they hardly regard each other as completely human. Conflict may or may not develop but if it does, the conflict is on a biological level. A system of barter, often beginning in a ceremonial exchange of gifts, is more characteristic of the first stage of social contacts. In the history of race and culture contacts, the European in-

---

[39] See E. Franklin Frazier, "Race Contacts and the Social Structure," *American Sociological Review*, XIV (1949), 1–11. See also E. Franklin Frazier, "The Theoretical Structure of Sociology and Sociological Research," *The British Journal of Sociology*, IV (1953), 293–311.

[40] The expression "stage or phase" has been used advisedly. It will be seen in the course of the study, that while the different "phases" of race and culture contacts tend to follow a chronological order in development, they may exist simultaneously. Therefore, while these different "phases" of the developmental process may not represent a chronological order of events, they indicate the "logical" steps to be followed in a systematic sociological treatment of the subject.

vaders have often changed the physical and biological environment of native races by the introduction of new plants and animals, as well as new diseases. As the result of European contacts, changes occur in the diet and clothes of native peoples. The introduction of firearms has made native wars more devastating. During the period of these changes symbiotic rather than social relations are established between European and native peoples. Out of these symbiotic relations there emerges an ecological organization which is generally reflected in the racial division of labor which arises and in the location of racial settlements with reference to each other.

The system of barter develops into slavery or some form of forced labor for the non-Europeans. After slavery is abolished or the system of forced labor is modified, the racial division of labor tends to break down, and in some cases an effort is made to preserve it through legal measures. But usually the racial division of labor cannot be maintained, partly because it is in the interest of European capitalists to use non-European workers in the skilled tasks that were originally reserved for Europeans. Then, too, within the non-European communities a division of labor and specialization have tended to modify the racial division of labor. In the case of the older civilizations of Asia, a native bourgeoisie early came into existence. This modified the racial division of labor but did not completely efface it as long as financial control remained in the hands of Europeans.

The establishment of an economic organization of any nature has always required the institution of some type of political organization or control. For example, the characteristic form of economic organization in the early stages of race and culture contacts has been the plantation which has also been a type of political organization. The plantation has generally been a governmental unit within a larger governmental authority. In fact, various types of colonial administration have been set up in order to maintain and control the different systems of economic exploitation. Even in the case of the United States where the Negroes were a part of the American economic order, special systems of social control, not always legal but nevertheless essentially of a political character, were set up for Negroes. As a reaction to political control, nationalistic movements have developed among native peoples. This type of resistance to European rule was first developed in the older civilizations of Asia, but during recent years it has spread all over Asia and has begun to appear in Africa.

When we come to analyze race and culture contacts from the standpoint of the social organization which is created to accommodate peoples with different racial and cultural backgrounds we come to the heart of the problem. Where race relations have advanced beyond the system of slavery, a caste system has been the classical form of social organization. Caste, which rests upon sacred social sanctions, has been characteristic of agricultural societies. Under the impact of urbanism and modern industrialism caste tends to break down. In the modern industrial societies the type of social organization which has evolved to accommodate peoples of different racial and cultural origins has been a type of biracialism in which the principle of caste is interwoven with class distinctions. In Russia the problem has been met by developing a type of cultural pluralism. In modern industrial societies characterized by the increasing mobility of the population, both biracialism and cultural pluralism tend to break down. Where this occurs, peoples of divergent racial and cultural origins enjoy complete social mobility and in the process of assimilation the different traditional cultures become fused in a common national heritage. The Brazilian nation has exemplified this process which we shall have occasion to analyze in the course of our study. Where assimilation does not occur nationalistic movements are likely to rise. Although they have an economic and political basis, they involve the question of a common racial and cultural heritage. Nationalistic movements represent in some cases the failure of people with different racial and cultural backgrounds to achieve a single social organization. In nationalistic movements the cultural values of the minority supersede those of the dominant group. Thus one arrives at the problem of culture and personality.

Contacts between Europeans and non-Europeans have resulted in the diffusion of many traits of European culture. The extent to which this has occurred has depended upon a number of factors. For example, the American Negroes, who have been immersed for more than three centuries in a community with European culture, have lost almost completely their African cultural heritage. On the other hand, in Asia and most of the areas of Africa the diffusion of European culture has been limited to certain areas and to certain classes of the native population. The diffusion of European culture has generally resulted in the adoption of some of the techniques of European civilization and in changes in habits and overt behavior. Consequently, this type of acculturation has not affected the deeper layers of the personalities of native peoples or changed their fundamental values and outlooks on life.

The relatively small number of individuals who have acquired the values and sentiments of Europeans have often become "marginal men" or cultural hybrids. It has been the marginal men who have become the leaders of the nationalistic movements. Although the concept of the marginal man is very broad, it does not include all aspects of the problem of culture and personality arising as the result of race and culture contacts. Our analysis, therefore, of the current phase of race and culture contacts will explore other aspects of the relations of culture to personality. For example, the expansion of European culture together with the increasing mobility of the peoples of the world is producing a type of cosmopolitan "culture." The bearers of this new culture represent new personality types as well as the latest phase in race and culture contacts.

Within the sociological frame of reference which has been outlined, an analysis of the phenomena of race and culture contacts as they have developed on various racial frontiers will be undertaken in the following chapters.

PART I

Ecological Organization

CHAPTER II

The Nature of Initial Contacts

INTRODUCTION

According to his *Journal*, when Columbus first landed on an island in the West Indies, large numbers of the natives assembled to receive the Europeans. Columbus states that since he knew that they could be converted to the Christian faith more easily by love than by force, he

gave to some of them red caps, and glass beads to put round their necks, and many other things of little value, which gave them great pleasure, and made them so much our friends that it was a marvel to see. They afterwards came to the ship's boats where we were, swimming and bringing us parrots, cotton threads in skeins, darts, and many other things; and we exchanged them, for other things that we gave them, such as glass beads and small bells. In fine, they took all, and gave what they had with good will.[1]

As Columbus sailed along the coasts of the other islands, he was greeted in a similar manner by the natives. It appears that mingled with these evidences of friendship there was a feeling of awe. For as Columbus relates in his

[1] Clements R. Markham (trans.), *The Journal of Christopher Columbus* (London: The Hakluyt Society, 1893), p. 37.

Journal, he and his crew understood that the natives had asked if they had come from heaven. "One old man came into the boat," his *Journal* records, "and others cried out, in loud voices, to all the men and women, to come and see the men who had come from heaven, and to bring them to eat and drink." [2]

FASCINATION OF THE UNKNOWN

Columbus' account of the manner in which he and his crew were received appears to be typical, since the reports of many other explorers provide similar evidence. For example, the accounts of the travels of Captain Cook contain abundant evidence of the friendly reception which Europeans met when they first had contacts with native peoples in various parts of the world. When Cook discovered Van Diemen's Land in 1777, he and his men were, as he wrote:

agreeably surprised, at the place where we were cutting wood, with a visit from some of the natives; eight men and a boy. They approached us from the woods, without betraying any marks of fear, or rather with the greatest confidence imaginable; for none of them had any weapons, except one, who held in his hand a stick about two feet long, and pointed at one end. [3]

Cook's account of the astonishment and lack of fear exhibited by the natives of Hawaii is even more important since it reveals a more fundamental element than friendliness in the initial contacts between members of different racial and cultural groups. Concerning the behavior of the Hawaiians, Cook wrote:

In the course of my several voyages, I never before met with the natives of any place so much astonished as these people were, upon entering a ship. Their eyes were continually flying from object to object; the wildness of their looks and gestures

[2] *Ibid.,* p. 41.
[3] *A Voyage to the Pacific Ocean,* prepared under the direction of Captains Cook, Clerke, Gore (London: W. and A. Strahan, 1784), I, 96.

fully expressing their entire ignorance about everything they saw, and strongly marking to us, that till now, they had never been visited by Europeans. . . .[4]

Behind the so-called friendly attitude which natives are reported to have exhibited toward Europeans, there is then the more fundamental attitude of fascination. The fascination which natives have exhibited in their first encounter with Europeans is similar to the attitude of young children and even adults, who have not been influenced by stereotypes, when they first meet individuals of a different race. They appear to be fascinated rather than truly friendly or hostile or fearful.[5]

Maunier has pointed out in discussing the first stages in the contacts of Europeans and native peoples that "We take one axiom for granted: the foreigner never fails to arouse interest, his coming is never meaningless. Sometimes the native is pleased and gratified. He may admire or despise the foreigner; he will never, or almost never be indifferent to his arrival." [6] The arrival of the European is not meaningless because the native attempts to define the coming of Europeans in terms of his own cultural heritage and experiences with strangers. It appears that the stranger is very often not regarded as a secular person.[7] When, as happens sometimes, he is regarded as a blessing from the gods, he is therefore treated in a friendly though an awesome manner. There are also cases where the stranger is regarded as an evil omen and consequently arouses feelings of hostility. But in either case the native attempts to establish a basis of communication and social intercourse. Cook noted in his accounts that some of the Hawaiians

[4] *Ibid.*, II, 194.

[5] We shall have occasion later to discuss in some detail this phase of race and culture contacts when we analyze the contacts of different races in modern civilized communities.

[6] René Maunier, *The Sociology of Colonies* (London: Routledge & Kegan Paul, Ltd., 1949) , I, 55.

[7] See Hunton Webster, *Taboo: A Sociological Study* (Stanford: Stanford University Press, 1942) , pp. 230 ff.

repeated a long prayer before they came on board; and others afterward sung and made motions with their hands, such as we had been accustomed to see in the dances of the islands we had lately visited.[8]

The attempts on the part of native peoples to establish a basis of social intercourse with Europeans often assume a ceremonial character. It may involve an exchange of names. This happened with Captain Cook on the island of Oahu when he exchanged his name of James for the names of the Hawaiian chief.[9] Sometimes it involves communal meals, in which the eating of the same food creates a feeling of communion with strangers. This attempt to establish communion with strangers may include the sharing of their wives or the gift of their daughters or sisters.[10]

Very often it is through the exchange of gifts that native peoples have attempted to establish a basis of communion with Europeans. Through the exchange of gifts and other rituals, Europeans or strangers have established friendly relations with native peoples. The French were especially successful in this respect among the North American Indians, and successful missionaries have first been "adopted" by native peoples before beginning their missionary efforts. On the other hand, the exchange of gifts represents an embryonic form of barter and may be regarded as the initial stage in the trade that soon develops between Europeans and native peoples.

THE SILENT TRADE AND BARTER

Much evidence has been collected and analyzed to show that because of hostility, fear, and distrust the initial contacts between strangers and members of primitive

[8] Cook, Clerke, and Gore, *op. cit.*, II, 195.

[9] Maunier, *op. cit.*, p. 61.

[10] Concerning this practice in various parts of the world see Edward Westermarck, *The History of Human Marriage* (London: Macmillan Company, Ltd., 1921) , I, 225 ff.

groups involved a type of exchange of goods known as silent trade.[11] Silent trade is a transaction involving an exchange of goods between people who do not even see each other. One party to the transaction leaves his goods and when he returns the next day he finds other goods opposite to the goods which he has left. If he is satisfied he accepts the other goods in exchange; if not he takes away the goods which he has left.

In Grierson's account of this type of trade, there is little information concerning such relations between Europeans and native peoples, but Grierson does refer to Livingstone's statement, in his *Missionary Travels*, that his men were told as they approached the coast of Loanda that the natives in trading with white men leave ivory on "the shore in the evening, and next morning the seller finds a quantity of goods placed there in its stead." [12] Grierson also includes Bastian's report that during one of his travels a primitive group in the Andes established relations with him by placing near his camp bananas that had been freshly gathered. After finding the fruit there in the morning, Bastian would leave what he considered a suitable exchange in the evening.[13]

However, from the beginning of European contacts with non-European peoples, it appears that trading was carried on in the manner of the silent trade. The Portuguese who began trading in gold dust and slaves on the coast of West Africa engaged in silent trade with the natives. This was due to the fact that Portuguese and Africans distrusted each other since the Africans feared that the Portuguese would enslave them and the Portuguese feared that they would be killed by the Africans. When Columbus landed in the new world, some trading was undertaken at least in so far as the exchange of gifts may

[11] P. J. Hamilton Grierson, *The Silent Trade* (Edinburgh: William Green and Sons, 1903).

[12] Quoted in *ibid.*, p. 44.

[13] Cited in *ibid.*, p. 47.

be considered an initial step in barter and trade. But trading was limited by the fact that the Spaniards were seeking precious metals and offered nothing in return. On the mainland of North America, trading was also restricted because the settlers lacked staples for trade. In fact, the whites were able to survive because they learned how to cultivate beans, corn, pumpkins, and tobacco from the Indians and because they adopted Indian articles of clothing. Nevertheless, some trading was carried on from the beginning. For example, the fur trade became one of the most important links between the Indians and European settlers, while trading in whiskey and firearms became one of the main causes of racial conflicts.

The slave trade stands out as the historically most significant case of trade involving Europeans and native peoples. The Europeans began with the bartering of goods and gradually engaged in the buying and selling of men. This developed into the famous triangular trade in which the English, as the chief owners of the slave ships, played the major role. Ships carrying English manufactures and gin and guns would sail to the coast of West Africa where they would trade these goods for gold and ivory as well as slaves. The slaves, gold, and ivory would be taken, to be sold in the West Indies and North America. In the West Indies the ships were loaded with sugar and other tropical products in exchange for the slaves, while in North America the slaves were sold for cotton and tobacco. The ships, which would complete the triangular trade in six or more months, carried the products of the West Indies and North America to England.

The slave trade was a constant source of conflict between European traders and the native Africans who engaged in the trade. Before the white man had established himself in West Africa, the civilization of this region, which had reached a high stage of development, was destroyed by the Moorish conquests from the North. The inauguration of the slave trade depopulated the country and completed the destruction of civilization in this part of Africa.

Bartering between Europeans and native peoples was a constant source of conflict. Some of the explorers complained that, when they first had contacts with natives, the latter either had no conception of trade or did not understand a system of exchange involving economic values. After analyzing the available evidence on this question, Herskovits concludes:

Though in non-industrial societies sparring between traders for advantages does, of course, mark their operations, sometimes even this seems to be absent where values in terms of goods exchanged by direct barter are fixed by traditional usage. Nonetheless, among nonliterate groups the conduct of business transactions has nothing of the impersonal quality that has come to be an outstanding characteristic of our economic system.[14]

Thus, there was the basis for genuine misunderstanding which led to conflicts between Europeans and native peoples. The conflict was especially likely to arise over the question of land. Nonliterate peoples generally do not regard land as an object of commerce. In South Africa, conflicts arose between the Dutch and the Hottentots over the title to lands. After the Hottentots and Bushmen were driven from the land desired by the Dutch, title to lands became one of the chief sources of conflict between the Dutch and the Bantu peoples. Conflicts over title to land have characterized contacts between Europeans and natives in other parts of Africa where whites have desired land for economic exploitation or settlement.

Of course, the conflicts between Europeans and non-Europeans over the title to lands was not due only to conflicts of concepts concerning the nature of landownership. From the beginning the British authorities assumed that

[14] Melville J. Herskovits, *Economic Anthropology* (New York: Alfred A. Knopf, Inc., 1952), p. 34.

the Indians had no title to the land in North America. The United States continued the policy of the English in regard to the possession of land. Thus there was continued a system of land robbery. Likewise in other dealings the whites engaged in all forms of cheating the Indians, whom they regarded as inferior people without rights. In New Zealand, the Maoris were deprived of their lands through so-called legal means based upon the theory that no native had title to land unless it had been granted by the crown. This led to wars between the Europeans and natives which in 1860 resulted in the destruction of the Maori as a people. Similar conflicts have characterized the dealings of Europeans with native peoples in other parts of the world. The conflicts over the slave trade were especially bloody and continued throughout its history.

CONFLICT ON A BIOLOGICAL PLANE

The important fact that should be noted in regard to the conflicts which arise during the first stage of race and culture contacts is that they are confined to the biological plane. Since the two parties in conflict are not members of a common moral order, generally they do not regard each other as human. Consequently, there is no basis for human sympathy or opportunity for human impulses to assert themselves and restrain the "savage" character of these conflicts. This explains, in fact, why civilized men with their greater imagination regarding human suffering and more efficient resources have been more savage than the so-called savages in these racial conflicts. Finally, there are no codes or contractual agreements such as exist between warring nations to regulate the character of the conflict.

The friendly intercourse that marked the initial contacts between the Indians and the crews of Columbus' ships was of short duration. When Columbus returned in 1493 to the island of San Domingo where he had built a fortress and left a garrison, he found the fortress demolished and the garrison destroyed. As far as he was able to learn, the garrison had failed to maintain discipline among themselves and had engaged in plundering and molesting the Indians. Although it appears that immediate reprisals were not taken against the Indians, from this time onward the conquest of the West Indians by the Spaniards was characterized by barbaric cruelty.[15]

The struggle between the Spaniards and the native population followed from the attempt of the former to establish a system of slave labor to work the mines. Although the Spaniards possessed firearms, which gave them an advantage over the natives, the Indians continued to offer resistance to a form of enslavement that gradually reduced their numbers. The Spaniards met this resistance by the use of every form of torture and punishment. For example, fierce dogs were used to hunt down and tear the natives to pieces. The systematic extermination of the natives was so great that by 1511, it was reported, the greater part of the native population had disappeared.[16] The same system of working the natives to death and subjecting them to torture was repeated from island to island. When the missionary, Las Casas, recommended the introduction of Negro slaves to save the native population and bring an end to the cruelties practiced upon them, it was too late to save the Indians. Moreover, he was making a recommendation, which he later regretted, that involved the subjection of another branch of humanity to similar tortures. As the Spanish conquest spread to Mexico and South America, the struggle on the biological plane continued but in these areas the native Indians, being more numerous than the West Indians and possessing a superior social organization, were able to resist complete annihilation.

[15] See P. Pierre-Françoise-Xavier de Charlevoix, *Histoire de l'Isle Lespaguale ou de S. Domingue*, 2 Vols. (Paris: 1780).
[16] *Ibid.*, I, 310–11.

The treatment of the Indians by the British colonists and later by the Americans was as brutal as that by the Spanish explorers. In New England the Puritans justified their barbarous treatment of the Indians by appealing to the example of the Hebrews in the Old Testament.[17] In Virginia, despite the friendly attitude of the Indians, as the English colonists moved westward they destroyed Indian tribes without sparing women or children. After the United States was established as an independent nation, the contacts between whites and Indians continued to be characterized by struggle on a biological plane. Soon after the American Revolution, an American army drove the Indians from their homes in Ohio around the Great Lakes.[18] Then in 1838 came the great atrocity against the Cherokees in which men, women, and children were slaughtered. During the 1840's when gold was discovered in California and Oregon, clergymen joined in the massacre of Indian women and children. Whites killed Indians "as a sport to enliven Sundays and holidays." [19] The so-called treaties which the government of the United States made with the Indians did not bring to an end the racial struggle. Despite the eighteen treaties which the American government made with the Indians in 1852 alone to provide reservations, the whites continued to encroach upon the areas reserved for Indians. The whites not only stole the land from the Indians but they engaged in every form of cruelty toward Indian women and children while the government refused to provide any protection for Indians.

Contrary to what might be inferred from Sir Harry Johnston's assertion that "the Negro in a primitive state is a born slave," [20] the African slave trade was characterized

17 A. Grenfell Price, *White Settlers and Native Peoples* (Cambridge: At the University Press, 1950) , p. 12.

18 *Ibid.*, pp. 15–16.

19 *Ibid.*, p. 17.

20 *A History of the Colonization of Africa by Alien Races* (Cambridge: At the University Press, 1913) , p. 151.

throughout its existence by violent resistance on the part of the Negro. In retaliation for this violent resistance, the Europeans subjected the Negro to every imaginable type of cruel punishment. For example, a surgeon in the Royal British Navy wrote in 1721 the following account of how the Negroes who revolted on board a slave ship were treated.

Captain Harding, weighing the Stoutness and Worth of the two Slaves, did, as in other Countries they do by Rogues of Dignity, whip and scarify them only; while three other, Abettors, but not Actors, nor of Strength for it, he sentenced to cruel Deaths; making them first eat the Heart and Liver of one of them killed. The Woman he hoisted up by the Thumbs, whipped and slashed her with knives, before the other Slaves till she died.[21]

During the slave insurrections in the West Indies, both Europeans and Negroes treated each other with barbaric cruelty. On the mainland of North America revolt on the part of the Negro slaves was suppressed with torture and burnings alive. The discovery of a plot among Negro slaves against the whites in New York City in 1741 resulted in the burning alive of thirteen of the 125 Negroes arrested. All during the period of slavery in the southern states, conflicts between whites and blacks were characterized by inhuman reprisals. In regard to these conflicts during slavery, it should be noted that where human relationships were established between masters and slaves, both slaves and masters were less likely to engage in barbaric cruelty toward each other. Racial conflict assumed an inhuman and barbaric relation between the Negro slaves on the one hand and the overseers, slave traders, and the patrollers on the other. The slave traders regarded the slave as a commodity while the overseers and patrollers, recruited

21 Elizabeth Donnan, *Documents Illustrative of the History of the Slave Trade to America* (Washington. D.C.: Carnegie Institute of Washington, 1935), IV, 266.

from among the poor whites, regarded the Negro as a subhuman species.

When the human and customary ties between masters
and slaves were dissolved as the result of the Civil War and
emancipation, so that Negroes and poor whites became
competitors, racial conflicts often became a struggle on a
biological plane. The class struggle between the planters
and the rising commercial and industrial class on one hand
and the poor whites on the other was resolved by uniting
both in a struggle for white supremacy. During this racial
struggle every kind of barbaric cruelty was utilized to reduce the Negro to a subordinate status or to practically
re-enslave him. When the northern armies were withdrawn
from the South, the whites resorted sometimes to whole-
sale slaughter of Negroes. The continuation of the racial
struggle on a biological plane is indicated by the thousands of lynchings in the South, involving the burning
alive of Negroes in an atmosphere of holiday-making on
the part of whites. In the race riots which have occurred
in the North, racial conflict has generally appeared to be a
struggle on a biological plane. In the South many whites
have simply wanted to put the Negro in his "place"; in the
North, where for a long time there was no "place" for
the Negro, European immigrants have joined the racial
struggle.

In Australia and Tasmania, where Europeans have
succeeded in establishing themselves, a racial struggle ensued from the beginning of European contacts and ended
in the practical extermination of the natives. Despite the
fact that the aborigines were timid and inoffensive, the
Dutch attempted to kidnap them and the English and
French fired upon them.[22] Then as the explorers advanced
inland and settlements were started, the natives were
hunted like wild animals and shot upon the least provoca-
tion. As the result of assaults on native women, atrocities

[22] Price, *op. cit.*, pp. 105–6.

were practiced by natives as well as whites, and the whites were quick to retaliate. It became an established rule that no white person could be tried for any kind of atrocity inflicted upon the natives. In Tasmania the peaceable natives were shot and bayonetted, and children were thrown into the fire. The hunting of the natives as wild beasts and the manner in which the wounded were killed aroused protests on the part of societies for the protection of the natives. Nevertheless, the native population of Tasmania was finally exterminated. In New Zealand the advent of the Europeans intensified native warfare and made it more destructive. At the same time, the conflict between European and Maori tended to be the same as that between whites and natives elsewhere. The coming of the missionaries tended to offset the destructive effects of the advancing European frontier.

In South Africa, the conflict between the Dutch settlers and the Hottentot and Bushman began soon after the Dutch had their first contacts with the natives. According to contemporary accounts, the Dutch or Boers regarded both Hottentots and Bushmen as wild animals, to be shot on sight. Hunting parties were organized for the purpose of killing the natives, who were accused of being "inveterate thieves." Bounties were also given for evidence of the death of the members of these tribal groups. The Hottentots were subdued and the Bushmen were driven into the desert. But when the Dutch met the better organized and more highly developed Bantu groups, a racial struggle began which is not yet settled.

Turning to the areas in which Europeans did not estabilsh sizeable white communities, one finds similar evidence of a struggle on a biological plane. When the Congo Free State in 1891 declared all vacant land the property of the State and reserved the principal products of the land, rubber and ivory, the natives became the victims of the private groups which were granted concessions to exploit the land and collect taxes. The natives, with their nomadic habits and primitive notions of land tenure, became the victims of a ruthless type of exploitation which aroused indignation in Europe and the United States. The native villages were required to supply a certain quota of labor and food. Moreover, natives were forced to pay taxes in the form of rubber which they collected. When they failed to supply the required amount of rubber, they were beaten and often mutilated. The natives were reduced to a type of slavery in which no account was taken of their human qualities.

It is unnecessary to add evidence from other parts of Africa or from the islands of the Pacific where, when conflicts developed between natives and Europeans, they assumed the character of a biological struggle. When initial contacts resulted in conflicts between Europeans and the peoples of the old civilizations of Asia, they could not become entirely a struggle on a biological plane because of the higher civilization of these peoples and their numerical strength. Although the peoples of the old civilizations of Asia were conquered because of the superior technique of the Europeans, the conquerors found it in their interest to conduct warfare according to some accepted rules.

In concluding this chapter, it may be pointed out that the first contacts between members of different racial and cultural groups are neither essentially friendly nor hostile. It appears that the so-called friendliness that has been manifested during first contacts between Europeans and native peoples was based, in fact, upon an attitude of fascination toward the stranger. The hostility which natives have manifested toward the first Europeans with whom they had contacts has been due to historical conditions or cultural attitudes which define the stranger as hostile or evil. Generally, from the beginning some kind of exchange of gifts or goods is established which develops into a system of barter or trade. Hostilities may arise from a conflict of interests and even from misunderstandings. When these conflicts arise they generally assume the character of a racial struggle on a biological plane. Rivalry is excluded and there are no codes to regulate the character of these conflicts. The natives may be exterminated or the strangers may be annihilated or expelled. Generally, some system of barter or exchange of goods is established. This system provides the basis for a symbiotic relationship which may be regarded as the first stage in the development of race and culture contacts.

CHAPTER III

Changes in Physical and Biological Environment

INTRODUCTION

In studying the first stage in the development of race and culture contacts, one must take account of the changes in the physical and biological environment of native peoples which result from the introduction of new physical objects and changes in plant and animal life. Thus the term "physical and biological environment" is used in a broad sense to include not only clothes, houses, and firearms, but microbes and alcohol, sugar and cattle. Some of these new elements were introduced through the system of barter which was established almost from the beginning between Europeans and native peoples. But, generally these new forms of animal and more especially plant life became the basis of a type of economic exploitation that established the basic pattern of race relations. Moreover, the new forms of plant and animal life became a part of the natural environment of the native population, changing their habits of consumption, affecting their health as well as their relations with Europeans. Therefore, it is essential to study these changes in the environment, thus broadly defined, since they provide the basis of the symbiotic relations which are characteristic of the first stage of race and culture contacts.

CHANGES IN PLANT AND ANIMAL LIFE

From earliest times man has introduced plants into all parts of the world. However, the extent to which human activities have been responsible for the dispersal of plants in various countries of the world has been dependent upon man's influence in these countries. Consequently, the dispersal of plants has been most intensive in recent centuries as European peoples have colonized different countries.[1] One of the earliest plants to be transported to various parts of the world as the result of European migrations was sugar cane. It appears from available evidence that sugar cane originated in India or some part of eastern tropical Asia and spread eastward and westward.[2] During the Middle Ages the Arabs introduced it into Egypt, Sicily, and southern Spain. Prince Henry transported it to Madeira, and thence it was carried to the Canary Islands in 1503. From the Canary Islands it was taken to Brazil and Haiti in the early sixteenth century, and from there to Mexico and Cuba. By the middle of the seventeenth century it had been introduced into Barbadoes and other islands in the West Indies.

The introduction of sugar cane into the West Indies doomed those islands to a system of Negro slavery which laid the foundation for the future pattern of race relations and racial survival.[3] This is made especially clear in the case of the island of Hispaniola, where French planters occupied the western part of the island and the Spaniards the eastern part. The Spanish exploited the land for pre-

---

[1] Ronald Godd, *The Geography of the Flowering Plants* (New York: Longmans, Green & Co., Inc., 1947) , p. 303.

[2] *The Encyclopaedia Britannica* (11th ed.) , XXVI, 35 ff.

[3] See Eric Williams, *Capitalism and Slavery* (Chapel Hill: University of North Carolina Press, 1944) , pp. 23 ff.

cious metals and in attempting to do so killed off a large proportion of the Indian population and mixed with the remainder as well as with the Negro slaves who were introduced into the island. On the other hand the French sugar planters introduced thousands of Negro slaves to work the sugar plantations on the fertile lowlands in the western part of the island. As a result, during the last decade of the eighteenth century the slightly more than 100,000 inhabitants of the Spanish half were almost equally divided into whites, free Negroes and mulattoes, and slaves. On the French half of the island there were nearly 500,000 slaves confronting 30,000 French and 28,000 free Negroes and mulattoes.

In 1640 the population of Barbados numbered approximately 37,000 whites and 6,000 Negro slaves. After sugar cane was introduced during the following year, the Negro population began to increase much more rapidly than the white population. By the end of the eighteenth century there were four times as many Negroes as whites, and at present whites form only about 7 per cent of a population of about 200,000. The introduction of sugar cane into northern Brazil led to the importation of a large number of Negro slaves, who have determined the racial composition of that region.

Although tobacco was a plant which Europeans found among the natives of the New World, it was European enterprise that transplanted it to many parts of the world. On the other hand, rice, which had been carried to Spain by the Arabs, was introduced into South Carolina in 1700. Rice cultivation was one of the reasons for the importation of Negro slaves into the colony, where for a period they outnumbered whites.

However, the cultivation of cotton was chiefly responsible for the growth of the Negro population in South Carolina and other southern states. Although this crop was cultivated extensively not only in the Orient but also was found in Mexico and Peru by the Spanish explorers, the United States has led the world in cotton production. When it appeared that Negro slavery might die out in the United States in the last decade of the eighteenth century, the invention of the cotton gin and the development of the European textile industry assured the institution of Negro slavery and the plantation system in the southern states. Thus was created one of the most important racial frontiers in the modern world. It was owing to the enterprise of Europeans that cotton cultivation has become important in the countries of South America, and more important still in Uganda, the Anglo-Egyptian Sudan, the Belgian Congo, and in French territories in Africa. The introduction of cotton into Africa is changing the environment of the natives and shaping the character of race relations in these areas.

The cultivation of coffee in various parts of the world is also the result of the expansion of European peoples. The early history of coffee as an economic product is obscure though there is record of its use in Abyssinia during the fifteenth century. Coffee drinking, in spite of the prohibition of coffee as an intoxicating beverage by the Mohammedans, spread throughout Arabia. Up to the end of the seventeenth century the entire world depended upon Arabia for coffee. Around this time coffee cultivation was introduced into Java, Ceylon, and Surinam, and not long thereafter the cultivation of coffee spread throughout the West Indies. In 1754 coffee was introduced into Brazil, where it became one of the chief products. Just as the introduction of sugar cane into northern Brazil was followed by the importation of large numbers of slaves, the growing importance of the commercial production of coffee has been responsible for the settlement of European immigrants in the coffee lands in southern Brazil.

Cocoa is another plant which has been transplanted to many parts of the world and has affected the relations of men with different racial and cultural backgrounds. The Spanish explorers found cocoa in Mexico where it was drunk in large quantities and used as a form of currency. It was introduced into Spain and other parts of Europe, including England, where it was a fashionable drink in the early eighteenth century. Since cocoa requires a warm and rainy climate in order to be cultivated as a commercial crop, it was transplanted to the West Indies, South America, and Africa.

The cultivation of rubber for commerce is another striking example of the effect of the introduction of new plants among native peoples. Although the existence of rubber was first observed in South America not long after discovery of the continent, the plant was not identified until the eighteenth century. A significant change in the rubber industry occurred where European exploiters ceased to depend upon wild rubber from trees and introduced rubber plants from South America into other parts of the world, particularly the Federated Malay States, Java, Sumatra, and Ceylon. More recently, as Liberia in Africa has become one of the important rubber-producing areas, the entire native life there has been affected.

Although the introduction of cocoa on the Gold Coast fitted into the established family economy,[4] it had a different effect among the people of the forest zone of the Ivory Coast. Before the introduction of cocoa and coffee, the natives of this tropical forest zone had cultivated annual crops—rice, manioc, ignames, and bananas—which formed the basis of a subsistence economy.[5] The chief was the depository and arbiter of the rights of the village to the forest. There was no ownership of land; instead, there was ownership of the harvest. Each year the chief might redis-

---

[4] Pierre Gourou, *Les Pays tropicaux* (Paris: Presses Universitaires de France, 1948) , p. 159.

[5] Raymond LeFevre, "Cacao et café, cultures 'révolutionnaires': d'évolution des peuples de la forêt," *La Revue de géographie humaine et ethnologie,* 1948–9, pp. 52–62.

tribute the areas to be burned and cleared for cultivation. The head of each patriarchal household would in turn distribute the tasks among the heads of families.

The introduction of cocoa and coffee plantations has created a revolution which is transforming the organization of Negro society in this area. First, under the plantation system it is necessary to prepare the land three or four years before production begins, and production does not reach its maximum for seven or eight years. Since ownership of land with definite boundaries thus becomes necessary, contacts must be made with the villages. These arrangements are often the source of misunderstanding and conflicts. Under the new condition of working, the patriarchal family is broken up and the ancestral household dissolved. The individual is emancipated and assumes responsibilities as an individual worker. This change in the native culture and social organization has changed the character of race and culture contacts in this region.

One of the most important consequences following the introduction of new plants and new forms of cultivation has been the erosion and exhaustion of the soil. The sugar cane and tobacco plantations exhausted the soils of Brazil and the West Indies. The erosion of soils resulting from the introduction of new plants by Europeans for commercial purposes has been extremely serious in the tropical regions.[6] This has been due principally to deforestation and the introduction of the plow. In Northern Rhodesia where it is estimated 16 per cent of the soil has been lost, erosion has followed the introduction of the plow. Likewise in Kenya, Uganda, and Tanganyika the introduction of the plow has been responsible for much of the erosion of the soil.[7]

[6] See Gourou, *op. cit.*, Chap. XI.
[7] G. V. Jacks and R. D. Whyte, *The Rape of the Earth. A World Survey of Soil Erosion* (London: Faber and Faber, Ltd., 1939), pp. 71 ff. See also Jean-Paul Harroy, *Afrique: terre qui meurt* (Bruxelles: Marcal Hayez, 1949), pp. 118 ff.

Although there was undoubtedly soil erosion before the coming of the European, most of the soil erosion in Africa is in Kenya and Southern Rhodesia where there are European colonies.[8] The destruction of the native social organization and traditional system of agriculture has disrupted the native methods of dealing with erosion. Moreover, the native system of shifting agriculture allowed sufficient time for the soil to recover, whereas with the introduction of the plow and the intensive cultivation under the Europeans the soil is constantly exhausted. For example, the cultivation of peanuts in Senegal has caused exhaustion of the soil. The erosion and exhaustion of the soil is perhaps as responsible for land hunger in South Africa among the native people as their increase in population. Likewise, the introduction of coffee into Kenya and the restriction of the Kikuyu to reserves have been responsible for conflicts with Europeans.

Changes in the plant life of the areas of race and culture contacts are closely related to changes in the animal life. For example, where pastoral peoples have had to change their nomadic pattern of life, as in the case of Kenya, overstocking may result since cattle continue to be regarded as a form of wealth. And since overstocking results in overgrazing, overstocking may be regarded as one of the causes of erosion.[9]

The most important changes in animal life in these areas have resulted from the importation of new types of animal life. We might begin with two well-known cases: the rabbit and the mongoose. The rabbit was introduced into Australia by the early European settlers and became very destructive as far as plant life was concerned. The mongoose, which was domesticated in the Orient and used to kill birds and snakes, was introduced into other parts of the world to kill rats and vermin. The mongoose was introduced into Jamaica and Hawaii especially for the pur-

[8] *Ibid.*, p. 257.   [9] Harroy, *op. cit.*, pp. 155 ff.

pose of killing rats on sugar plantations. It not only multiplied greatly and therefore became a burden from the standpoint of numbers, it also became a pest, killing poultry, useful birds, and mammals.

The introduction of the horse into the New World, first by the Indians and later by the Spaniards, is an outstanding example of the influence of new animal life on race and culture contacts. The horse had become extinct before the arrival of Columbus in the New World.[10] The Spanish explorers who followed Columbus brought the horse with them, and from the Spanish settlements horses were spread over the southern plains.

Later the English brought the horse to the eastern seaboard. It was in the steppe-like areas of North America and South America that the horse influenced the native cultures. The horse had three main influences on the culture of the Indians. First, in providing a new means of transport for goods and men it increased the mobility of the Indians and thereby widened the area of their contacts. Secondly, the horse tended to change the character of wars among the Indians and gave a new character to the wars between the Indians and the white men. Finally, the horse changed the entire manner of hunting the buffalo and thereby hastened its extermination.

The disappearance of the buffalo or, more correctly, the bison together with their confinement on reservations caused the collapse of the Indian culture. Before the coming of the white man the bison ranged in countless numbers over a third of North America. The completion of the Union Pacific Railroad divided them into northern and southern herds. During the period from 1870 to 1875 about 2,500,000 bison, according to estimates, were destroyed. When the Northern Pacific Railroad was com-

[10] See Clark Wissler, *Man and Culture* (New York: Thomas Y. Crowell Co., 1923), pp. 115 ff. See also Clark Wissler, *Indians of the United States* (New York: Doubleday, Doran and Co., Inc., 1940), pp. 261 ff.

pleted in 1880 the destruction of the northern herd began, and within a few years it had been completed. The opening years of the twentieth century found the vast majority of the bison, numbering less than 1,200, in public parks and zoological gardens.

In concluding this section, we shall refer to the introduction of sheep into Australia. Until the end of the eighteenth century Spain had a monopoly on the production of fine wool. The monopoly was broken as specimens of the merino breeding stock were given to members of royal houses of Europe and the Napoleonic wars finally dispersed the stock. The English took sheep to America and later to Australia, where they played a crucial role in European settlement.[11] It is of special interest to note that whereas the natives in Australia have been exterminated or shunted from the stream of European life, some of the native males find employment as "rough hands" with sheep.[12]

IMPACT OF NEW DISEASES

Contrary to the romantic notion of the "noble savage," whose "innocence" and contact with "nature" had enabled him to escape the diseases of civilized man, the various non-European peoples were subject to diseases before contact with the white man. It is generally accepted that the yellow fever was of African origin and was carried to the New World by the Negro slaves. Nevertheless, it is true that one of the worst consequences of the contacts of Europeans with native people was the spreading of new diseases among the latter by the whites. In the conquest of Hispaniola and other West Indian islands by the Spanish, the new European diseases were as devastating as the firearms of the white men.

11 See Griffith Taylor, *Australia: A Study of Warm Environments and Their Effect on British Settlement* (London: Methuen & Co., Ltd., 1940) , pp. 306 ff.
12 *Ibid.*, p. 424.

The Indians on the mainland of North America were also subject to the devastating effects of European diseases. It is possible that the plague which destroyed so many Indians before the arrival of the Pilgrim fathers had spread southward as the result of the Indians' contacts with Europeans who followed upon the discoveries of Cabot along the Newfoundland banks.[13] Among the most fatal diseases was smallpox which carried off thousands in Massachusetts. As the Europeans spread westward, their advance was marked by great epidemics of smallpox and measles. Although there may have been some tuberculosis before the coming of the white man, the disease acquired epidemic proportions as the result of contacts with whites. Throughout the period of contacts with whites there were periodic epidemics which destroyed tribes from coast to coast. Syphilis was also responsible for the decimation of the Indian population. After the Indian was confined to reservations, the European diseases continued to take their toll. The number of Indians declined as the result of measles, diphtheria, and tuberculosis in addition to bad rations and condemned foodstuffs.[14]

The Negroes who were brought to the United States as slaves became subject to a number of European diseases, of which tuberculosis and syphilis made greatest inroads on the Negro population. Although reliable data on the health of the Negro during slavery do not exist, there is evidence that because of his isolation during this period these diseases were not as widespread as during the decades following emancipation. For example, during the Civil War, of the 315,620 white and 25,828 colored recruits examined, those rejected for tuberculosis amounted to 11.4 per 1,000 for the whites and 4.2 per 1,000 for the Negroes.[15]

[13] A. Grenfell Price, *White Settlers and Native Peoples* (Cambridge: At the University Press, 1950), p. 10–11.

[14] Wissler, *Indians of the United States*, p. 82.

[15] S. J. Holmes, *The Negro's Struggle for Survival* (Berkeley: University of California Press, 1937), p. 75.

It should be noted, however, that although the incidence of tuberculosis was lower among Negro recruits than among white recruits, the death rate among Negro soldiers was four times as high as among white soldiers.

After emancipation the incidence of tuberculosis and respiratory diseases among Negroes and the deaths resulting from these diseases increased to such an extent that one student of the Negro concluded that these diseases would result in the extinction of the race.[16] Likewise, syphilis became a scourge among Negroes as the result of their mobility and the social disorganization following emancipation. Not until the second decade of the twentieth century did it appear that these two diseases among Negroes were being brought under control.

In Mexico and the countries of Central America the advent of the Spaniard resulted in the spread of European diseases among the Indians. Since the Indian had not developed an immunity to measles and smallpox, these new diseases had devastating consequences. It is reported that whole communities were wiped out as the result of the diseases brought by the Spaniards. In South America the Indians suffered the same consequences of Spanish conquest. They were constantly ravaged by European diseases for which they had developed no immunity. Smallpox carried by prospectors and missionaries helped to depopulate the Amazon Valley.[17] In Brazil the imported Negro slaves as well as the Indians became the victims of European diseases.

The history of the conquest and settlement of Australia and New Zealand shows that, as in other parts of the world, European contact resulted in the spread of tuberculosis, influenza, measles, smallpox, and venereal dis-

---

[16] Frederick L. Hoffman, *Race Traits and Tendencies of the American Negro* (New York: The Macmillan Co., 1896), p. 329.

[17] Gourou, *op. cit.*, p. 145.

eases.[18] Since the natives of these islands, like the Indians in the Americas, had not developed an immunity to these diseases, they often succumbed in large numbers while the whites suffered only slight effects. Since European males have been the forerunners in the conquest and settlement of areas inhabited by non-European peoples, the spread of European venereal diseases has been an inevitable consequence of initial race and culture contacts. For example, Captain Cook left a record of his efforts to prevent the crews of his ships from introducing venereal diseases among the Hawaiians. He wrote:

The order not to permit the crews of the boats to go on shore was issued, that I might do everything in my power to prevent the importation of a fatal disease into this island, which I knew some of our men laboured under, and which unfortunately, had been already communicated by us to other islands in these seas. With this same view, I ordered all female visitors to be excluded from our ships.[19]

But from Captain Cook's reports it appears that he did not succeed in restraining his crew, who possessed little knowledge of the fatal consequences of venereal diseases and who felt no responsibility toward native peoples. Throughout the Pacific, European contact resulted in the decimation of the native populations by European diseases. For example, in 1875, 40,000 died on the Fiji Islands as the result of measles introduced by the crew of a European ship.[20] In Hawaii approximately a tenth of the population died in 1848 and 1849 as the result of epidemics of measles, whooping cough, influenza, and diarrhea, and in 1853–4 nearly 2,500 died from smallpox alone.[21] In

18 Price, *op. cit.*, 117–21.
19 *A Voyage to the Pacific Ocean,* prepared under the direction of Captains Cook, Clerke, and Gore (London: W. and A. Strahan, 1784) , I, 96.
20 Gourou, *op. cit.*, p. 145.
21 Andrew W. Lind, *An Island Community* (Chicago: University of Chicago Press, 1938) , p. 98.

fact, one of the chief legacies of the Europeans throughout the islands of the Pacific has been the diseases which they introduced among the natives.[22]

In Africa the native population also was affected by the diseases brought by the white man. For example, the Hottentot population was drastically reduced as the result of the outbreak of smallpox in 1713. Venereal diseases introduced by the European have spread among the African population in tropical Africa. The impact of European diseases had a less disastrous effect upon the older civilizations of Asia since contacts with Europeans were restricted on the whole to the ports.

INTRODUCTION OF FIREARMS

Not only did the Europeans introduce diseases among native peoples. They also introduced firearms, which probably had as disastrous an effect upon native peoples as the new diseases. When the English first settled in Virginia in 1607, anyone teaching Indians to use firearms or selling them firearms was subject to the death penalty.[23] But it appears that the law was constantly broken and that Indians were taught to use firearms and were employed as hunters. Attempts in the other colonies to prevent the Indians from learning the use of arms failed likewise in their purpose.[24] The introduction of firearms among the Indians changed the nature of warfare among them. Because the Indians acquired firearms the Iroquois were able to crush other tribes. As the use of firearms spread among the Indian tribes and nations, warfare became more devastating. In North America the French, the English, and the Americans provided their Indian allies with arms with the result

[22] Douglas L. Oliver, *The Pacific Islands* (Cambridge: Harvard University Press, 1951), *passim.*

[23] William C. Macleod, *The American Indian Frontier* (New York: Alfred A. Knopf, Inc., 1928), p. 319.

[24] *Ibid.,* pp. 309, 312.

that they exhausted or destroyed each other.[25] Moreover, the Indians destroyed the fur-bearing and other animals and thereby impoverished themselves. In Latin America, where the Europeans subjugated the Indians with firearms, the natives did not learn to use them for their own destruction.[26]

The natives of Australia and Tasmania, who were practically exterminated by the European settlers, never had an opportunity to learn the use of firearms. On the other hand, the Maori on the neighboring islands of New Zealand used firearms with devastating effect in their native wars. In fact, one native chief, who had visited England where he acquired muskets and ammunition, undertook to emulate the achievements of Napoleon. For nearly twenty years he ravaged large areas of the North Island.[27] As a result of the conquests of this chief and other warriors who had acquired firearms, there was a decline in the native population.

The Hawaiians, who placed a high value upon iron in trading with Europeans, generally demanded iron in the form of firearms in order to carry on the bloody wars which were largely responsible for the decline in their population.[28] In Africa, the Arabs as well as the Europeans introduced firearms. However, as the slave trade was developed by Europeans, the natives who engaged in the traffic in slaves were eager to secure firearms in order to carry on more effectively the intertribal wars which provided the slaves. As one African chief stated in the early nineteenth century, "We want three things, powder, ball, and brandy; and we have three things to sell, men, women, and chil-

[25] Price, *op. cit.*, pp. 78–9.
[26] This was due, according to Macleod (*op. cit.*, p. 312) , to the fortunate circumstance that their country was not supplied with fur-bearing animals.
[27] Price, *op. cit.*, pp. 153–4. See also I. L. G. Sutherland, "Maori and Pakeha," in Horace Belshaw (ed.) , *New Zealand* (Los Angeles: University of California Press, 1947) , p 55.
[28] Lind, *op. cit.*, p. 95.

dren." [29] In fact, it was slavery not firearms that was responsible for the decline in the population of Africa. Moreover, Africans never utilized firearms for self-destruction to the same extent as did the Indians in North America. In South Africa, where in the early nineteenth century the advancing European frontiers met the disciplined warriors of the Bantu tribes who were warring among themselves, the natives did not use firearms on a large scale to settle differences among themselves or to resist the advance of the white man.

But in a number of the Pacific islands the introduction of firearms reduced the population and kept the islands in poverty. After firearms were introduced into Fiji, Tonga, and Samoa, these islands became armed camps.[30] It was said that the history of Samoa was a "saturnalia of blood" until the end of the nineteenth century. Likewise in the Solomons and the New Hebrides, the slaughter resulting from the introduction of the musket and later carbines and the repeating Winchester caused a loss of man power and of women and children that affected adversely the future labor supply in these islands.

The introduction of firearms among the peoples who comprised the older civilizations of Asia did not have the same effects as it had on peoples with a preliterate culture. The introduction of firearms was accompanied by other aspects of European technology which changed, of course, the relations of Asians to Europeans. These changes will be included in the discussion of developments in race relations resulting from the changes in the economic relations.

    [29] T. F. Buxton, *The Slave Trade and Its Remedy* (London: John Murray, 1840), p. 280.
    [30] Stephen H. Roberts, *Population Problems of the Pacific* (London: George Routledge & Sons, Ltd., 1927), pp. 66–7.

CHANGES IN FOOD, CLOTHING, AND SHELTER

In considering the changes which have occurred in the food habits of native peoples as the result of contacts with Europeans, we turn first to the effects of the introduction of alcohol among non-European peoples. The Incas had only light beers, while the Mayas, although they fermented corn and the juice of pineapple, did not have a problem of drunkenness. On the other hand, the Aztecs had had to deal with the problem of drunkenness resulting from the use of a powerful alcoholic beverage. After the Spanish conquest, the Aztecs were unable to control the problem and, it is said, the Mexicans became "almost a nation of drunkards." [31] Somewhat similar results followed the introduction of brandy by the Spaniards among the Indians of South America. Although the Spanish government and the missionaries made some attempt to stop or control the consumption of alcohol by the Indians, it is believed that brandy killed more Indians than labor in the mines.

In North America, where the Indians had never known alcohol, the introduction of alcoholic beverages had worse effects than in Mexico and other parts of the Americas. Immediately after alcoholic beverages were introduced, it appears that the Indians acquired an uncontrollable craving for alcohol. As the result of their excessive drinking, they were weakened physically and acquired tuberculosis and lung diseases. Although the chiefs among the Indians recognized the bad effects of alcohol and attempted to control it, their efforts were almost in vain. The opportunity to profit from the sale of alcohol to the Indians encouraged the white traders to violate the laws enacted by the Europeans as well as the regulations inaugurated by the Indians to control the acquisition of al-

[31] See Macleod, *op. cit.*, pp. 28 ff.

cohol. Then, too, both the English and the French used liquor to weaken the Indians who were unfriendly or neutral in the struggle between these two nations for the possession of North America.

As the white frontier advanced in Australia and the neighboring islands, the natives became the victims of alcohol. Especially during the 1840's there was much drunkenness in South Australia, while on Flinders Island and in the city of Hobart, Tasmania, many of the natives suffered from alcoholism.[32] Nearly a hundred years later, it was stated in official reports that the natives in Australia were the victims of alcohol as the result of calculated action on the part of the whites.[33] In the New Hebrides entire districts were depopulated as the result of alcoholism among the natives.[34] In Hawaii, where whole villages were sometimes in a condition of helpless intoxication, the use of alcohol was an important factor, it is said, "in undermining native production and native ability to compete in the economic struggles." [35]

When one turns to Africa, one finds that there also the introduction of alcohol has affected adversely the physical survival of the natives. From the beginning of European contacts with the natives of West Africa, rum was one of the main articles in the slave trade. Moreover, the Negroes were intoxicated in order that they would not resist their enslavers, black or white, and alcohol was used to induce the natives to surrender their right to their lands. The high mortality among the natives on the Gold Coast in the middle of the nineteenth century has been attributed mainly to infant mortality and the enormous consumption of alcohol.[36] During the last decades of the

[32] Price, *op. cit.*, pp. 118, 120.

[33] *Ibid.*, p. 141.

[34] W. H. R. Rivers (ed.) , *Essays on the Depopulation of Melanesia* (Cambridge: At the University Press, 1922) , p. 29.

[35] Lind, *op. cit.*, p. 96.

[36] See R. R. Kuczynski, *Demographic Survey of the British Colonial Empire* (New York: Oxford University Press, Inc., 1948) , I, 475–6.

nineteenth century, there were official reports on the deleterious effects of alcohol on the native population of Kenya,
Swaziland, and Basutoland.[37] Although at the present time
alcohol does not seem to have the same devastating effects
as in the past, it nevertheless has played an important role
in Africa as in other parts of the world in changing the
biological relations of native and European races.

The changes in the plant and animal environment of
native peoples which have resulted from European contacts have affected their sources of food supply and dietary
habits. The advance of the white frontier, as we have seen,
caused the destruction of the buffalo which was the Indian's staff of life. Moreover, many Indians who were dependent upon agriculture were reduced to starvation as
the result of the loss of their lands and the advance of
white civilization. In fact, as it became an established policy of the United States to confine the Indian to reservations, the Indian was doomed to slow starvation for more
than a century.[38] The specific effect of European contacts
upon the dietary habits of non-European people is revealed more clearly in other parts of the world. In Melanesia, for example, the introduction of canned meats and
fish or the substitution of rice and meat for the native veg-
etable diets had a deleterious effect upon the health of
the natives.[39] In Africa, widespread malnutrition among
the natives has resulted from European contact. One of the
primary causes of malnutrition has been the driving of the
natives from their lands and their confinement to areas inadequate for their needs. This has been true, for example,
in the case of the Basuto, a pastoral people in South Africa.[40] European contact has also affected the dietary habits of African peoples by destroying their traditional social
organization which provided the labor and system of culti-

[37] See *ibid.*, II, 25, 69, 215.
[38] Macleod, *op. cit.*, pp. 439 ff.
[39] See Rivers, *op. cit.*, pp. 21, 30. See Roberts, *op. cit.*, p. 68.
[40] See Kuczynski, *op cit.*, II, 69.

vation necessary for securing a proper diet.[41] Moreover,
wherever urban and industrial areas have developed in
Africa, the problem of the malnutrition of the natives has
become acute.[42] In South Africa the urbanized native does
not earn enough to buy the minimum food necessary for a
healthful existence.[43] This aspect of the influence of European contacts upon the dietary habits of native peoples
will be analyzed in more detail in the section of this study
dealing with the economic aspects of race and culture contacts.

In some areas of the world changes in the mode of
dress introduced by Europeans have seemingly affected the
survival of native peoples and therefore should be considered in connection with physical changes. It seems that
among the natives on the islands of the Pacific the adoption of European attire had serious consequences for their
health. According to one observer, "Of all the evil customs introduced by civilization [among the Melanesians]
the wearing of clothes was probably the greatest." [44] The
wearing of European clothes by the natives has had bad effects from the standpoint of both hygiene and health. The
natives adopted European clothes without regard for the
warmth of the body or the exclusion of cold. Often, as the
result of permitting wet clothes to dry on their bodies, they
fell victims to influenza and colds.[45] The adoption of European dress had similar consequences among the Hawaiians.[46] From available sources of information the adoption
of European dress by African natives did not have the
same serious consequences as in the islands of the Pacific.

[41] For one of the most fundamental studies of this broad aspect of
the problem see Audrey I. Richards, *Land, Labour, and Diet in Northern
Rhodesia* (New York: Oxford University Press, 1939).

[42] See Kuczynski, *op. cit.*, I, 10, and I, II, *passim*.

[43] See Ellen Hellmann (ed.), *Handbook on Race Relations in South
Africa* (New York: Oxford University Press, 1949), p. 388.

[44] Rivers, *op. cit.*, p. 7.

[45] *Ibid.*, p. 8.

[46] Lind, *op. cit.*, p. 96.

Nevertheless, the African has generally shown a great craving for European clothes and often he has sweltered in the heavy European clothes which he has worn as an indication of his new status.[47] This is especially true in urban areas where it sometimes happens that worn-out shoes that let in water may be the cause of colds. However, such conditions will be treated under the section dealing with economic conditions.

We turn next to the question of the effects of new types of habitations which have been the consequence of European settlement. In the Pacific, often when the Europeans established plantations, native villages which were located on healthy heights were shifted to swamp lands. This has occurred in Fiji, Hawaii, and New Zealand.[48] In Melanesia, the natives have often abandoned their native type of houses and imitated the European constructions—a change which has contributed to the propagation of tuberculosis among the natives.[49] In Africa, housing has become one of the most serious problems of the natives who have been influenced by European civilization. The inadequate housing of natives who have migrated to urban and industrial centers has been a major factor in the morbidity and mortality of the African.[50] The discussion of this phase of race and culture contacts goes beyond symbiotic relations and will be considered in the section dealing with the economic aspects of race and culture contacts.

However, before analyzing the economic aspects of our problem, we shall consider in the next and final chapter of this part of our study the ecological aspects of race and culture contacts.

[47] See, for example, Richards, *op. cit.*, pp. 216–17.
[48] Roberts, *op. cit.*, p. 84.
[49] Rivers, *op. cit.*, p. 92.
[50] See K. A. Busia, *Report on a Social Survey of Sekondi-Takoradi* (London: Crown Agents for the Colonies, 1950). See also Ellen Hellmann, *Rooiyard, A Sociological Survey of an Urban Slum Yard* (Cape Town: Oxford University Press, 1948).

CHAPTER IV

Ecological Organization and Symbiotic Relations

INTRODUCTION

As we have noted in the Introduction to this book, there are three main areas of race and culture contacts which have come into existence as the result of the economic expansion of Europe: communities composed of both European and non-European peoples; tropical dependencies; and the older civilizations of Asia. These three areas of race and culture contacts have become differentiated both because of climatic conditions, and because of differences in the social organization and social development of the non-European peoples. However, considered from the standpoint of human biology the relations which developed between European and non-European peoples in all these areas became a form of symbiotic relationship. This section of our study is not concerned with symbiotic relations on a world scale, but with the symbiotic relations which developed within smaller areas of contacts. The symbiotic relations within these smaller areas have been conditioned partly by climate and partly by the growth in numbers and distribution of racial and cultural groups with respect to each other. Therefore, in this chapter our analysis will be concerned with the symbiotic relations which have developed within the various colonial areas and within the cities over the world where the phenomena of race and culture contacts are brought into sharp relief. As a first step in analyzing the symbiotic relations in the smaller areas, it is necessary to consider the relation of racial settlement to climate.

RACIAL SETTLEMENT AND CLIMATE

From the beginning of their expansion European peoples realized that climate would limit their settlement. When they attempted to establish themselves in the tropics, they were defeated by diseases and dietary difficulties.[1] As the result of our better understanding of the problem of European settlement, we recognize that these difficulties were related often to maladministration as well as climatic conditions. Thus the problem of racial settlement and climate is extremely complex since the adjustment of Europeans to a tropical climate involves more than what is included in the term climate.[2] Much study has been devoted to this problem and in recent years the results have been analyzed and summarized in a single volume.[3]

The Portuguese, who were especially fitted by their

[1] At the opening of the present century Sir Harry H. Johnston stated that from the standpoint of European settlement there were "three classes of territory into which Africa falls when considered geographically." In North Africa where climatic conditions were not "wholly opposed to healthy European settlement," the competition and numerical strength of the natives prevented European settlement. In tropical Africa, white settlement was impossible. Consequently, there remained only small restricted areas at high altitudes outside the Tropics where white settlement was possible. See *A History of the Colonization of Africa by Alien Races* (Cambridge: At the University Press, 1913), pp. 443–5.

[2] Max. Sorre, *Les Fondements de la géographie humaine* (Paris: Librairie Armond Colin, 1951), I, 94 f.

[3] A. Grenfell Price, *White Settlers in the Tropics* (New York: American Geographic Society, 1939).

"environmental experience and racial history" to establish
colonies in the tropics, failed in the Eastern Hemisphere
whereas they succeeded in the Western Hemisphere. In the
East they not only were compelled to adapt themselves to
a tropical climate, but they were confronted by millions of
colored peoples in densely populated areas. However, the
geographic environment played an important role in their
failure to establish settlements in that their numbers were
constantly reduced by the terrific toll of diseases. Because
of their ignorance of hygiene, thousands died in India and
in Africa from tropical diseases. The Dutch, French, and
British were no more successful than the Portuguese in establishing themselves among the dense colored populations in the tropical areas of the East. The English in India
and Malaya and the Dutch in Java remained numeri-
cally insignificant among teeming millions of colored
peoples.

In the Western Hemisphere the history of European
settlement was different. The Portuguese succeeded in establishing themselves in Brazil, while the Spaniard
founded communities in South America, and the French as
well as the Spanish established communities in the West
Indies. The British founded relatively large communities
in Barbados, Jamaica, and St. Kitts. The British experienced considerable difficulty in establishing permanent
communities because of the ravages of dysentery and yellow
fever. Of the nearly 20,000 British soldiers who were sent in
1796 to the West Indies, 85 per cent died within five years,
many having succumbed to yellow fever. The survival of
the Portuguese in Brazil and of the Spanish in the remainder of South America has been associated with racial mixture on a large scale involving both the Indian and the
Negro. Only in Cuba and Puerto Rico has a large element
of the surviving Spanish population remained unmixed.
In the British West Indies, the European population has

declined over the years while the Negro population has steadily increased.[4]

It is difficult to assess the relative influence of the climatic factor as opposed to economic, social, and political factors in accounting for the failure of Europeans to maintain settlements of significant size in the tropical areas of the Western Hemisphere. The devastating effects of tropical diseases during the early years of attempted settlement were partly the result of the ignorance of hygiene and probably were partly the result of the physical condition of the whites. Moreover, it appears that the dissolute habits of Europeans were partly responsible for their lack of resistance to disease and for their high death rate. The plantation system of agriculture with slave labor, which found a congenial soil in the tropics, was also responsible for the decline of the white population. The plantation system created a small leisure class of whites having nothing in common with the poor whites who were the victims of a system of slave labor. At the same time the plantation was a commercial type of agriculture which tended to exhaust the soil and bring about its own eventual destruction. Political factors also played a part since the West Indies was constantly involved in European wars. In San Domingo the French population was practically exterminated by the revolt of the Negroes.

The progress of science and the development of technology have ushered in an era which has been called the "scientific invasion of the tropics."[5] The development of modern means of transportation has broken down the isolation of the tropics, while the advances in medicine and sanitation have enabled Europeans to cope more efficiently

[4] See Vincent T. Barlow, *A History of Barbados 1625–1685* (Oxford: The Clarendon Press, 1926). See also Lowell J. Ragatz, *The Fall of the Planter Class in the British Caribbean 1763–1833* (New York: The Century Co., 1928).

[5] Price, *op. cit.,* pp. 33 ff.

with tropical diseases. Modern facilities for transportation enable Europeans in the tropics to circumvent the effects of summer rains and to supply themselves with the amenities and the foodstuffs of the European world. During the last quarter of the nineteenth century, a number of discoveries laid the basis for the control of malaria and of trypanosomiasis of cattle, which results from infection by the tsetse fly. About 1900 the great battle against yellow fever began in earnest.

The results of the "scientific invasion of the tropics" have been studied by Price in respect to a number of white settlements.[6] In Florida the European has maintained himself, but he still needs to carry on a fight against malaria and hookworm and to raise the standard of Negro health to the level of his own. The experiment of white settlements in northeastern Queensland, Australia, has made progress, but the results are not conclusive. It seems certain that there is no chance for successful white settlement in the northern arid region of Australia. In the West Indies, despite the fact that white communities can survive in regions of high temperature, the whites cannot withstand the economic competition of Negroes and must therefore be absorbed. However, in Costa Rica the Europeans who have inhabited the plateaus have maintained and expanded their numbers. The only menace to this progress is the prospect of invasion of Negro workers in the lowlands. In Panama the Americans have succeeded in making white settlement possible through the application of medical science, hygiene, and sanitation, as well as through control of housing, clothing, diet, and alcohol. But here, too, the presence of the Negro population, which is increasing, raises doubts as to permanent white settlement.

In some parts of tropical Africa, as for example Nairobi, Salisbury, and Kimberley, the problem of European

6 Price, *op. cit.*, pp. 41–168.

settlement is similar to that of Costa Rica. But in tropical Africa as a whole, European settlement is limited in two ways by climatic conditions: first, climatic factors influence the activity, health, and comfort of Europeans because of the reaction of their bodies to the heat and humidity of the tropics; and secondly, such climatic factors as temperature and rainfall influence the distribution of organisms which are responsible for tropical diseases in men and animals.[7] It appears that, as the result of the advances in medical science, limitations of European settlement due to diseases are more important than those due to heat and humidity. One of the diseases limiting European settlement has been malaria, which is endemic in areas climatically suitable for European settlement. If European settlement were limited to areas free from malaria, it would be restricted to the plateau regions of South Africa and the highlands of Kenya. Much progress has been made in rendering safe for European settlement the areas where anopheles mosquitoes breed.

There remains then, the problem which Europeans face in large areas of Africa in regard to the reaction of their bodies to heat and humidity. In the Sudan and Congo and even in other areas of Africa the European runs the risk of heatstroke. On the basis of studies dealing with this phase of the problem, it is possible to divide the climates in Africa into four types: 1) unsuitable for Europeans throughout the year; 2) unsuitable for a season of eight months' duration; 3) unsuitable for four months; and 4) suitable for more than eight months.[8] Classification of the climatic regions of Africa in this way indicates that there is little chance for extensive European settlement in the tropical areas of Africa. The Congo Basin and much of the upper and lower Guinea coasts are unsuitable for Eu-

[7] S. P. Jackson, "Climate," in South African Institute of International Affairs, *Africa South of the Sahara* (Cape Town: Oxford University Press, 1951) , p. 1.

[8] *Ibid.*, p. 2 ff.

ropeans throughout the year, while the Sudan and the East Coast are unsuitable for eight months of the year.

This survey of materials on the relation of racial settlement and climate indicates that climate has played an important role in determining the location of European peoples in the various parts of the world. However, the need to study the influence of climatic factors in conjunction with economic, political, and social factors is emphasized when the differential growth of non-European and European populations is considered in various parts of the world.

DIFFERENTIAL GROWTH OF EUROPEAN AND NON–EUROPEAN PEOPLES

The favorable climate of the part of North America that became the United States, together with the social organization of the Indians, ensured its settlement by whites. Unlike the Indians who had built the great civilizations of Mexico, Guatemala, and Peru, the Indians of the United States were for the most part seminomadic agriculturalists and food gatherers. The Pueblos in the Southwest had an agricultural culture derived largely from the civilization of Mexico; the Indians of the Central Plains did not practice agriculture but hunted the buffalo and antelope. Along the Gulf of Mexico were located the Creeks and other tribes that engaged in hunting and agriculture. North of this area were the Mound Builders of Ohio, and the Iroquois who formed the League of the Five Nations. In the Far West were found the least developed group of Indians, though there were some exceptional tribes. Consequently, taken as a whole, the Indians had not achieved a political and economic organization that could long withstand the advance of the white settlers.

Although there is considerable doubt concerning estimates of the size of the pre-Columbian Indian population, it is certain that the number of Indians declined considerably after the settlement of the country by whites. According to the most reliable estimates, the Indian population in the United States at present is about one tenth of what it was when the conquest of the continent began.[9] The decrease in the Indian population was due to the disappearance of the buffalo, to the policy of direct extermination of the Indians, and to the restriction of the Indians to reservations. As the result of a more enlightened and humane policy in regard to the Indians, their numbers have shown a steady increase during the last two decades.

In contrast to the Indian population which declined until recent decades and which has been segregated from the white population, Negroes have constantly increased in numbers and have become increasingly dispersed among the whites. During the colonial period the Negro population grew in response to the demand for slave labor to work the rice, indigo, and tobacco plantations in the southern colonies.[10] For a period the slave population of South Carolina outnumbered the whites, but by the time the first federal census was made in 1790, the whites outnumbered the Negroes. At the first census, 40 per cent of the entire Negro population was concentrated in Virginia, while 50 per cent was located in three other southern states—Maryland, North Carolina, and South Carolina. When cotton became the chief commercial crop in the South and the plantation system spread westward, the Negro population followed the course of this expansion.

At the first census Negroes constituted about 20 per cent of the entire American population. Since then, not only has the proportion of Negroes declined, but the Negro rate of increase has been less than that of whites, except for three decades, 1800 to 1810, 1930 to 1940, and

[9] William C. Macleod, *The American Indian Frontier* (New York: Alfred A. Knopf, Inc., 1928), pp. 15–16.

[10] E. Franklin Frazier, *The Negro in the United States* (New York: The Macmillan Co., 1949), pp. 171 ff.

1940 to 1950. During the first period the importation of
Negroes was accelerated in anticipation of outlawing the
slave trade in 1808. The slower rate of urbanization of
Negroes and the decrease in European immigration account for their higher decennial rate of increase during the
last two decades. The greater rate of increase of the white
population has been associated with European immigration on a large scale. At the same time, as we have seen in
the preceding chapter, the greater incidence of disease and
a higher death rate have restricted the increase of the Negro population. Although the proportion of Negroes in
the American population has declined and their rate of
increase has been less than whites, the Negro population
has increased twenty-fold since 1790.

Changes in the distribution of Negroes in the United
States have been tied up with the economic development
of the country and the demand for Negro labor. Until
World War I nine tenths of the Negro population was
concentrated in the South. But the proportion of Negroes
in the total population of the South showed a marked decline from more than a third in 1880 to less than a fourth
in 1950.[11] During this period of 70 years, the so-called
Black Belt decreased in area and in Negro population.
The decline in the proportion of the Negro population in
the South has been partly due to the migration of Negroes
to northern industrial centers beginning with World
War I. Changes in southern agriculture as well as the demand of northern industries have been responsible for
these northward migrations. The migrations of 2,000,000
or more Negroes from the South did not increase signifi-
cantly their proportion in the total population of the
North as measured by any census before 1950, when the
proportion amounted to 5 per cent. The location of war

---

[11] U. S. Bureau of the Census, *U. S. Census of Population: 1950*
(Washington, D.C.: U. S. Government Printing Office, 1953), Vol. II,
Characteristics of the Population, Part I, United States Summary, p. 106.

industries in the West tended to redirect Negro migration during World War II.

Two facts are of primary importance in regard to the number and location of Negroes in the United States. The first is the urbanization of the Negro population which has followed the general trend of urbanization. The mass migrations since World War I have created vast urban Negro communities in the midst of the metropolitan areas of the North. Second, the rate of increase of the Negro population is due partly to the fact that all persons with even remote Negro ancestry are included in the Negro population. The proportion of mulattoes or persons of mixed ancestry increased from 11.2 per cent in 1850 to 20.9 per cent in 1920. Between 1870 and 1890 the number of mulattoes doubled, and it nearly doubled again between 1890 and 1910. The figures for 1920 showed a decline in absolute and relative number of persons of mixed ancestry in the Negro population. While the number of primary crossings probably declined during the later period, the decline can only be explained by attributing it to faulty census enumeration or to the fact that, with the increasing movement of Negroes to cities, especially to northern cities, mulattoes have "passed" for white or have become a part of the white population. In fact, there are indications that not only has the latter occurred but also that intermarriage between Negroes and whites has increased in recent years as the result of urbanization.

In Mexico the 30,000 Negroes who were brought in to work on the sugar plantations have gradually been absorbed in the Mexican population.[12] The large percentage of mixed bloods or mestizos is due to the facts that the Spanish population was partly absorbed by Indians and that few whites have entered Mexico since its independence. San Salvador, to the south of Mexico, has a larger

[12] See Gonzalo A. Beltrán, *La Poblacion Negra de Mexico, 1519–1810* (Mexico, D.F.: Ediciones Fuente Cultural, 1940) .

percentage of mixed bloods, while the pure Indian population has become predominantly Spanish in culture. The pure or near pure Spanish population, which amounts to about 8 per cent, constitutes a sort of aristocracy from the standpoint of wealth and political power. Guatemala is essentially a nation of Indians since the majority of the population is of pure Indian descent with a minority of mixed Indians and white ancestry having political ascendancy. Nearly three fourths of the population of Honduras is of mixed Indian and white ancestry while Negroes constitute less than 10 per cent of the population. In Honduras, the political control of the country is in the hands of the white minority. Although the Indian population of Nicaragua was reduced considerably during the Spanish conquest, nearly four fifths of the population is of mixed Indian and white ancestry. The small, pure Indian population along with the Negroes, who were introduced because of banana culture, constitutes about a tenth of the population. Costa Rica differs from these other countries in that the small original Indian population was absorbed or deported to Peru and Panama. The whites were too poor to import Negroes and, therefore, worked the land themselves in an area which has a cool and healthful climate.[13] Panama also shows certain distinctive characteristics from the standpoint of population. Like the other Central American countries it has a large proportion of mixed bloods, about 50 per cent, but Negroes constitute nearly a third of the population, with pure Indians amounting to only 10 per cent. In the Canal Zone Negroes comprise about 70 per cent of the population. In Panama as well as the Canal Zone the majority of these Negroes are of West Indian origin and were introduced as laborers in the construction of the Canal.

When Europeans first settled in Australia there were, according to estimates, close to 300,000 aborigines. At the

[13] Price, *op. cit.*, p. 123.

present time there are about 52,000 aborigines of unmixed blood and 26,000 half-castes or mixed bloods.[14] The decline in the aboriginal population has been due largely, as we have seen, to a policy of extermination carried out by the whites. There are indications of a continued decline in the unmixed native population while the number of half-castes is increasing. During this period of decline in the native population, the European population has increased to more than 7,000,000. In recent decades the European population has increased as the result of the immigration of Italian and other non-British peoples.[15]

In New Zealand, as the result of European contact, the Maori population first underwent a period of decline for several reasons: [16] the spread of European diseases and drunkenness among the natives; intertribal wars as well as wars between natives and Europeans which were all the more devastating as the result of the introduction of firearms; and finally, a land policy which robbed the natives of their lands on a large scale. During the period of native decline the Maori population was reduced from an estimated 200,000 to less than 40,000 where it remained until the first decade of the twentieth century. From 1906 onward the Maori population showed an increase. Between 1906 and 1936 it increased from 50,000 to 82,000, and in 1947 it had reached more than 100,000. This increase was associated with the isolation of the Maori population, with the institution of an educational system suited to the culture of the natives, and with a program of housing, health, and sanitation. During the period of growth of the Maori population, the increase in the number of mixed bloods was greater than that among the full bloods.

[14] A. Grenfell Price, *White Settlers and Native Peoples* (Cambridge: At the University Press, 1950) , pp. 99–101.
[15] See Griffith Taylor, *Australia: A Study of Warm Environments and Their Effect on British Settlement* (London: Methuen and Co., Ltd., 1947) , pp. 425 ff.
[16] See Price, *op. cit.,* Chaps. VIII, IX.

When one turns to South Africa, where the population is composed of Europeans, natives (Bantu), the Coloured group, and Asians, one is struck by "the stability of their relative numerical strength." [17] From 1904 to 1946 Europeans constituted about 21 per cent of the total population, while the proportion of natives remained about 68 per cent. Likewise, the Coloured group remained about 8 per cent and the Asians between 2 and 3 per cent. During the entire period the relative increase in the entire non-European population was only 1 per cent. From the standpoint of numbers, the European population increased from 1,116,806 to 2,335,460 or more than doubled during these years, the increase having been due primarily to natural increase despite the immigration of Europeans. The native population showed a similar rate of increase (from 3,491,-056 to 7,735,809) though there is reason to believe that more thorough enumerations in recent censuses account partly for the rate of native increase. There are even greater difficulties involved in knowing the real increase in the Coloured group because of the phenomenon of passing into the European population and the existence of race mixture without as well as within marriage. According to the available statistics, the Coloured group increased from 445,228 in 1904 to 905,050 in 1946. The Asian group, which numbered 122,734 in 1904 and which increased rapidly between 1904 and 1911, numbered 282,539 in 1946. We shall have occasion to refer to the numerical strength of these racial elements in the African population during the succeeding sections of this study.

We shall turn now to the demographic aspects of race and culture contacts in the tropical areas of Africa, Southeast Asia, and the Pacific Isles.

Although the native African population did not suffer from the introduction of European diseases to the same

[17] See Ellen Hellmann (ed.), *Handbook on Race Relations in South Africa* (New York: Oxford University Press, Inc., 1949), pp. 9–26.

extent as the natives in the Pacific and America, there is reason to believe that the native population declined as the result of European contact during the eighteenth and nineteenth centuries.[18] According to official censuses and estimates, in Africa south of the Sahara there are around 110,000,000 Africans, about 500,000 Europeans, and 250,-000 Asians including Arabs.[19] In view of the incomplete censuses, it is difficult to know whether the African population is increasing.[20] In fact, it has been stated that growth in the native population has been prevented by the high mortality resulting from the spread of diseases.[21]

The largest concentration of Europeans is in Southern Rhodesia where they number more than 100,000. This represents an increase of 100 per cent since 1936 in the European population which regards the country as its home. These Europeans draw their living not only from mining, in which many natives are employed, but also from farming, which is concentrated in the high veld plateau.[22] On the other hand, in Northern Rhodesia where the economy is based upon copper mining, there is a European population of less than 50,000. The Portuguese colony of Angola contains the second largest concentration of Europeans outside the Union of South Africa. The European population, numbering about 45,000 as compared with a native population of nearly 4,000,000 has not increased much in spite of encouragement by the Portuguese government. The European population of Mozambique is about one half that of Angola, and the native population is about

[18] See A. M. Carr-Saunders, *World Population* (Oxford: Clarendon Press, 1936), p. 301.

[19] See South African Institute of International Affairs, *Africa South of the Sahara* (Cape Town: Oxford University Press, 1951), Appendix A, "Population Table."

[20] See Carr-Saunders, *op. cit.*, p. 302. See also R. R. Kuczynski, *Demographic Survey of the British Colonial Empire* (New York: Oxford University Press, Inc., 1948), I, pp. 2–5.

[21] See Carr-Saunders, *loc. cit.*

[22] Lord Malcolm Hailey, *An African Survey* (New York: Oxford University Press, Inc., 1938), p. 1380.

5,000,000. Although the European population in the Belgian Congo has nearly tripled since 1935, its numerical significance is small (76,000) as compared with a native population of 10,000,000 or more. Europeans are also found in significant numbers in the highlands of Kenya (about 30,000) and in Tanganyika (about 16,000). In both of these territories the Asian population outnumbers the Europeans. There is only a sprinkling of Europeans in the remaining English and French territories in Africa south of the Sahara. There are about 9,000 Europeans, for example, in Nigeria, and about the same number in French Ivory Coast.

When one turns to Southeast Asia, which is entirely tropical, one finds a situation similar to tropical Africa in regard to the numerical relations of Europeans and native races. In Netherland East Indies there are somewhat less than 280,000 Europeans in a native population numbering nearly 70,000,000. But probably 80 per cent of these Europeans are Eurasians since the mixed bloods are classified as Europeans.[23] In addition to the European population there are 1,500,000 Chinese and 133,000 other Asians. In Malaya the population doubled between 1911 and 1939 but this increase was due largely to immigration. There are only 18,000 Europeans in a population of nearly 2,500,000, of which the native Malayans form only 42 per cent while the Chinese form 43 per cent and the Indians 14 per cent. In Indo-China and the islands of Southeast Asia, the Europeans are negligible from the standpoint of numbers. Under the Spaniards, who were inconsequential in number, the native population of the Philippine Islands increased rapidly until 1877, and after the American occupation it doubled in thirty-five years.

In tropical Oceania the native population suffered a decline as the result of white contact. According to the best

[23] Warren S. Thompson, *Population and Peace in the Pacific* (Chicago: University of Chicago Press, 1940), pp. 253-4.

estimates the total population of these islands, which numbered 3,500,000 when the white man arrived, is about 2,700,000 at the present time.[24] The native population of Polynesia declined from more than 1,000,000 to 180,000 in 1890 and then rose to 330,000 in 1938. In Micronesia, composed of the Carolines, Marshalls, and Marianas, the native population declined from an estimated 200,000 at the end of the eighteenth century to 80,000 by 1900. During this period the native population in New Guinea and neighboring islands extending as far east as Fiji declined from about 2,200,000 to about 1,200,000 but had increased to about 1,400,000 in 1939. However, on a number of islands in the Polynesian group it appears that the native population is still declining. The nonnative population in tropical Oceania numbers about 700,000, of whom 230,000 are Japanese. There are about 98,000 Indians (in Fiji), 52,000 Filipinos (in Hawaii), and 40,000 Chinese (nearly three fourths of whom are in Hawaii). There are about 142,000 whites, nearly three fourths of whom are in Hawaii. The remainder of the nonwhite population consists largely of mixed bloods and some Malayans and people from Indo-China.

In Hawaii, where the coming of the whites marked the beginning of the decline of the native population, the tide of native decline was stemmed by the emergence of a part-Hawaiian population.[25] The native Hawaiian population declined steadily from 300,000 in 1778 to less than 70,000 in 1853. Then there began a native revival, largely as the result of the increasing number of offspring of native women and foreign men. However, the decline in the pure native stock continued until the beginning of the present century when there set in a revival which is continuing today. At the present time these pure Hawaiians constitute

[24] See Thompson, *op. cit.*, pp. 36–7.
[25] See Andrew W. Lind, *An Island Community* (Chicago: University of Chicago Press, 1938), pp. 24 ff.

about 3 per cent and the part-Hawaiian about 15 per cent of the total population. Japanese make up little more than a third of the total population and Caucasians about 25 per cent. The Filipino population which increased from 2,400 in 1910 to 63,000 in 1930 declined to 53,000 or 13 per cent of the total in 1940. The Chinese population, which constitutes about 7 per cent of the population, has increased more slowly. The remainder of the Hawaiian population includes Koreans, Puerto Ricans, and Portuguese.

All three of the countries included under the older civilizations of Asia, that is, India, China, and Japan, have experienced an increase in population during the past hundred years. When the first census was taken in India in 1872, the returns showed a population of 203,000,000, though there is reason to believe that the correct figure was about 256,000,000.[26] By 1941 the population of India had reached nearly 400,000,000. Although it is more difficult to secure reliable figures on the population of China, it appears certain that its present population of 350,000,000 to 450,000,000 reflects a growth over the past century.[27] The population of Japan, for which reliable figures are available, began to increase rapidly after 1872, rising from 32,000,000 in that year to 73,000,000 in 1940.[28] While the increase in the populations of these countries has relevance for the ecology of race and culture contacts, its principal significance is that it has affected the "political geography" of the world by changing the man-power relations of the European and non-European peoples.[29] Moreover, as these countries attempt to solve their economic problems, they threaten such areas reserved for white settlements as Australia and New Zealand. Therefore, the relations of these

26 Thompson, *op. cit.*, p. 219.
27 *Ibid.*, pp. 177–8.
28 *Ibid.*, pp. 94.
29 See Quincy Wright, "Population Trends and International Relations," in Hans W. Weigert and Vilhjamar Stefansson (eds.), *Compass of the World* (New York: The Macmillan Co., 1945), pp. 408–28.

older civilizations to European peoples are of special importance in the sections of our study dealing with the economic and political aspects of race and culture contacts.

This brief summary of the differential growth of European and non-European peoples indicates that in areas where climate and economic opportunity have been favorable to permanent white settlement, the white population has grown more rapidly than the colored population, as in the United States, Australia, and New Zealand, or has multiplied at the same rate as the non-European population, as in South Africa. In the case of Australia, however, the political factor has enabled the white population to multiply without competing with the Asian. In Mexico and Central America where Europeans encountered a settled Indian population and Negro slaves were imported to work plantations, a measurement of the differential growth is impossible since the relatively small European population has become racially mixed to a great extent. An exception to this pattern is found in Costa Rica, where the white population, due to its settlement in the highlands, has remained unmixed.

In the tropical regions the native colored populations diminished at first as the result of European contact. These non-European populations have shown signs of increase in recent years as uncontrolled economic exploitation of native peoples has diminished and the native peoples themselves have offered greater resistance to exploitation. This is especially marked in tropical Africa where the native peoples have not only benefited from the advanced medical knowledge, improved sanitation, and increased agricultural productivity brought by whites; but also an indigenous nationalism has been created among them. Only in the highlands of East Africa, where the white man has found a congenial environment, have the European peoples increased in sufficiently large numbers to create the problems inherent in a biracial community.

ECOLOGICAL BASIS OF RACE RELATIONS

On the basis of our discussion in this chapter and in those preceding it, we shall attempt to show the ecological basis of race relations and their essentially symbiotic character. This phase of race and culture contacts may logically be considered the first stage in their development. The ecological basis of race relations is concerned with the manner in which the relations of men to their environment determine relationship patterns which develop between men with different racial and cultural backgrounds.[30] Although the adjustment of men to their environment is always achieved in terms of a cultural heritage, it happens that when men with different racial and cultural backgrounds confront each other, the accommodation which is established between them is on a physical and biological plane. Superior technology in warfare and biological adaptation to the geographical environment become decisive factors in the conflict which generally arises. The symbiotic nature of their relations is indicated by the spatial separation of their habitations and the "subsocial" character of the competition which develops between them. Although we are dealing with a stage or phase of race relations which may be considered an "ideal type" relationship, this is nevertheless necessary if one would gain a clear conception of the nature of race and culture contacts.

Beginning with those areas of the world where people with different racial and cultural backgrounds have been brought together in the same community, we may see how the ecology of race relations is revealed in the spatial distribution of their habitations. In the West Indies, where

[30] See James A. Quinn, *Human Ecology* (New York: Prentice-Hall, Inc., 1950), Chaps. I, II. See also Everett Cherrington Hughes and Helen MacGill Hughes, *Where Peoples Meet* (Glencoe: The Free Press, 1952), Chap. IV.

African slaves supplanted the native Indian population that was annihilated, European settlements arose about the "great house," which was often an imposing structure on an elevation facing the sea.[31] In Latin America generally, the distribution of Spanish settlements was determined by the location of the Indian population since for the Spaniards, whose chief motivation in the New World was "Greed, Gold, and God," the sedentary Indians possessed the treasures which they sought.[32] However, variations in the pattern of racial settlement may be found in particular countries owing to topographical features and economic factors. In Mexico, where an overwhelming majority of the population is Indian, the Spaniards settled first in Guadalajara and Mexico City in the Mexican Highlands.[33] From the first of these two centers, the Spaniards spread out "northwestward along the Pacific Coast into the southwest of what is now the United States," and from Mexico City they spread to various parts of Latin America and even to the Philippine Islands. On the other hand, in Costa Rica, where Indians could not be employed as laborers on the haciendas, an unmixed Spanish population occupied the highlands on the Pacific side and became farm owners. In the lowlands on the Caribbean side, the Spaniards managed the plantations worked by Jamaican Negroes.[34] The settlement of Brazil by the Portuguese was carried out in three regions, each of which owed its importance to one of Brazil's three chief products—sugar, gold, and coffee.[35] The importation of Negro slaves and their settlement in the northwest of Brazil and in Minas Gerais were for the production of sugar in the former and of gold in the latter region. The production of coffee was re-

---

[31] Ragatz, *op. cit.*, pp. 5 f.
[32] Preston E. James, *Latin America* (New York: The Odyssey Press, Inc., 1942) , p. 14.
[33] *Ibid.*, p. 591.
[34] *Ibid.*, pp. 706–7.
[35] *Ibid.*, p. 401.

sponsible for a new migration of Europeans—Italians, Portuguese, Spaniards, and Germans—to southern Brazil and for the rise of the city of São Paulo, which has become today the leading manufacturing center in Brazil.

The growth and spread of the Negro population in the southern part of the United States was in response, first, to the demand for labor on tobacco, indigo, and rice plantations and later to the advance of the "Cotton Kingdom" towards the southwest.[36] The Black Belt which came into existence became the basis of a broad pattern of race relations which has continued to the present time. Included in the general pattern of race relations was the distribution of Negroes who were free before the Civil War. These Negroes, who owed their freedom largely to the decline of the plantation system, were concentrated in the upper South and in cities.

It is in the studies of American cities that the ecological basis of Negro-white relations have been most clearly revealed.[37] In the older cities of the South the location of the Negro population is the result of historical factors. The Negro communities are the outgrowth of the Negro quarters which were located near the dwellings of the white planters. On the other hand, the location of the Negro communities in northern cities, and in fact in the newer cities of the South, is due to economic factors inherent in the growth of these cities. Negroes and other

[36] Frazier, *op. cit.*, pp. 30 ff.

[37] Of the numerous studies which have been made, the following may be cited: Robert E. Park, "The Urban Community as a Spacial Pattern and a Moral Order," in Ernest W. Burgess (ed.) , *The Urban Community* (Chicago: University of Chicago Press, 1926) , pp. 3–18. Ernest W. Burgess, "The Determination of Gradients in the Growth of the City," *Publications of the American Sociological Society*, XXI (1927) , 178–84. Ernest W. Burgess, "Residential Segregation in American Cities," *The Annals of the American Academy of Political Social Science*, CXL (November 1928) . Robert D. McKenzie, *The Metropolitan Community* (New York: McGraw-Hill Book Co., 1933) . E. Franklin Frazier, "Negro Harlem: An Ecological Study," *The American Journal of Sociology*, XLIII (July 1937) , 72–88. E. Franklin Frazier, *The Negro in the United States*, Chap. XI.

racial groups have settled in the "vulnerable" areas of cities—vulnerable in the sense that they are no longer residential areas and that the rentals are low. The Negro communities have expanded as the cities have expanded, and the Negro has found a dwelling place that fits his economic circumstances. Conflicts have occurred when his increasing numbers and his demand for housing have met the resistance of white neighborhoods. This has been, in brief, the history of the Negro settlements in relation to the ecological organization of American cities. From these areas in which European and non-European peoples are part of a single community, let us turn to the tropical areas where Europeans have settled in small numbers.

Europeans form, in the tropical areas where they have settled, only small enclaves among the native peoples. They are generally concentrated in coastal cities which are centers of administration, and from these cities they control the commerce and other forms of economic life introduced by the Europeans. In French West Africa, they are concentrated in Dakar, and in French Equatorial Africa, in Brazzaville. Likewise, in British West Africa the European population is to be found mainly in Accra and Lagos. Or if one turns to Southeast Asia, one finds that the Europeans and Eurasians, who together form 1 per cent of the Malayan population, are concentrated on Singapore Island.[38] In the islands of the Pacific, the Europeans, who still look to Europe as their home, occupy the healthiest areas and are more or less segregated from the native population. An exceptional situation exists in Honolulu, Hawaii, where the dissolution of the various racial ghettoes, which once formed the ecological basis of race relations, is indicative of the new social organization, with its new indigenous culture, which is emerging.[39]

[38] See E. H. G. Dobby, *Southeast Asia* (New York: John Wiley and Sons, Inc., 1951) , p. 136.
[39] See Lind, *op. cit.*, pp. 308 ff.

We come finally to South Africa where an attempt is being made to change through political means the spatial pattern of race relations which has grown up. Here we are interested in the spatial pattern only as a phase of the ecological basis of race relations; we shall postpone to a later chapter an analysis of the political attempt to change this pattern. South Africa is a country in the temperate zone in which Boer, English, Hottentot, Bushmen, Bantu, and Indians have struggled to survive. During this struggle the Bushmen were hunted as wild beasts and driven into the desert while the Hottentots became a dying race. The advance of Boers in search of water and grass brought them into conflict with the Bantu who sought the same sources of existence.[40] Then in the closing years of the eighteenth century came the English with their ideas of freedom. Their attempt to apply these ideas by keeping white and black apart failed. Each advance of the European frontier failed to drive the Bantu away; each advance ended in making him a settler on European farms. The Great Trek of the Boers beyond British control only established new racial frontiers and made impossible the separation of white and black.[41] The introduction of Indian laborers on the sugar plantations of Natal added to the complexity of the racial pattern of South Africa.

The pattern of racial settlement was finally determined by industrialization and urbanization. The diamond fields changed the competition of whites and blacks for land and cattle into competition for a place in industry.[42] Then came the gold rush on the Rand which made Johannesburg the largest city in Africa. Before 1923 the native population was ignored; but in that year an act was passed to segregate Europeans and natives.[43] Despite sub-

[40] See C. W. DeKiewiet, *A History of South Africa* (New York: Oxford University Press, Inc., 1946) , pp. 24 ff.
[41] *Ibid.*, pp. 56 ff.
[42] *Ibid.*, p. 89.
[43] Hellmann, *op. cit.*, p. 229 ff.

sequent acts the natives continued to enter Johannesburg and other cities. By 1946 nearly 1,800,000 natives were in the cities of the Union of South Africa. Of the 371,000 natives in Johannesburg, 90,000 were in locations, 53,000 in native areas, and 11,000 in municipal hostels. However, within the city were 69,000 domestic servants and 38,000 housed on employers' premises. The dynamic nature of the economic life of South Africa had nullified attempts to exclude natives from cities while urbanization was even reducing the segregation of the 3,000,000 or more Africans on reserves.

The differential growth of European and non-European population, as we have seen, is another aspect of the ecology of race relations. Therefore, it will not be necessary to restate the situation in the different areas of the world. It is, however, necessary to make more precise this phase of the ecological processes involved in race and culture contacts. The differential growth of European and non-European people is constantly changing as the result of economic and social factors. The cessation of native wars may cause an increase in the native population, but this may be offset by the introduction of new diseases and changes in dietary habits. Or the introduction of hygienic and sanitary measures reduces the death rate of native peoples; while at the same time their employment in industries may increase their death rate, and urbanization may decrease their birth rate. All of these factors are a part of the ecology of race relations. The ecological process also involves a racial division of labor, discussion of which belongs in the next section on economic organization of race relations.

In concluding this chapter, which also concludes the first part of our study, it is necessary to bring to a clear focus the nature of human relationships which develop out of the purely ecological organization of race and culture contacts. The ecological organization forms a "symbiotic substructure" upon which the higher levels—economic, political, and cultural—of the existing society rest.[44] On this level or in this stage of race and culture contacts, the relations between members of different groups are subsocial in the sense that they do not regard or treat each other as human. The competition which exists between them is without legal, or customary, or moral restraints. In the conflicts which arise between them, the struggle is on a biological plane without codes or moral regulations. This stage of relationships is summed up in such statements as "the only good Indian is a dead Indian," or "the only good Bushman is a dead Bushman." This type of relation exists not only between Europeans and pre-literate natives. It is also characteristic of the relations between Europeans and the peoples of the older civilizations of Asia. The terrorism of Da Gama against the people of India and his burning of Moors alive were justified on the ground that the right to navigate the seas belonged only to Europeans.[45] Even as late as 1870, the President of the Hong Kong Chamber of Commerce declared: "China can in no sense be considered a country entitled to all the same rights and privileges as civilized nations which are bound by international law." [46]

From the ecological organization of race relations we shall turn in the next section of this study to the types of economic organization which result from race and culture contacts.

[44] See "Human Ecology," in Robert E. Park, *Human Communities* (Glencoe: The Free Press, 1952), p. 157.

[45] K. M. Pannikar, *Asia and Western Dominance* (New York: The John Day Book Co., n.d.), p. 42.

[46] Quoted in *ibid.*, p. 43.

Economic Organization

CHAPTER V

From Barter to Slavery

INTRODUCTION

In chapter II we have seen the role of barter or the exchange of goods in the symbiotic relations which developed between European and non-European peoples during the initial stage of contacts. In this chapter we shall go more deeply into the nature of barter which involved, as we shall see, not only the exchange of goods for goods but also the exchange of goods for labor. In the exchange of European goods for the labor of the natives one can see the transition from the initial stage of race and culture contacts to the second stage during which organized economic relations emerged. The transition was, in fact, the process by which the system of barter developed into a system of slavery in response to the demand for a continuous and disciplined labor force. This process in Brazil has been analyzed in a study which has provided the title of this chapter.[1] However, the process has not been characteristic solely of race and culture contacts in Brazil; it may be re-

[1] Alexander Marchant, *From Barter to Slavery* (Baltimore: The Johns Hopkins Press, 1942).

garded as typical of a phase of race and culture contacts in other parts of the world.

BARTER AMONG FREE MEN

It was not long after the discovery of Brazil in 1500 that Portuguese traders began to occupy points along the Brazilian coasts.[2] As agents of the Crown these traders had come to Brazil to secure brazilwood, which provided a dye-stuff similar to that which was used in the production of textiles in Europe. Almost from the beginning they had to compete with the French who also recognized the value of brazilwood. In a country lacking animals that could be used for transporting the brazilwood, which was heavy as well as hard, both the French and the Portuguese were dependent upon the native Indians for labor. From the available records of the French and Portuguese ships which were engaged in the brazilwood trade, one learns that the European traders exchanged trinkets and, what was more important, cutting tools for the brazilwood which was cut and loaded on their ships. In addition to securing brazil-wood, the Portuguese obtained food and other wares from the Indians through barter. Through the system of barter, as Marchant points out, the European received not only the material objects—brazilwood, food, and other wares—but also the labor of the Indians.[3] As a consequence, the Portuguese who came later to Brazil faced two possibilities in dealing with the natives: 1) the exchange of goods for goods; 2) the exchange of goods for labor. The latter possibility provided the means for inducing the Indians to cultivate crops in exchange for goods, and it led, as we shall see, to the establishment of slavery.

In Spanish America the period of barter between the Europeans and Indians involving the exchange of goods for goods was of short duration. According to European

---

[2] *Ibid.,* pp. 28 ff.   [3] *Ibid.,* p. 47.

political theories that were current when the Spaniards entered the New World, they did not come as conquerors but as pacifiers of a region which had been granted to the Spanish crown by the Pope.[4] Therefore, it was only necessary to inform the Indians that they were the subjects of the Spanish crown, and if they refused to acknowledge the Spaniards as their overlords, they were guilty of treason. Within two years after the arrival of Columbus, the island of Haiti was pacified and each adult Indian was required to pay a stipulated head tax to the crown. Indians who could not pay the tax in goods were required to work for the Spanish colonists who paid the tax. In the face of the growing demand for Indian labor, the colonists were not satisfied with this arrangement and soon the Indians were organized into labor gangs.

In Australia, the natives, who were hunters and fishermen, could not be disciplined for agricultural labor; consequently the transition from barter to slavery did not occur. The conflict which developed between the Europeans and the natives ended in the partial extermination of the latter. There was a brief period of barter with the natives on New Zealand which included the trading of "tools, hatchets, and large nails" for the wives and daughters of the natives. However, as we have seen in chapter III, the advancing European frontiers in New Zealand dispossessed the natives of their lands and resulted in bloody wars which left the Maoris impoverished and demoralized.[5] In South Africa, which also became an area of European settlement, the initial contacts between Europeans and the native Hottentots involved a system of barter. However, when the Dutch colonists sought a cheap and disciplined labor supply, they had to turn to the Dutch colonies in India and to the West African slave markets. In this re-

[4] William C. Macleod, *The American Indian Frontier* (New York: Alfred A. Knopf, Inc., 1928), pp. 69 ff.

[5] A. Grenfell Price, *White Settlers and Native Peoples* (Cambridge: The University Press, 1950), p. 153.

spect they followed a course similar to that of the European colonists in what became the southern states of the United States.

The system of barter which characterized the initial contacts of Europeans and natives in the tropical areas of the world where white settlement was impossible did not always lead to the enslavement of the native on his native soil. In West Africa, which was the source of slaves for the colonizing European powers in the Western World, natives were bartered by native rulers, merchants, and conquerors for the products of European industry. In the Gold Coast, for example, the monopoly of supplying slaves was jealously guarded by the Africans, and the king of Dahomey refused to permit European traders to enter his kingdom.[6] Africans on the coast acted as middlemen and sent their agents inland to purchase slaves. Likewise in Nigeria, the Africans supplied slaves to satisfy the ever-increasing demands of Europeans for labor on overseas plantations.[7] Thus, in the case of West Africa, the Africans who bartered their brethren into slavery for rum and firearms were not subjected at the time to any form of forced labor.

When European peoples established contacts with the older civilizations of Asia, barter quickly developed into commercial relations which differed from the economic relations with nonliterate peoples. In the East Indies, for example, the Dutch could not deal with individual traders but were forced to deal with established governments. "They were forced, before they knew it," as Day wrote, "to become politicians, seeking their commercial ends through diplomatic channels, and warriors, upholding the gains that had been given them by treaty." [8]

[6] W. E. F. Ward, *A History of the Gold Coast* (London: George Allen and Unwin, Ltd., 1948), p. 82.

[7] Sir Alan Burns, *History of Nigeria* (London: George Allen and Unwin, Ltd., 1951), pp. 65 ff.

[8] Clive Day, *The Policy and Administration of the Dutch in Java* (New York: The Macmillan Co., 1904), pp. 45–6.

However, as the Dutch extended their trade, commercial relations were combined with military conquests. These military conquests became necessary in order to transform commercial relations between free people into a type of exploitation. Likewise, when Europeans entered into economic relations with the people of China, India, and Japan, it was on the basis of commercial relations with peoples who lived under established governments. Moreover, the extent and character of their commercial relations depended upon the extent to which the peoples of these countries could resist the domination of European peoples. Let us see, therefore, how commercial relations between European and non-European peoples developed into a system of exploitation, which became in fact a form of slavery.

FROM COMMERCE TO EXPLOITATION

The Indians in the island of Haiti, as we have seen, were organized into labor gangs in order to secure a disciplined supply of labor. The significance of this in the transition from barter to slavery is made clear in Marchant's study of Brazil. The first step in the direction of exploitation was taken when the Indians of Brazil ceased to exchange their possessions for the artifacts of European manufacture and began to exchange their labor for goods—food, clothing, and housing.[9] At first, the Indians bartered food, which they had grown, for articles supplied by the Portuguese. Then, they were induced to grow food especially for the Portuguese, and gradually the Indians were induced to supply their labor for new agricultural tasks.

The system of barter continued under the *donatarios* but the Indians became dissatisfied with the cheap articles which they received in exchange for their labor, and the

[9] Marchant, *op. cit.*, pp. 67 ff.

Portuguese had to bid against each other for the labor of the Indians. Since the *donatarios* had come to Brazil in order to establish plantations, it was inevitable that the system of barter would not supply their need for cheap and disciplined labor.[10] In the beginning it was possible through barter to secure labor for their plantations and for building mills, but often after the Indians had acquired the goods which they wanted, they refused to work. Then the Portuguese were compelled to engage in aggressive wars in order to secure labor. In some cases the Indians carried on wars against the Portuguese in retaliation for the attempts to enslave them, while in other cases the Portuguese participated in the intertribal wars for the purpose of obtaining labor.

Although in South Africa the European had to turn to the slave markets of West and East Africa for slaves, he nevertheless undertook to exploit the labor of the native Hottentot and colored population. During the first decade of the nineteenth century vagrancy laws were passed in order to compel Hottentots to work for the white farmers. The Europeans could not subjugate the Bantu as easily as they had done in the case of the Hottentot. Nor could the advancing white frontier exterminate the native population as the Europeans had done in North America. As the white frontier advanced the native Bantu became increasingly incorporated into the white community, where he worked first on farms and later in factories.

In the tropics the transition from commerce to exploitation coincided with the introduction of a plantation system of agriculture for the production of staples for exportation. The "parks" or estates which were distributed among the Dutch in Java for the production of nutmeg for the European market were worked by the Bandanese peons who were brought from a neighboring island. The enslavement of the natives of the Philippine Islands soon

[10] *Ibid.,* pp. 71 ff.

followed the establishment of Spanish rule.[11] Although the system of barter with the natives of tropical Africa often resulted in disputes and conflicts because of cheating, exploitation did not begin on a broad scale until Europeans began to utilize native labor in the production of commercial staples and minerals for exportation.

Our discussion of the evolution of economic relations between Europeans and peoples of Asia will be reserved for later chapters, since the economic relations between Europe and the older civilizations of Asia began on the level of commercial relations and the later changes were due mainly to the political and military dominance of Europe, which eliminated the Asian peoples as the suppliers of manufactured goods in world trade.

FREE MEN BECOME SLAVES

The final stage in the establishment of forced labor or slavery under the Spaniards began in 1505 when the labor gangs were reorganized into new gangs each of which was assigned to a colonist. Each of these gangs was known as an *encomienda* and the colonist to whom it was assigned, an *encomiendere*.[12] Although the missionaries were able to secure laws against the creation of new *encomiendas*, the planters were able to circumvent the laws and in the end the *encomienda* became the policy of the Spanish crown. As the result of the operation of the *encomienda* and of diseases and massacres, the Indian population of the West Indies was exterminated and Negro slaves were imported to work the plantations.

The final stage in the evolution from barter to slavery in Brazil was brought about as the result of the introduction of plantations. Despite the wars which were carried

[11] Bruno Lasker, *Human Bondage in Southeast Asia* (Chapel Hill: University of North Carolina Press, 1950), pp. 36 ff.

[12] Macleod, *op. cit.*, pp. 80 ff.

on to enslave the Indians, they could not be utilized completely for plantation labor. They were able to escape from the coastal areas where the plantations were established, and they were generally supported by the Jesuits and the government in their resistance to slavery. With the establishment of the sugar plantations in northern Brazil, slaves from Africa began to supplant the Indians as plantation laborers. Likewise, the system of Negro slavery which developed in the English colonies and later in the United States was the result of the failure of Europeans to reduce the native population to slavery.

Turning to other parts of the world, we find that the economic relationship which began in barter often ended in a system of compulsory labor or slavery. Since the *encomienda* had become the policy of the Spanish crown, it was introduced into the Philippine Islands. In Java the Dutch introduced slavery for plantation labor, and it is estimated that there were 27,000 slaves in Java in 1815 and 3,000 slaves were brought to Batavia each year.[13] Although slavery, as generally defined, did not become widespread, the *culture system* which was established in Java was essentially a type of compulsory labor.[14]

In this chapter we have undertaken to trace the processes by which initial contacts involving barter between European and non-European peoples developed into organized economic relationships. The distinguishing fact in this process is that the barter of goods between free men became a system of exploitation when the labor of non-Europeans became an object of barter in their relations with Europeans. Although the exchange of their labor for European goods on the part of native peoples began in some cases on a voluntary basis, it was generally through the use of force that Europeans were able to change the system of barter into organized economic relationships. It was thus that a system of compulsory labor in-

[13] Lasker, *op. cit.*, p. 35.   [14] See Day, *op. cit.*, Chap. VIII.

volving the exploitation of native peoples came into existence. There were variations in the systems of compulsory labor depending largely upon the stage of social development of non-European peoples. In the next chapter, we shall consider the different forms of compulsory labor which came into existence.

CHAPTER VI

Systems of Forced Labor

INTRODUCTION

The simplest and most primitive system of compulsory labor that developed as the result of the contact of European and non-European peoples was slavery. Slavery developed primarily in response to the demand for cheap labor in a plantation system of agriculture which produced staples for export. When the earlier forms of slavery were abolished partly as the result of the growth of humanitarian sentiment but more fundamentally as the result of economic and political forces, the conscription of native labor in colonial areas provided a substitute for slavery. Even in those areas where a system of recruitment of "free" labor gradually emerged, the element of compulsion has not been absent. And in still other areas the element of compulsion has been disguised under some such arrangement as "quota" assignments of production for native peoples.

THE PLANTATION AND SLAVERY

According to Nieboer, slavery has developed in those areas with "open resources" which are defined as those areas in which "every one who is able-bodied and not defective in mind can provide for himself independently of any capitalist or landlord." [1] Hence, in order to secure a cheap and disciplined labor supply for capitalistic exploitation it has been necessary to introduce a system of forced labor. The establishment of the plantation system of agriculture with slave labor by Europeans in various parts of the world has provided the confirmation of this hypothesis. Thompson has made probably the best succinct statement of the common characteristics which this institution exhibits wherever it has existed.

For one thing, and most obviously, it produces some kind of agricultural staple—cotton, rice, sugar, tobacco, bananas, coconuts, rubber, coffee, tea, sisal, etcetera—for an outside, usually an overseas, market. Incident to plantation development the production of these staple crops is shifted away from relatively inaccessible original habitats, perhaps in the interior of continents, nearer to the ocean's edge where they may be more cheaply transported to consuming populations. Hardly a single staple is plantation produced in areas native to the plants or trees. The shifting of wild rubber tapping from the interior of Brazil and the Belgian Congo to plantation planting in Malaya and elsewhere is an example of what the plantation does in the production of these staples generally. The history of rubber since 1900 repeats in telescoped fashion the similar histories of cotton and tobacco and sugar over a considerably longer period of time. . . . The chronic need of the plantation as an institution is not only for ample labor but for cheap labor. A continuous supply of cheap labor is a chief desideratum of every plantation society. It is to meet this need that labor has been recruited half way around the world, and almost every plantation society has put some new combination of men to work—generally, but not always, under white planters or overseers. Thus it is that another characteristic of the plantation institution is a labor problem which everywhere tends to be defined also as a race problem. Some kind or degree

[1] H. J. Nieboer, *Slavery as an Industrial Institution* (The Hague: Martinus Nijhoff, 1910), p. 385.

of race problem seems about as indigenous to the plantation as the staple which it produces.[2]

In the preceding chapter we have seen how the natives of the island of Haiti were reduced to slavery in order to insure a cheap and disciplined supply of plantation labor. After the native population of Haiti and other islands was killed off, African slaves were introduced on the West Indian plantations. While it is true that indentured white servants were utilized to some extent as a source of forced labor, Negro slaves soon became the only source of labor for the sugar plantations of the West Indies. The sugar colonies in the West Indies became the main source of wealth for the British empire and at the end of the eighteenth century the annual income from the West Indies, according to Pitt, amounted to £4 million as compared with £1 million from the rest of the world.[3] Likewise, more than a sixth of the entire commerce of France by the middle of the eighteenth century consisted of the sugar produced by Negro slaves on West Indian plantations.[4] The sugar supplied to the refineries of Rouen, Nantes, La Rochelle, Bordeaux, and Marseilles was re-exported to all of Europe. Thus the labor of Negro slaves became one of the main economic supports of European civilization in the eighteenth century.

On the American mainland Negro slave labor supplanted indentured white labor soon after the settlement of the Virginia Colony in 1607. Although the Negroes introduced in 1619 had the same status as the indentured

[2] Edgar T. Thompson, "The Plantation as a Race-Making Situation," unpublished statement before the Conference on Race Relations in World Perspective (Honolulu: University of Hawaii, 1954). Quoted with the permission of the author. See George McCutchen McBride, "Plantation," in Edwin R. A. Seligman and Alvin Johnson (eds.), *Encyclopaedia of the Social Sciences* (New York: The Macmillan Co., 1930), XII, 148–53.

[3] See Eric Williams, *Capitalism and Slavery* (Chapel Hill: University of North Carolina Press, 1944), pp. 52–3.

[4] Gaston-Martin, *Histoire de l'esclavage dans les colonies françaises* (Paris: Presses Universitaires de France, 1948), p. 105.

white servants, as the demand increased for cheap disciplined labor for the cultivation of tobacco, rice, and indigo, the enslavement of Negroes became an established policy.[5] The substitution of black slavery for white servitude in Virginia was clearly due to the economic advantages of the former. During the closing years of the eighteenth century when there was a decline in the profits from tobacco plantations, it appeared that Negro slavery might disappear. But as a consequence of the invention of the cotton gin and technological developments in the textile industries of England, cotton plantations with Negro slavery became the basis of the economic life of the southern states of the United States.

Since slave labor was utilized primarily in the production of sugar in the West Indies and in the hot coastal regions of the Americas, the plantation system of agriculture did not develop on a large scale in the Spanish colonies. On the other hand, in the Portuguese settlement of Brazil, "The milieu and the circumstances called for the slave." [6] What was the milieu and what were the circumstances? The Portuguese crown sought to obtain colonial wealth in a vast jungle area where the climate was too harsh for European settlement on a large scale.[7] This could be attained only through sugar production and slave labor on plantations. When the Indian because of his lack of ability and his slothfulness failed to supply the necessary labor, the planters imported Negro slaves. Through this type of colonial economy based upon sugar production, Portugal was able to compete with other imperial European nations.

In the East the Portuguese imported African and Oriental slaves into Malacca and their other possessions. But

[5] E. Franklin Frazier, *The Negro in the United States* (New York: The Macmillan Co., 1949), Chap. II.

[6] Gilberto Freyre, *The Masters and the Slaves* (New York: Alfred A. Knopf, Inc., 1946), p. 250.

[7] *Ibid.*, pp. 250–3.

when the Portuguese were ousted from their main conquests, the Dutch introduced systems of forced labor which were only disguised forms of slavery.

CONTROL OF NATIVE PRODUCTION

At first the Dutch East India Company established factories and carried on trade with the natives in Java. But the trade relations developed into a system of "contingents" and "forced deliveries." Theoretically, "the contingents were fixed amounts of products due annually from the native rulers for a small return or for nothing, while the forced deliveries varied in amount." [8] As a matter of fact both the contingents and the forced deliveries were political in character since they were based upon Dutch power. The Dutch stimulated the growth of coffee, which had been introduced from Arabia, "through commands laid on the native agents to furnish the amounts required as contingents and forced deliveries." In the case of sugar, which had to be manufactured before being placed upon the market, a different system was necessary, so the Dutch used their power to secure land, labor, and the necessary supplies for the Chinese who acted as middlemen. After the failure of the East India Company the Dutch continued the system of the contingents.

While Java was occupied for a brief period by the British, the system of forced deliveries was modified and subjected to regulation. Upon the restoration of the Dutch, the coffee plantations were leased to the native village governments which were required to pay a tax or rent, amounting to one third to one half of the product. For a time there was an unsettled economic policy. Finally as the result of a new policy there was instituted what was known as the "culture system." [9] Despite the advantages

[8] Clive Day, *The Policy and Administration of the Dutch in Java* (New York: The Macmillan Co., 1904), pp. 62 ff.
[9] See *ibid.*, Chaps. VII, VIII, IX.

which the culture system was supposed to have over the previous systems, it too was a system of forced labor. It was based upon compulsion on the part of the Dutch government which provided for its own profits first, and the laborers received as wages only what was left. Between 1860 and 1865 the least lucrative culture systems which had been organized for the production of tea, tobacco, indigo, pepper, and cinnamon were given up. This paved the way for capitalistic enterprise based upon a system of "free" labor although the European employers often depended upon official pressure in order to secure native labor.

The only similar system of forced labor established by a European government during the early years of European colonization was that instituted by the Spanish government in the Philippine Islands during the last quarter of the eighteenth century. However, during the last decade of the nineteenth century the Belgian government in the Congo instituted a system of forced labor that was similar to that of the Dutch in Java. Beginning as a territory governed by the International African Association and later becoming the Congo Free State following the Conference of Berlin in 1885, the Belgian Congo became in fact a Belgian colony within two decades.[10] The Congo Free State reserved for itself the best lands in the Congo and proceeded to collect and export rubber. The natives who collected rubber above Stanley Pool were required to pay the state a tax in rubber not to exceed one fifth of what they collected and in addition to perform certain *prestations* for the state. The amount of labor and rubber required from the natives was not the same for all regions.[11] When the government changed its policy to a requirement of forty hours of labor from each native, the new decree was administered so as to secure the maximum amount of rub-

[10] See Raymond L. Buell, *The Native Problem in Africa* (New York: The Macmillan Co., 1928), II, 415 ff.
[11] *Ibid.*, II, 429.

ber. As an example of the manner in which the natives
were subjected to a large number of obligations in addition to the forty hours of labor, Buell cites the situation in
the Cheffery of Bumba.

Thus the Cheffery of Bumba, composed of one hundred huts,
was obliged to furnish every month five sheep or pigs, or fifty
chickens, sixty kilos of rubber, one hundred and twenty-five
loads of manioc, fifteen kilos of maize or peanuts, and fifteen
kilos of sweet potatoes. Moreover, one man out of every ten
was obliged to serve as a laborer at the government post, and
one man from the Cheffery was obliged annually to go to the
Force Publique—the military organization. In addition, the
whole population of the Cheffery was obliged to work one day
out of every four on public works.[12]

Not only the government officials but also commercial
agents required the labor tax of forty hours a month from
the natives. Consequently, the system resulted in the continuous servitude of the natives. When the villages failed
to produce the required amount of rubber the chiefs were
arrested. Moreover, armed native sentinels—some strangers and other natives of the villages—were employed to
see that the rubber was collected according to requirements. The natives were whipped and in some cases
women and children were killed. This situation continued
in the Congo Free State from 1891 to 1906.[13]

In 1906 native laborers were forced to work on the
construction of the Great Lakes Railway when the state
declared that the construction of the railroad was a work
of public utility.[14] Although in 1908 the king was not permitted to issue a Royal Arrete again, declaring that work
on this railroad and on automobile roads was of public
utility, railway construction was still considered necessary
and natives were forced to work. Even as late as 1926 when
there was a demand for laborers to work on the railroads,
laborers who thought that they were being recruited to

---

[12] *Ibid.*, II, 430. Reprinted by permission of the Bureau of International Research.   [13] *Ibid.*, II, 434.   [14] *Ibid.*, II, 502 ff.

work on a cotton farm were sent to Leopoldsville with ropes around their necks. Despite the opposition of the Belgian Cabinet to such practices, the illegal conscription of labor for private enterprise continued, largely because of the zeal on the part of officials to industrialize the Congo.

CONSCRIPTION OF LABOR

The system of labor tax instituted by the Congo Free State as a source of profit for the state also provided the means for private commercial enterprises to profit from a system of compulsory labor. This has not been peculiar, however, to the Belgian Congo since, as we shall see, wherever European governments have conscripted labor mainly for public services, private enterprises have not failed to profit from the system of compulsory labor.

In the French colonies in Africa, natives were subject to a labor tax in addition to taxes proper.[15] Each native was thus required to work a certain number of days for the government without pay. In West Africa, this labor, which was known as a *prestation,* included work on roads, bridges, and the cleaning of wells, while in French Equatorial Africa the *prestation* included the establishment of roads and markets as well as their maintenance. Likewise, in most of the British colonies in Africa, the natives have been compelled to work for four weeks during the year on the maintenance of roads and paths. The Portuguese government was the only European government that openly engaged in a system of forced labor for private enterprises.[16] As the result of criticisms of the inevitable abuses incident to a legalized system of forced labor and of the influence of the League of Nations, the Portuguese government abolished compulsory labor for private enterprises but declared that such labor could be employed for the public good and in cases of urgency. Although the

[15] *Ibid.,* I, 1037-8.   [16] *Ibid.,* I, 31.

German government did not openly engage in a system of forced labor, when it introduced cocoa, palm, and rubber plantations in the Cameroons, the government assumed responsibility for the recruitment of labor for the plantations.[17] The system of labor recruitment by the government was abandoned when the British took over the colony after World War I.

A good example of the close relation between conscription of labor by the European governments and the conscription of labor for private enterprise is provided by the former system of concessions in the French Congo.[18] In 1899 there were forty concessionaire companies holding about 250,000 square miles of land in the French Congo, which were required to pay 15 per cent of their profits to the government in addition to rent for the land. These concessionaire companies had rights to all the resources of the soil though they were supposed to respect the native villages and their culture. But soon the companies complained of the shortage of labor and demanded the conscription of native labor or a head tax to accomplish the same end. The French government refused to give the companies the right to conscript labor but agreed to the head tax. When the companies argued that the natives could not pay the tax in kind because the products of the soil belonged to the companies, the government ruled that the tax could be paid in money. This did not prevent the companies from conscripting native labor. Some of the administrators forced the natives to collect rubber, the value of which was many times the amount of the tax. The companies not only gained a profit from the system of taxation, but they also profited from the system of forced labor which they were able to impose upon the natives. After a number of native revolts, and the arousal of public opinion in France, in 1906 the government compensated the natives for the rubber tax which they paid. Three years

---

[17] *Ibid.*, I, 685.   [18] See *ibid.*, II, 229 ff.

later the system of rubber tax was abolished and the payment of tax in money was substituted.

As late as 1925, however, the French administration in the Sudan was conscripting labor for commercial and transport firms there.[19] In 1923 the conscription of agricultural laborers for the plantations in the Sudan was described as follows:

The conscript is designated by the village chief, which means that he is always recruited from the least desirable element of the population. Ordinarily, he is a former slave or son of a slave. He does not know where he is sent nor what will be his new condition. Having only a vague notion of the passage of time, the length of his employment will seem to him interminable. If he is a bachelor, he knows that he will soon return to his village without having saved anything, with the result that the long exile will be a waste of time for him; and if he is married—and the case is frequent—he will be anxious about the welfare of his family. His morale is also very bad. Many conscripted laborers die from simple neurasthenia. Their food upon public and private works is, however, better than what they receive in their villages. The plantations of the Compagnie de Culture Cotonniere du Niger enjoy, moreover, an excellent reputation in this respect. As to the regular and assiduous work which must be carried on, the lack of enthusiasm to serve under European employment is many times due to the constant restrictions imposed upon the natives.[20]

The policy of the Portuguese government of conscripting labor for private enterprise was influenced largely by the needs of South African mines for native labor. The recruiting of native labor in Mozambique was carried out by an organization established by the Chamber of Mines and known as the Witwatersrand Native Labor Associa-

19 *Ibid.*, II, 27-8.
20 E. Belime, *La Production du coton en Afrique occidentale française* (Paris: Publications du Comité du Niger), p. 254, as quoted in Buell, *op. cit.*, II, 28. Reprinted by permission of the Bureau of International Research.

tion.[21] This organization had branches throughout Mozambique which employed native recruiters and native runners to procure native workers. The Portuguese government gained from the recruitment of native laborers through the revenue received from emigration fees. During the 1920's, the government of Liberia which was supposed to be representative of the interests of the African natives yielded to the financial inducements offered by the Firestone Company to provide native workers for its plantations.[22] Although the English government was opposed from the beginning to the conscription of native labor for private enterprises, the system of recruitment of "free" native labor in territories under British control has often involved an element of compulsion.

RECRUITMENT OF "FREE" LABOR

The recruitment of "free" native or colored labor in many parts of the world where Europeans have settled or gained political control has often concealed a system of forced labor. The element of force becomes apparent when one examines the method of recruitment, the terms on which the workers have been engaged, and the control which Europeans have exercised over native or colored workers during the period of their employment. The most primitive form of the so-called recruitment of "free" laborers has involved the kidnapping of natives to work in European enterprises. The method of recruiting so-called "free" labor for the early plantations in the South Seas may be cited as an example of this primitive type of recruitment.[23] The native Polynesians were unsatisfactory as laborers because their subsistence economy satisfied their needs and they were not conditioned to the requirements

21 Buell, *op. cit.*, I, 30.
22 *Ibid.*, II, 833-4.
23 Douglas L. Oliver, *The Pacific Islands* (Cambridge: Harvard University Press, 1951) , pp. 93 ff.

of organized labor under foreign masters. Although the Negroid people of the Fiji Islands were more tractable, they could not supply the needs of the plantations. The white settlers in Australia experienced similar difficulties in securing a supply of labor. Therefore, they and the planters turned to the New Hebrides for laborers. Masters of vessels would anchor in the bays or lagoons of these islands and "induce" the natives to contract to "work hard and faithfully at a distant island or plantation" in return for which they were to be fed, paid, and sent home. These Pacific blackbirders became notorious as slavers who destroyed villages and held chiefs as hostages until they "signed up" enough laborers.

The recruitment of "free" labor has involved an element of compulsion wherever the development of large-scale European industry has required a supply of labor that was not available locally. From the beginning of their occupation of the Congo, the Belgians were faced with a shortage of available labor. Although the Belgian government introduced reforms after taking over the administration of the Free State, the labor requirements of the owners of mines and agricultural concessions tended to nullify these reforms.[24] In order to satisfy the owners' demands for thousands of workers, organizations were set up to recruit native labor. Recruiters were sent out to scour not only the villages of the Congo but to seek native workers in Northern Rhodesia and Angola. Although the Belgian government prohibited the forceful recruitment of labor for private enterprises, as late as 1922 the Governor-General of the Congo declared in a circular that it was a mistake to believe that after a native had paid his taxes and other legal obligations he could remain inactive. Therefore, natives should be "encouraged" to work in private enterprises if they did not voluntarily accept employment. This encouragement included pressure upon the

[24] See Buell, *op. cit.*, II, 533 ff.

chiefs to provide labor; if they did not do so, their status was reduced together with a concomitant reduction in salaries.

The recruitment of "free" native labor has involved some form of compulsion in the British territories in Africa. In 1894 the Cape Province imposed a tax of ten shillings on native males who had not been employed out of their district for three months.[25] This tax was repealed in 1905. However, three years later the Transvaal government imposed a tax of £2 upon each native who was not a farm laborer. In the compounds connected with the mines the industrialized native was placed under the strict control of a European manager and the police boys, and if the native deserted his employment and broke his contract he was liable to imprisonment.[26] The most important single factor responsible for the entrance of the native into European employment has been the lack of land on which he could provide food for himself and his family.

In Kenya, European settlers had difficulty from the beginning in securing native labor. After 1903 when white settlers began to arrive in large numbers, the British administration aided the settlers in securing native labor.[27] When certain restrictions were placed upon the methods of recruiting native labor, the settlers demanded that a tax be placed upon the natives to force them to enter European employment. In 1913, the governor was reported to have stated that he considered taxation as "the only possible method of compelling the native to leave his reserve for the purpose of seeking work." When ex-soldiers were given farms after World War I, the problem of securing native labor became more acute. In 1919, the governor declared that "The white man must be paramount. . . . For the good of the country and for his own welfare he [the native] must be brought out to work. . . . Our policy, then, I believe, should be to encourage voluntary work in

25 *Ibid.*, I, 19.   26 *Ibid.*, I, 41-2.   27 See *ibid.*, I, 329 ff.

the first place but to provide power by legislation to prevent idleness." [28] After much controversy over the question of compulsory labor, the European settlers had their way. Consequently, up to the 1920's, native labor was secured through government pressure and through recruiters who used a form of "persuasion" which generally concealed an element of force. Moreover, the machinery which was used to adjust European employees and native wage earners created a new category of crimes. The method of dealing with these new crimes, including detention camps, created in fact a system of peonage from which private employers profited.

Peonage has existed in other parts of the world where European employers have needed native labor. When the *encomiendas* were abolished towards the end of the Spanish rule in the American colonies, the whites continued a system of peonage to hold the Indian laborers in a form of involuntary servitude.[29] This was achieved by involving them in debt and keeping them in the service of their employers until they had paid their debts. These debts consisted of the tribute imposed upon the Indians, the cost of food and clothing which were supplied the Indians, and money advanced to them for marriages, funerals, and other ceremonial occasions. The system of peonage was continued in many of the republics which were established after Spanish rule was overthrown, and it became notorious in Mexico where one third of the rural laborers worked under a system of peonage. It was not until the revolution in Mexico that an effective fight against peonage in Latin America was initiated. In the Philippine Islands, the system of peonage introduced by the Spaniards continued to be widespread as late as 1930 despite the fact that it had been outlawed by the Congress of the United States.

[28] Quoted in *ibid.*, I, 333.
[29] See George McCutchen McBride, "Peonage," in Edwin R. A. Seligman and Alvin Johnson (eds.), *Encyclopaedia of the Social Sciences* (New York: The Macmillan Co., 1930), XII, 69–72.

On the mainland of the United States, peonage developed as the result of the abolition of Negro slavery.[30] At first, Negroes who were charged with vagrancy and petty crimes were allowed to pay their fines by working for some white employer. It was not long before Negro workers who had become indebted to white employers for food, clothes, lodging, and tools were forced to work long periods in order to pay for such materials. Negro farm laborers and even tenants who were under yearly contracts were likewise caught in the net of indebtedness to the white planters and were forced to work until they had paid their debts. The laws of the southern states protected the white planter against the violation of these contracts by defining violations as criminal offenses. Often Negro workers were forced to work under armed guards, and the white planter did not resort to the courts to settle complaints against his black workers but took the law in his own hands. Although the Congress of the United States enacted anti-peonage legislation in 1875, not until 1919 were state laws upholding peonage declared unconstitutional by the Supreme Court. Nevertheless, vestiges of peonage remained in the southern states until World War II.

Although during the nineteenth century a number of international agreements dealt with the problem of slavery, only after the organization of the League of Nations was an effort made to deal with the broader problem of forced labor on an international level.[31] The Covenant of the League of Nations did not contain any reference to forced labor, but there were specific provisions in both B and C Mandates prohibiting forced labor. An inquiry held by the League of Nations in 1922 revealed that private enterprise availed "itself of the native labour obtained by

[30] See Edward B. Reuter, *The American Race Problem* (New York: Thomas Y. Crowell Co., 1927) , pp. 238–40.
[31] See *Report of the Ad Hoc Committee on Forced Labor* (Geneva: United Nations and International Labour Office, 1953) , Appendix I.

the application of compulsory labour laws." [32] The International Labour Office, which had also been interested in the labor problem in the colonies and mandated territories, reported in 1929 that various methods of direct or indirect compulsion had been used to overcome "the difficulties of an inadequate labour supply." [33] States adhering to the Convention adopted by the International Labour Conference in 1930 agreed to "suppress the use of forced or compulsory labour in all of its forms within the shortest possible period." [34] The International Labour Office was also concerned with the questions of recruiting, of written contracts for native workers, and of penal sanctions for breach of contracts. In regard to these issues the International Labour Office was only able to secure the adherence of the various states to rules governing the conditions of recruitment and the definition of breach of contract.

Because of the growth of public opinion against compulsory labor but more especially because of the growing unrest among the colored colonial peoples who were drawn into two world wars to defend democracy and the principle of racial equality, the United Nations was compelled to give some attention to the problem of compulsory labor. On the whole, however, the declarations of the United Nations have been concerned with generalities. In Article 56 of the Charter all members of the United Nations pledge themselves to work for the achievements of Article 55 which states that the United Nations shall promote "conditions of economic and social progress and development" and "universal respect for, and observance of, human rights and fundamental freedoms for all without distinctions as to race, sex, language or religion." Even the Declaration of Human Rights contains no reference to compulsory labor but only forbids slavery and affirms the universal right to "free choice of employment."

Our discussion so far of the different forms of forced

[32] *Ibid.*, p. 133. [33] *Ibid.*, p. 139. [34] *Ibid.*, p. 142.

labor as they concern the relations of the white and colored races in the world provides an introduction to the economic relation of the industrially advanced European peoples to the colored peoples who lack the technology and capital required by modern civilization. We shall turn our attention to this broader problem in the next chapter.

CHAPTER VII

White Capital and Colored Labor[1]

INTRODUCTION

This chapter is concerned with the most important phase of the economic relations which have developed between the European and the colored races: the relationship of white capital to colored labor. One aspect of this relationship has been a conflict between European and non-European conceptions concerning the ownership and utilization of land and its resources and concerning the meaning and ends of labor. From the standpoint of the organization of labor, the relation of white capital to colored labor has generally resulted in a system of white management. In some areas a class of colored middlemen has existed from the beginning, while in other areas this class has only come into existence at a later period. In either case, ultimate control of economic development in modern times has been in the hands of white owners of capital. As the result of the growing resistance of the colored peoples to

[1] This title is taken from the title of the well-known book by Lord S. H. Olivier, *White Capital and Coloured Labour* (rev. ed.; London; The Hogarth Press, 1929).

this kind of control, some countries have ceased to be areas for uncontrolled investments by white capitalists. Even in those parts of the world where resistance to the domination resulting from the investment of European capital has been weaker, the problem of white capital and colored labor still exists and has become largely the problem of aid to underdeveloped areas.

FOREIGN INVESTMENTS

From the standpoint of race and culture contacts, foreign investments or the export of European capital became important when the African slave trade was inaugurated. In the beginning the importance of black Africa in the relation of white capital to colored labor was due to the fact that the European trading settlements in Africa supplied colored labor to overseas capitalistic operations. The European merchants and investors supplied the ships and the goods which were required in the operation of overseas plantations. The returns from the investments in the West Indian sugar plantations were higher than from any other form of cultivation of Europe or America.[2] With the growing industrialization of the European world, investments in plantations worked by servile colored labor became less important, and the export of European capital was increasingly devoted to the extraction of minerals and other raw materials which were required by an industrial civilization.

When the Portuguese and other Europeans first established contacts with the Japanese in the sixteenth century, it appears that the Japanese were on the verge of establishing themselves in Formosa, the Philippines, and Indonesia.[3] Moreover, Japan welcomed foreigners at first

[2] Eric Williams, *Capitalism and Slavery* (Chapel Hill: University of North Carolina Press, 1944), p. 53.

[3] G. B. Sansom, *The Western World and Japan* (New York: Alfred A. Knopf, Inc., 1950), pp. 169 ff.

and exhibited an interest in the outside world. It was because of the fear of foreign aggression that the Tokugawa Shogun inaugurated a policy of exclusion that lasted until the nineteenth century. Then it was the Russians who first revealed to the Japanese people their weakness in relation to the West.[4] But before the Russians could establish normal diplomatic relations with the Japanese, Commodore Perry had already opened Japan to the West.

From the opening of Japan to the West until the later years of the nineteenth century, the import and export trade was in the hands of foreign merchants.[5] But Japan soon learned the trading and financial methods of the West and assumed control of her economic life. The Japanese were wary about encouraging foreign investments to industrialize the country and, except for two small foreign loans, it was not until after the turn of the century that they engaged in foreign borrowing.[6] When the war with Russia occurred in 1904, Japan had established her security and prestige to the point that she was in a position to make large loans in the West.[7] During World War I, Japan increased her gold holdings and balances in London and New York. The defeat of the Japanese empire in her struggle with the American empire in the Pacific in World War II has reduced Japan to economic dependence upon the United States. This economic dependence is, however, tied up with the role of Japan in the political struggle between the United States on the one hand and China and Russia on the other.

China offers a marked contrast to Japan in regard to the role of foreign investments in their respective relations with the West. In the absence of a strong national govern-

[4] *Ibid.*, pp. 243 ff.
[5] George C. Allen and Audrey G. Donnithorne, *Western Enterprise in Far Eastern Economic Development: China and Japan* (New York: The Macmillan Co., 1954), pp. 196 ff.
[6] *Ibid.*, p. 224.
[7] *Ibid.*, pp. 232 ff.

ment and of institutional foundations for economic development in China, the Western peoples provided through the "unequal treaties" the necessary legal and institutional basis for their investments.[8] From the time of the Roman Empire the West had drained off the precious metals and goods of China without finding a market in China for the goods of the West. In fact, up until the nineteenth century the West possessed no technical superiority over China. Since China had no national government when contacts were first established between Europeans and Chinese, trade between the West and China was in the hands of the East India Company and an association of Chinese merchants. When the Chinese government attempted to prohibit the importation of opium in 1836, this action led to the Opium War with England. The defeat of the Chinese resulted in the Treaty of Nanking in 1842 which opened China to Western trade.

After the Treaty of Nanking the Western powers gradually took over the control of the political and economic life of China so far as their interests were concerned.[9] Through a number of treaties the foreign powers gained control of the shipping, of the maritime customs, and of mining and railways. The defeat of China by Japan in 1894 revealed the extent of China's weakness and inaugurated the dividing up of China by the Western powers and Japan.[10] The economic penetration of China was carried out through foreign settlements or through concessions which were under foreign control. The number of Treaty Ports increased from five to eighty, while foreign concessions numbered more than twenty by 1913.[11] Between 1911, when the revolution broke out in China, and

    [8] *Ibid.*, pp. 14 ff.
    [9] *Ibid.*, pp. 15 ff.
    [10] See C. F. Remer, *Foreign Investments in China* (New York: The Macmillan Co., 1933).
    [11] Allen and Donnithorne, *op. cit.*, p. 14.

1937, when the Japanese invaded the country, there was civil war in China. During this internal struggle the Chinese were able to recover some of their autonomy and to force the Western powers to surrender their control over her economic life. However, the Japanese seized control of the economic life of the eastern part of China. It was not until the establishment of Communist rule that the Chinese were able to completely control their economic destinies.

In India, the earliest English investments can scarcely be distinguished from a form of tribute imposed upon the country. When Lord Robert Clive obtained in 1765 from the Great Moghul a charter making the East India Company the administrators of Bengal, an economic policy was inaugurated by which India was drained of its manufactures and Indian workers were forced to work in the company's factories.[12] The success of this policy, which was meant to discourage or destroy Indian manufactures, was assured when the power loom was invented in Europe. Millions of Indian artisans were deprived of their means of livelihood and became agricultural laborers. At the same time, as the result of the decline of Indian manufacture of silk and cotton, the people of India were forced to buy goods manufactured in England.[13] Then later, when Indian capitalists set up cotton mills in their own country, English manufacturers were able to have an excise imposed upon cotton goods produced by Indian industries.

One of the most important features of the economic policy of the English in regard to India concerned the land of the country. Under Warren Hastings, India became a great estate which was to be exploited for the benefit of the East India Company and its servants.[14] Before the Eng-

[12] Romesh Dutt, *The Economic History of India Under Early British Rule* (London: Routledge and Kegan Paul, Ltd., 1950), pp. 35 ff.

[13] *Ibid.*, pp. 256 ff.

[14] *Ibid.*, pp. 54 ff.

lish gained control in India there had been exploitation by the landlords. Nevertheless, the peasants had certain customary rights which had to be respected. But under the East India Company the welfare of the agricultural population and the rights of the Indian rulers were subordinated to the profits of the company. The revenues from the land were drained off in the form of commodities which went to Europe. This policy proved disastrous to the company and it was necessary to introduce reforms.

These reforms were first carried out in Bengal where a fixed percentage of the rental from the land was paid by the landlords to the crown.[15] Although the crown took the major proportion of the rentals, a fixed policy benefited the entire agricultural population, the peasants as well as the landlords. Similar reforms were not extended, however, to other parts of India. When the rule of the East India Company was ended in 1858, the first Viceroys under the crown undertook to bring about reforms that would have respected the hereditary rights of the Indian cultivators and increased their welfare. But British policy was determined by a school of thought that favored the Indian landlords and at the same time increased the taxes of the peasant. As a result, the masses of Indian peasants remained in an impoverished condition while about a fourth of the revenues derived in India went to England.[16]

Since India has achieved her political independence, the land problem has become a domestic problem and has ceased to be a factor in the economic relations of Indians with the European races. The same is true of the other countries of Asia which have achieved political independence. Land has, however, continued to be an important factor in race relations in the Pacific, with impoverished

15 *Ibid.,* pp. 81 ff.
16 See Romesh Dutt, *The Economic History of India in the Victorian Age* (7th ed.; London: Routledge and Kegan Paul, Ltd., 1950), Preface and *passim.*

Asians looking to Australia and other vacant areas where they hope to improve their economic condition.[17] In these areas, land as a factor in race and culture contacts is bound up with world politics. As we shall see, it is in the tropics and in areas of white settlement that land together with labor has become a major factor in the economic relations of races.

After the Napoleonic wars, Great Britain achieved first place among the European nations as an exporter of capital. It was much later that France, Germany, and the United States became large net capital exporters.[18] English foreign investments doubled during the thirty years preceding World War I and in 1914 amounted to $20,000,000-000, or about one fourth of the national wealth of Great Britain. The foreign investments of France in 1914, which had doubled during the previous twenty years, were valued at $8,700,000,000, or about 15 per cent of the nation's wealth.[19] Germany did not begin to export capital until the 1880's; however, just before the opening of World War I, the nation's foreign investments amounted to about $6,000,000,000.[20] Belgium and the Netherlands, whose foreign investments were largely in Dutch colonies, were also exporters of capital on a smaller scale.

Before World War I, these nations exported capital for the building up of backward regions or countries. The people of these backward countries were considered

from the point of view of modern civilization, socially immature. They have had no experience in handling large sums of money. They are without established traditions of financial

---

[17] See Radhakamal Mukerjee, *Races, Lands and Food* (New York: The Dryden Press, Inc., 1946).

[18] M. Palyi, "Foreign Investment," in Edwin R. A. Seligman and Alvin Johnson (eds.), *Encyclopaedia of the Social Sciences* (New York: The Macmillan Co., 1930), VI, 367.

[19] *Ibid.*, VI, 369.

[20] *Ibid.*, VI, 370.

trusteeship. They have developed no national credit to inspire confidence in investors. Their social institutions are so weak as to be subject to disruption by any ephemeral social theories which happen to come their way.[21]

Not all the backward regions or countries were inhabited by colored peoples. Some of the foreign investments were in Europe, about 20 per cent were in the United States, and an equal proportion in Latin America.[22] A considerable proportion of the investments in Latin America were, of course, in countries in which Indians or Negroes or both formed a large proportion of the population. The English had invested about £250,000,000, or somewhat more than their investments in Europe, in Egypt, Turkey, China, Japan, and other parts of the world. However, nearly a half of the English foreign investments were within the British empire. Of the English investments within the empire slightly more than a half were in Canada, Newfoundland, Australia, and New Zealand. South Africa absorbed more than a fifth of the investments within the empire while India and Ceylon absorbed even more than South Africa. The remainder of the investments within the empire were in West Africa, the Straits settlements, North Borneo, Hong Kong, and other colonies. Up to World War I, the vast majority of French capital was exported to European countries, especially Russia, despite the fact that France had a large colonial empire.[23] Likewise, nearly a half of the German foreign investments were in Europe, and only a small proportion of the investments were in African and Asian colonies.[24]

Following World War I, the United States became the

[21] Henry K. Norton, "Backward Countries as a Field for Investment," in *Foreign Investments* (Chicago: University of Chicago Press, 1929), p. 208.

[22] See Herbert Feis, *Europe: The World's Banker, 1870–1914* (New Haven: Yale University Press, 1931), p. 23.

[23] *Ibid.*, p. 51.

[24] *Ibid.*, p. 74.

leading creditor nation in the world as the result of her excess of exports over imports, Allied debts, and her large stock of gold reserves along with the expansion of credit based upon it. A large part of the foreign investments of the United States was in Europe and Canada. At the same time, however, the United States achieved a dominant economic position in certain South American and Central American countries. From the standpoint of our study the most important aspect of the increase in the foreign investments of the United States was the phenomenal growth of investments in Africa, Asia, and Oceania. Between 1914 and 1935, the foreign investments of the United States, direct and portfolio (financial institutions), increased from $17,000,000 to $413,100,000 in Oceania; from $245,900,-000 to $915,300,000 in Asia; from $13,200,000 to $125,-800,000 in Africa.[25] These were the areas in which the leading European nations had carved out colonial empires for economic exploitation, though the economic policies of the European powers in regard to their colonies varied. For example, the Dutch, who invested vast sums in the Netherlands East Indies, maintained an open-door policy in regard to investments, while the French with small investments in Indo-China placed restrictions upon foreign capital.[26] However, the economic policies in regard to their colonies did not change the fact that in these same areas were located the raw materials which were required by an industrial civilization. The need to regulate the distribution of these raw materials was recognized as one of the major conditions for re-establishing the world economy on a peaceful basis.[27]

[25] See Cleona Lewis, *America's Stake in International Investments* (Washington, D.C.: The Brookings Institution, 1938), Table, p. 606.

[26] See Thomas E. Ennis, *French Policy and Development in Indochina* (Chicago: University of Chicago Press, 1936), pp. 3–5.

[27] See *Raw Material Problems and Policies* (Geneva: League of Nations, 1946).

LAND AND LABOR

From the beginning of the contact of the Europeans with the Indians in the Americas, there was a conflict of ideas concerning the nature of land tenure. The two conflicting conceptions of the relationship of men to the land are generally designated as the individual and the collective conception of land tenure. Large grants of individual holdings, which reflected the European conception of land tenure, were made to the subjects of Spain and Portugal in America. Likewise, the English, disregarding the rights of the Indians to ownership of the land, made large land grants to soldiers and noblemen. The conception of individual ownership of land is opposed to the collective conception, according to which the land

belongs to a group of persons all of whom are bound together by ties of kinship or by common rights acquired after long established residence in a particular community. Each member of the group enjoys the privilege of sharing with his fellows the land and other natural resources of the holding, including pasture, game, wood, water and rock, and of being allotted a small piece of tillable land which may be held indefinitely and even passed from one generation to another, or may be reassigned different members of the community.[28]

Where the collective conception of land tenure exists, the relation of men to the land and their rights in regard to the products of the soil are, as Labouret has pointed out, of an essentially religious nature.[29] The individual conception of land tenure introduced by Europeans tends to secularize the relationship of natives to the land and effects fundamental changes in their habits and customs. This is

[28] George McCutchen McBride, "Land Tenure," Latin America, in Edwin R. A. Seligman and Alvin Johnson (eds.), *Encyclopaedia of the Social Sciences* (New York: The Macmillan Co., 1933), IX, 119. Reprinted by permission of the publisher.

[29] Henri Labouret, *Paysans d'Afrique occidentale* (7th ed.; Paris: Gallimard, 1941), p. 59.

achieved first by a transition from a subsistence economy to a commercial system of agriculture with marketable crops.[30] Another stage in the process of secularization is attained when land acquires a "transferable value" and rights in the land are commercialized. It is also important to point out that this transformation is accompanied by changes in the organization of labor and changes in the meaning of labor for native peoples.

The economics of dual societies, or societies which have had the Western capitalistic money economy imposed upon their traditional communal economy, has been studied by Boeke in the case of Indonesia.[31] In his study, Boeke shows that a knowledge of the sociological aspects of the village community, which is primarily a social and religious unit, is necessary in order to understand the economic life of the Indonesian village.[32] In fact, the village community was an original community or what Tönnies has called a *Gemeinschaft* or communal body. In addition to the genealogical and religious factors, subsistence agriculture provided the basis for communal life and determined the physical limits of the village. Under the system of subsistence agriculture, land was not regarded as an article of commerce. The introduction of the culture system, which was described in the previous chapter, disturbed native industry by forcing the natives to work on government plantations and stimulated the need for money. And as the natives became wage earners, private employers were able to build up large landed estates.[33]

A number of factors determine the manner in which land affects the economic relations which are established between European and native peoples. There is, first, the

[30] See Introduction by Lord Malcolm Hailey to C. K. Meek, *Land Law and Custom in the Colonies* (New York: Oxford University Press, Inc., 1949).

[31] J. H. Boeke, *Economics and Economic Policy of Dual Societies* (New York: Institute of Pacific Relations, 1953).

[32] *Ibid.*, pp. 21 ff.

[33] *Ibid.*, p. 78.

nature of the crops which are cultivated.[34] Some crops require the plantation type of agriculture for the profitable investment of capital. The cultivation of sugar has required the plantation type of agriculture, which has developed from individually owned plantations to large company-owned estates. On the other hand, the cultivation of cocoa as in the Gold Coast has been carried on successfully on the basis of peasant proprietorship. Then climate has affected the nature of land tenure though the influence of climate has been minimized by irrigation schemes. Systems of land tenure are also influenced by the type of marketing. Peasant producers may have to depend upon middlemen and become the victims of debt-servitude and lose their lands. Finally, the attitude of the natives toward the land based upon certain indigenous systems of inheritance may have some effect upon the economic relations which are established with Europeans.

In Malaya, a country with a climate suitable for the cultivation of almost every kind of tropical product, rubber and tin have been the chief sources of wealth. About two thirds of the more than 3,000,000 acres planted with rubber in 1938 were in large estates, and Europeans owned three fourths of the large estates.[35] Likewise, British capital controlled most of the tea and rubber plantations in Ceylon, where much of the land has come under European control.[36] In Africa, after the policy of establishing reserves to provide for the needs of the natives in Northern Rhodesia proved unsatisfactory, a new policy was inaugurated in 1942 to make larger provisions for the natives. At the same time, however, the new policy made provision for the alienation of crown lands for railroads and industrial developments.[37] As a result of the close association between Europeans and Africans in Nigeria and the freedom to deal with land, English systems of tenure

[34] Meek, *op. cit.*, pp. 2 ff.   [36] *Ibid.*, pp. 59 ff.
[35] *Ibid.*, p. 33.   [37] *Ibid.*, pp. 121 ff.

have been adopted and native family rights have been confirmed by English law.[38] The crown has placed certain restrictions upon the alienation of native lands to nonnatives. The crown has also placed certain safeguards about the native rights to land in the Gold Coast where the prosperous cocoa-growing industry is based upon peasant proprietorship.[39] Similar changes are occurring in French Africa. In Upper Guinea where, before the arrival of the European, the Kissi had a subsistence economy, not only has rice been a commercial crop for exportation but money and markets are changing the economic life of the people.[40]

The conflicting interests of Europeans and Africans in regard to land in Kenya have resulted in open racial conflict.[41] Because of the suitability for European settlement of the land in the Highlands, most of the land in this area has been taken from the natives, who have become squatters and labor-tenants on the European estates. Moreover, the land problem has become more acute because of the demand of urbanized Africans for agricultural land. In South Africa, which is the most important area of white settlement in Africa, land has been of primary importance in the establishment of economic relations between Europeans and Africans.[42] Land has been alienated for both industrial and agricultural purposes, and the native has increasingly found it necessary to work for the European, either as an industrial or agricultural worker, in order to gain a livelihood.

In considering land as a factor in the economic aspects of race relations, one should give some attention to the sit-

[38] *Ibid.*, pp. 146 ff.

[39] *Ibid.*, pp. 169 ff.

[40] Denise Paulme, *Les Gens du riz* (Paris: Librairie Plon, 1954), pp. 65 ff.

[41] Meek, *op. cit.*, pp. 76 ff. See also L. S. B. Leakey, *Mau Mau and the Kikuyu* (London: Methuen and Co., 1953). See also Jomo Kenyatta, *Facing Mount Kenya* (London: Martin Secker and Warburg, Ltd., 1938), Chap. II.

[42] See Ellen Hellmann (ed.), *Handbook on Race Relations in South Africa* (New York: Oxford University Press, Inc., 1949), Chaps. VII, VIII.

uation in the southern part of the United States.[43] Unlike
Kenya and South Africa, the southern states have not been
an area where there was a struggle between whites and
blacks for land. Nevertheless, land has played a major role
in the pattern of economic relationships between the two
races. After the emancipation of the Negro, the ex-slaves
did not realize their dream to become peasant proprietors.
They, along with many of the landless poor whites, continued in the same relation to the southern white planters as
the Negroes before emancipation. The attempt during the
agrarian unrest in the South in the nineties to bring about
an alliance between the landless whites and Negroes failed.
The extent of land ownership among Negro farmers increased up until the first decade of the twentieth century,
but it did not exceed 25 per cent. The land they held was
the poorer and least desirable land and it was generally under heavy mortgage to white men.

The problem of native labor is closely tied up with
changes in land tenure. As Boeke points out in regard to
Indonesia, "just as the native community is hostile to capital, so too in the native market we find a dislike for the
position of a wage-earner." [44] In the native village, the different kinds of wages which are involved in reciprocal aid
and other forms of mutual aid enable "a man to work for
another without entering into capitalistic wage relations"
and without surrendering his freedom in becoming subject to the "discipline prescribed by another." The problem of the employment of native labor in European enterprises arises then from the fact, as Noon has stated in
regard to Africa, that the aims of economic existence for
the native are different from those of the European.[45] The
African conception of work must be considered in its re-

<hr />

[43] See E. Franklin Frazier, *The Negro in the United States* (New
York: The Macmillan Co., 1949), pp. 117–22, 140–1, 151–5, 164–8.

[44] Boeke, *op. cit.*, p. 138.

[45] John A. Noon, *Labor Problems in Africa* (Philadelphia: University of Pennsylvania Press, 1944), p. 9.

lation to the family group since kinship ties are at the base of all economic activities.[46] Labor is performed, exchanged, and evaluated in relation to the family group for which the individual works and which aids him in his labor. The collective organization of labor extends beyond the small family group to the village, clan, and tribe. Labor for the African is not only a collective activity based upon family relations; it has certain religious attributes. The techniques which are employed are enmeshed in rites, prayers, and magic. And the notions and the emotions associated with them are opposed to the individualistic, secular, and purely economic conception of labor of the European who employs native labor.

Although in the older civilizations of Asia the handicrafts had developed to a high degree of perfection, the masses of peasants exhibited the same hostility as other peasant peoples to the capitalistic wage system. This has been shown in a study of Chinese workers in a Western type of factory during World War II.[47] The author of this study concludes that the problems in the factory were due to "the conflict between Chinese tradition and a modern organization of industry mainly copied from the West." [48] Traditionally, the Chinese handicraft worker was never separated from the rural community, whereas in the Western type of factory he has become an isolated worker like the workers in the cities of the West. As in other peasant cultures, the Chinese worker's subsistence was assured by the family system. This was true despite the fact that there was a labor surplus, since there was no unemployment as in a capitalistic labor market. The inefficiency of the Chinese worker under Western factory conditions, his lack of

[46] J. Cl. Pauvert, "La Notion de travail en Afrique noire" in *Le Travail de l'Afrique noire.* ("Presence Africaine 13") (Paris: Editions du Seuil, n.d.) , pp. 92–107.

[47] Kuo-Heng Shih, *China Enters the Machine Age* (Cambridge: Harvard University Press, 1944) .

[48] *Ibid.,* p. 154.

punctuality, and his lack of incentive are all due, as pointed out by the author of this study, to the transplantation of the worker from an integrated society to an agglomeration of workers for whom work means nothing except the wages he derives from it.

Industrialization in Africa has taken four principal forms:

the introduction of mining, leading to the settlement of labour in company camps or villages near the mining area; the development of plantations, involving the employment of a large proportion of seasonal workers; the large-scale development of industrial crops grown by African small-farmers with African hired labour, e.g., cocoa in the Gold Coast, cotton in Buganda; and finally the development of transport, factory industries and commerce which has led to the growth of a diversified wage-earning class of which a portion differing considerably from one area to another, is settled permanently in town.[49]

In West Africa and the western part of the Belgian Congo all four types of industrialization exist. On the other hand, in East Africa industrialization has "meant, primarily, the development of plantations run by Europeans or Indians and worked with African labor." Mining is the chief source of wealth in Northern Rhodesia and Katanga and is of importance in Southern Rhodesia where most of the natives in agricultural employment are on European farms. In the Union of South Africa the hundreds of thousands of native workers in the gold mines are drawn not only from the Union but also from Basutoland, Swaziland, Bechuanaland, and Mozambique.

A survey of Sekondi-Takoradi, a leading commercial center and the chief port of the Gold Coast, reveals some of the problems of the African worker in the urban areas

---

[49] Merran McCulloch, *Industrialization in Africa* (a report prepared by the International African Institute, in London, December 1950, for the Social Science Division of UNESCO), p.1.

that are developing in Africa.[50] The African worker faces first the problem of securing adequate housing. Because of the lack of housing there is not only much overcrowding but many workers sleep in the streets. Then the African worker experiences unemployment and destitution which were unknown in his traditional society. In order to meet the new problem of existence, the African forms various associations. Some of these associations are based upon occupations or they are modeled after the trade unions of the West. But very often the economic aims of the occupational associations are subordinated to social and religious aims, e.g., to provide mutual aid at funerals and other celebrations. The effort to maintain the traditional basis of social life is manifested in the associations based on tribal loyalties which undertake to deal with the new economic and social problems faced by the African worker.

Some African workers do not break completely with the subsistence economy when they become wage earners. Failure to do so usually represents, however, a transitional stage inasmuch as there are growing restrictions upon the subsistence economy and an ever increasing demand on the part of government for money payments for taxes. The mobility of African workers is often responsible for their inefficiency and their low wages. However, there is much evidence showing that the African worker responds to wage incentives in much the same manner as workers in the West.[51] The stabilization and increased efficiency of the African is not achieved, however, by economic incentives alone. The experience of the Union Minière in the Belgian Congo shows that the stabilization and increased efficiency of Africans was achieved by the reduction of illness and mortality, and by providing conditions favorable to

[50] Kofi A. Busia, *Report on a Social Survey of Sekondi-Takoradi* (London: Crown Agents, 1950).
[51] See Noon, *op. cit.*, pp. 16 ff.

normal family life, improved vocational education, and social services.[52]

The problem of the migrant African worker is still of great importance in the economic organization of race relations. The decrease in the proportion of recruited to non-recruited labor has meant that the costs of recruitment have been shifted from private industry to colonial governments, since it is the colonial administration that must look after the needs of the hundreds of thousands of African workers who constantly seek work in European enterprises. Moreover, it is the colonial administration which must safeguard the family and native social organization that are affected by the migration of workers.

When Negro workers in the United States were first drawn into modern industry on a large scale during World War I, many of them reacted in a manner similar to that of the peasant peoples of Asia and Africa. Because of social but more especially because of economic conditions in the South as well as because of the attraction of northern industry, thousands of Negroes migrated from southern plantations to the industrial centers of the North.[53] In the North they filled the vacuum created by the cessation of European immigration and the return of European immigrants to their homes. They found places mainly as unskilled workers in the heavy industries—iron and steel, shipbuilding, and meat packing. Many of these workers, who were unaccustomed to the habits and discipline of modern industry, had little understanding or appreciation of punctuality and continuous labor. Moreover, since they received a larger money remuneration than they had ever known, they lacked the incentive to work at tasks that had no meaning for them, thus creating a serious problem of

[52] L. Toussaint, "L'Avenir de la population bantoue du Haute-Katanga Industriel," in *Comptes Rendus du Congres Scientifique* (Bruxelles: Comité Spécial du Katanga, n.d.), pp. 31–44.

[53] See Sterling D. Spero and Abram L. Harris, *The Black Worker* (New York: Columbia University Press, 1931), Chap. VIII.

labor turnover for the industries. Their behavior was interpreted as evidence of laziness or as proof that the Negro because of his racial traits could not become an efficient industrial worker. But as the Negro worker became accustomed to the discipline of modern industry, he showed the same efficiency as white industrial workers.

WHITE MANAGERS

The investment of foreign capital by Europeans in countries inhabited by the colored races has always resulted in a system of white management. This has been inevitable since Europeans have brought to these countries not only the necessary capital but industrial techniques and methods of business enterprise that were unknown to non-European peoples. Western merchants who established enterprises in the Treaty Ports in China after 1842 had to assume responsibility for a type of commercial society that was unknown to the Chinese.[54] In establishing the shipping trade, they had to form banking institutions and insurance companies. In fact, the Chinese merchants found it more economical to send their goods in Western ships which were insured than in their junks that were menaced by piracy. Moreover, in order to establish trade relations with the Chinese economy, Western merchants had to organize the supply of goods for the export trade. The Western merchant became a privileged person in the foreign trade of China despite the fact that China had long carried on trade with Southeast Asia.[55] As a consequence, the foreign trade of China was dominated by the great Western commercial houses and the foreign chambers of commerce in the various Treaty Ports.

The dominant position of the Western merchant is shown by his role in the export of tea and silk. Because of

[54] See Allen and Donnithorne, *op. cit.*, pp. 18 ff.
[55] *Ibid.*, pp. 31 ff.

the limitations upon the ownership of land outside the Treaty Ports, Westerners could not establish tea plantations. With the exception of the Russians, who soon acquired control of the tea trade in Central Asia, the Westerners did not go into the country to purchase the tea. The control of tea by Westerners did not begin until the tea reached the Treaty Ports. Despite the efforts of the Chinese to share in the tea trade with the West, the trade remained in the hands of Europeans until China was able to free herself from Western domination. The Western merchant was not as successful in the silk trade as in the tea trade. In the case of silk it was necessary not only to organize the trade but to improve the methods of production and the quality of the product. In the end the Westerners failed because of the competition of the Japanese, who were able to supervise the production of a superior type of silk. The role of the European in the development of railroads, of the mining industry, and of various types of factories can not be recounted here. In each case it reveals the dominant role which the European played because of his knowledge of Western business organization and superior industrial skills.

Although in Japan the role of the European merchant was different from his role in China because of the reaction of Japan to the West, he nevertheless played a part in the modernization of Japan.[56] While the Japanese had a well-developed internal trade, they lacked the skill necessary to manufacture goods for export as well as the technical knowledge required in foreign trade. Consequently, nearly all the import and export trade of Japan remained in the hands of foreign merchants until the last decade of the nineteenth century. On the other hand, the Japanese in contrast to the Chinese were soon able to take control of their banking, and they gradually built up a merchant marine.

[56] *Ibid.*, pp. 196 ff.

In tropical Africa white managers were an indispensable part of the economic regime which was inaugurated by Europeans. Moreover, African natives had not reached the stage of civilization which the Europeans encountered in Asia. Under the system of concessions in the Congo, in French Equatorial Africa, and in the German Cameroons, Europeans became the masters of native labor. As the industrialization of Africa has advanced, the white man has continued to occupy managerial positions. The majority of the Africans employed in European enterprises are unskilled workers, while a few may occupy minor clerical positions and work in skilled occupations, depending upon the pressure of the white working force. In Leopoldville, the *Chantiers Navals et Industriels du Congo,* which includes two naval workshops and establishments for assembling tractors and electric machinery, employs about 200 Europeans and 3,000 to 3,500 Africans.[57] About two thirds of the Africans are employed as unskilled workers, while the remainder are employed as riveters, draftsmen, and in other skilled occupations. In Nigeria, where the educated African has gradually assumed a more responsible role in the economic life of the country, about 3,500 of the 34,500 Africans employed by the United Africa Company in trading, transport, plantation, and forestry were in the office organization and another 3,500 were in skilled labor.[58] Except for 1,100 Africans employed as storekeepers, the remainder worked in unskilled occupations. On the other hand, in the mines of Northern Rhodesia, Africans are confined almost entirely to unskilled occupations, and their promotion to even skilled occupations is opposed by white workers.[59]

In South Africa where, as we shall see in the next chap-

[57] *Industrialization in Africa* (a report prepared by the International African Institute for the Social Science Division of UNESCO) (London: Her Majesty's Printing Office, 1954), p. 49.

[58] *Ibid.,* p. 11.

[59] *Ibid.,* p. 105.

ter, there is a color bar in respect to employment, the dominant position of white managers is not based solely upon their economic position and cultural differences but is supported by law. For all racial groups in South Africa agriculture has been the chief occupation.[60] However, all but 3 per cent of the Europeans engaged in agriculture are farmers or sons of farmers whereas practically all of the Africans are peasants restricted to cultivating small parcels of lands in the reserves and to working as laborers on European farms. In the mining industry, Europeans act as managers, engineers, supervisors, and qualified miners.[61] In 1942–3 in private manufacturing industry, 5,695 Europeans were "working proprietors" as compared with 16 Africans, 164 Coloured, and 419 Asians.[62] Likewise, there were on the salaried staffs of private manufacturing industry 25,138 Europeans, 89 Africans, 28 Coloured, and 167 Asians. In commercial occupations, the managers and proprietors were predominantly Europeans with a fairly large proportion of Asians.

In the United States, where the dominant position of white managers has been based largely upon economic and cultural factors but has not been supported by law, the Negro has nevertheless been subject to white management in all phases of his economic life. The operation of a quasi color bar in industrial and other occupations in the United States will be discussed in the next chapter.

COLORED MIDDLEMEN

The establishment of economic relations between the European and colored races has generally resulted in the emergence of a class of colored middlemen. When the Europeans established the slave trade in Africa, the chiefs in what is now Nigeria engaged in the slave raids in order to

[60] See Hellmann, *op. cit.*, pp. 112–15.
[61] *Ibid.*, p. 116.
[62] *Ibid.*, p. 119.

supply slaves for the white dealers in black flesh.[63] Both on the Slave Coast and on the Gold Coast the supplying of slaves to the European ships was entirely in the hands of the native Africans.[64] The small African states on the Gold Coast encouraged Europeans to build forts on the coast in order to protect their monopoly of the supply of slaves from the more powerful inland kingdoms. As a result, the supply of slaves from the interior was controlled by the Accra and Fante middlemen who sent their agents to buy slaves in towns in the interior which specialized in the slave trade.

The role of the colored middleman in the economic relations of European and colored peoples achieved its classical form in the *comprador* who was a nominal employee of the Western business firms in China.[65] When Europeans began trading with China, it was necessary to employ a Chinese who could speak English, since the Europeans were ignorant of Chinese and very few Chinese could speak English. This nominal employee played a more important role than that of interpreter since he recruited the members of the Chinese staff and, more important still, he had charge of the purchases and sales involving Chinese dealers. These *compradors* acquired wealth through their transactions, and they often became traders in their own right. As the Chinese became educated in Western ways of doing business, as Westerners began to learn Chinese, and as Japanese firms became more important in China, the system of *compradors* began to decay.

The colored middleman has made his appearance in Africa as the result of the development of Western enterprise. On the Gold Coast, where goods manufactured

[63] Sir Alan Burns, *History of Nigeria* (London: George Allen and Unwin, Ltd., 1951) , p. 67.
[64] W. E. F. Ward, *A History of the Gold Coast* (London: George Allen and Unwin, Ltd., 1948) , p. 82.
[65] See Allen and Donnithorne, *op cit.*, pp. 47 ff.

abroad are channeled to the native consumers through European importers, these goods are distributed to native retail dealers.[66] Likewise, in Nigeria, where the bulk of import trade is handled by nonresident companies, these companies dispense "goods through their own widely distributed factories and through African middlemen who in turn supply local shops and markets or themselves retail." [67] The nonresident companies also "handle over 90 per cent of purchases for export of palm oil, palm kernels, groundnuts, and cocoa." The African has increasingly shared in the distributive trade in recent years. This development is in harmony with the Ten Year Plan of Development and Welfare which aims to secure "a larger share of Nigeria's trade for Nigerians and to accelerate the industrial development of Nigeria by methods which ensure the maximum participation of Nigerians." [68] Under the present economic relations of Europeans and Africans in South Africa there is no place, as we shall see, for the colored middleman.

Although there has not existed among the Negroes in the United States a class which might be designated middlemen in the sense in which we have used the word, those who have engaged in what is generally known as "Negro business" have played in a restricted sense a somewhat similar role. Whereas the colored middleman has generally derived his profit from procuring the goods produced by the colored masses for the white capitalist and trader, the Negro businessman in the United States has been restricted to providing those services for Negroes which the white businessman did not want to provide. Some of the Negroes who were free before the Civil War engaged in small business ventures based upon the skills which they

[66] Colonial Office, *An Economic Survey of the Colonial Territories, 1951* (London: His Majesty's Stationery Office, 1952), III, 33–4.

[67] *Ibid.*, p. 63.

[68] *The Nigerian Handbook* (2d ed.; London: Crown Agents for Oversea Governments and Administrations, 1954).

had acquired in domestic services.[69] Often they provided services for whites when they operated livery stables and taverns, and they became famous as caterers in southern as well as northern cities. It was only after the Civil War when the Freedmen's Saving and Trust Company was established that the Negro acquired the spirit of modern capitalism and undertook to establish banks and other forms of business enterprise. In fact, Negro business was held up to the masses as the solution of their poverty and unemployment and as the means to equality in a country where white men held economic power.[70] But the faith in Negro business only proved a delusion, since after more than a half century of preaching the necessity for Negroes to engage in business and the necessity for the Negro masses to be loyal to Negro business, Negro business enterprises are still of no significance in the American economy or in providing employment for Negroes.[71] The total assets of all the Negro banks in the United States amount to less than the assets of a single white bank in a small city, and the majority of Negro businesses are devoted to supplying personal services for Negroes which whites do not want to supply.[72] The new role of the Negro in the American economy will be discussed in the section dealing with the problem of social organization.

AID TO UNDERDEVELOPED AREAS

At the close of World War I, the Allied powers were faced with the struggle between, on one hand, the imperial

[69] See Abram Harris, *The Negro as Capitalist* (Philadelphia: The American Academy of Political and Social Sciences, 1936), pp. 10 ff. See also W. E. B. Du Bois (ed.), *The Negro in Business* (Atlanta: Atlanta University Press, 1899), pp. 8–13.

[70] See Harris, *The Negro as Capitalist,* pp. 49–50.

[71] See Frazier, *op. cit.,* Chap. XVI.

[72] For the present status of Negro business see Joseph A. Pierce, *Negro Business and Business Education* (New York: Harper & Brothers, 1947).

forces that wanted to annex outright the colonial possessions of the defeated nations, and, on the other, the advocates of the international administration of these colonies. Out of this struggle came the compromise which is known as the mandate system under the League of Nations. The mandate system was concerned especially with European possessions in Africa.[73] Although the idea underlying the system of mandates—namely, that the European imperial powers were to be regarded as trustees for backward peoples—did not change the economic relations of the European powers to the colored colonial peoples, it did represent a fundamental change in the nineteenth-century doctrine of colonies as underdeveloped imperial estates.

World War II completed the destruction of the world economy which had already been undermined by the impact of World War I. The European colonies, in which the colored peoples provided the source of labor, had played an increasingly important role in the world economy during the two world wars. Consequently, in any attempt to rebuild the world economy, it was necessary to recognize that the colonialism of the nineteenth century was no longer possible. In 1925 it became the official policy of Russia to "proletarize" its colonial peoples, and in its struggle with the West, Russia became the champion of the colonial peoples.[74] Moreover, the United States, as the leading industrial and financial power in the world, was opposed to colonial barriers and favored free markets. In the Atlantic Charter, in 1941, the position of the United States was expressed in Article 3 which declared that every people has the right to choose the form of government under which it desires to live.[75] This was a tardy recognition

[73] See Rayford W. Logan, *The Operation of the Mandate System in Africa, 1919–1927* (Washington: The Foundation Publishers, Inc., 1942). See also Lord S. H. Olivier, *op. cit.*, Chaps. XXIV, XXV.

[74] See Hubert Deschamps, *La Fin des empires coloniaux* (Paris: Presses Universitaires de France, 1950), pp. 76 ff.

[75] *Ibid.*, pp. 74 ff.

of the fact that Asia was in open revolt and that the people of Africa were voicing their opposition to colonial exploitation.

As a result of the Yalta Conference in 1945, a "new colonial charter" became a part of the Charter of the United Nations.[76] Article 73 of Chapter XI of the Charter stated that the members of the United Nations

which have or assume responsibilities for the administration of territories whose peoples have not yet attained a full measure of self-government recognize the principle that the interests of the inhabitants of these territories are paramount, and accept as a sacred trust the obligation to promote to the utmost, within the system of international peace and security established by the present Charter, the well-being of the inhabitants of these territories, and, to this end:

d. to promote constructive measures of development, to encourage research, and to cooperate with one another, and when and where appropriate, with specialized international bodies with a view to the practical achievement of the social, economic, and scientific purposes set forth in this Article; and

e. to transmit regularly to the Secretary-General for information purposes, subject to such limitation as security and constitutional considerations may require, statistical and other information of a technical nature relating to economic, social, and educational conditions in the territories for which they are respectively responsible other than those territories to which Chapters XII and XIII apply.

Chapters XII and XIII were concerned with the International Trustee System which included the mandated territories, territories which might be detached from the enemy as the result of World War II, and territories voluntarily placed under the trusteeship system. Article 76 of Chapter XII stated that one of the basic objectives of the

[76] See Henri Labouret, *Colonisation, colonialisme, decolonisation* (Paris: La Rose, 1952), pp. 49 ff.

trustee system was to promote the political, economic, social, and educational advancement of the inhabitants.

Although it was one of the principal aims of the United Nations to bring about cooperation on the part of its members in the economic development of the underdeveloped areas, the various European nations in control of these areas inaugurated their own plans of economic development, and they have drawn upon the financial resources of the United States. This is seen in the case of Africa which, as the result of political events in Asia, has become the most important underdeveloped area in the world. Under the Colonial Development and Welfare Act, $143,000,000 of the $336,000,000 voted by the British Parliament in 1945 was assigned to Africa south of the Sahara. Additional sums were set aside from the same source for public works in Africa not including other investments voted by Parliament. In France the government made grants to the Fonds de Développement Économique et Social (FIDES) in addition to contributions from the territories for African development. By the end of 1950 public development plans involving $264,000,000 had been financed almost entirely by metropolitan France. In addition to financing public development plans, the government made loans and grants amounting to $50,000,000 to public, semipublic, and private concerns in Africa. The Belgian Congo began in 1950 a ten-year plan in which metropolitan Belgium did not play a direct role. This plan provided for the industrialization of the Congo, for the development of native agriculture, and for education and hygiene.[77] Between 1946 and 1949 metropolitan Portugal made grants amounting to $66,000,000 in Angola and Mozambique.

In carrying out these developments, some of the African territories have been aided by the Marshall Aid to Eu-

[77] See Guy Malengreau, "Recent Developments in Belgian Africa," in C. Grove Haines (ed.), *Africa Today* (Baltimore: The Johns Hopkins Press, 1955) , pp. 337–57.

rope or out of the dollar credits which were set aside by the Economic Cooperation Administration for the development of overseas territories. Long-term loans were also made by the Economic Cooperation Administration in order to stimulate the production of scarce raw materials.[78] While it is difficult to estimate the extent of private investments, it appears that a large part of the profits in the various African territories is used for the expansion of existing enterprises or capitalization of new enterprises. Not much private foreign capital has been used in recent years in the development of these territories. About $11,500,000 of private foreign capital was invested between 1946 and 1949 in the French territories, while approximately $1,200,000, mostly from the United States, was invested in the Belgian Congo between 1947 and 1949.[79]

The problem of aid to underdeveloped countries was the subject of a study by a group of experts appointed by the Secretary-General of the United Nations at the invitation of the Economic and Social Council.[80] While the terms of reference of the resolution of the Economic and Social Council were concerned primarily with economic development in relation to unemployment and underemployment, the report of the group of experts analyzes the technological, economic, and to some extent, sociological factors involved in the problem of economic development of underdeveloped countries. Therefore, although this study does not deal specifically with the problem of the relation of white capital and colored labor, it contains much material on this problem. The report takes account of the low level of technological development in underdeveloped countries and the difficulties from an economic standpoint involved in capital formation. The problem of population

[78] *Investments in Overseas Territories South of the Sahara* (Paris: Organization for European Economic Cooperation 1951) , p. 51.

[79] *Ibid.,* p. 53.

[80] See *Measures for the Economic Development of Under-Developed Countries* (New York: United Nations, 1951) .

growth in relation to resources and productivity and the problems incident to planning are also considered. The report of the experts also shows how problems of economic development are related to the fact that some underdeveloped areas are dependent upon the export of one or two staples. Finally, the report shows that the economic development of the underdeveloped countries can not be carried out through private investments. Of special relevance to our study is the fact emphasized by the experts that in order to improve economic conditions the governments of underdeveloped countries must "spend large sums in improving the human factor—on schools, on agricultural extension services, on university training, on technical education, and on public health." [81] Also pointed out in the report is the fact that one of the serious obstacles to further expansion of direct foreign investment is the fear on the part of underdeveloped countries of foreign control of important sectors of their economies. In the conclusion, the experts face the fact that the implementation of their recommendations will depend upon political forces in the international situation. This will be dealt with in the third part of our study which is concerned with the political aspects of race relations.

81 *Ibid.*, p. 84.

CHAPTER VIII

The Color Bar and Labor

INTRODUCTION

The previous chapter was concerned primarily with the economic relations which have developed between European and colored peoples in areas where non-Europeans have been the chief source of labor. In this chapter our purpose will be to consider the economic relations which have developed between Europeans and colored peoples in those areas where white as well as colored peoples provide the labor of the community. Consideration will be given first to the racial division of labor which has grown up within these communities, either as the result of an impersonal competitive process or as the result of historical circumstances, or both. Then the discussion will be devoted to the attempts which have been made to maintain a color bar in employment in order that white and colored workers could not compete, or in order that colored workers could not enter skilled and white-collar occupations. This will be followed by a consideration of the role of management and organized labor in the maintenance of the color bar, or in removing racial barriers. Finally, our discussion will be concerned with the role of the state in maintaining or in breaking down the color bar in labor.

RACIAL DIVISION OF LABOR

In the first part of our study, which dealt with the ecological organization of race relations, we were concerned primarily with the manner in which the European and colored races had achieved a modus vivendi on the biological plane or in the struggle for existence. Where the different races have been brought together in the same community, this struggle for existence has resulted in a racial division of labor. The racial division of labor which characterizes the ecological organization of race relations grows out of an impersonal competitive process.[1] However, in the racial division of labor, as in all human divisions of labor, the particular labor status which a group has acquired is not due, as in certain animal forms, to biological specialization. So far as the racial division of labor is an impersonal process, the labor status of a race is determined by certain socially acquired characteristics. The habits and attitudes of slaves, or the attitudes of a racial group that occupies a certain caste position in a society, are the result of psychological and social adaptations to a particular status.

Where labor status is not predetermined by birth as it is in the case of slavery and caste, the cultural backgrounds and skills and the psychological make-up of races have determined their position in the existing division of labor. This may be noted in the case of the racial division of labor in Jamaica.[2] The Negro population of Jamaica increased from nearly 300,000 in 1844 to 1,000,000 in 1943.

[1] See Edward B. Reuter, "Competition and the Racial Division of Labor," in Edgar T. Thompson (ed.), *Race Relations and the Race Problem* (Durham: Duke University Press, 1939), pp. 47 ff.

[2] Based upon materials collected as part of an unpublished study by the author of race and culture contacts in the Caribbean area. This study was made possible by a grant-in-aid from the American Philosophical Society. The facts concerning Jamaica are also based upon a subsequently published study by Leonard Broom, "The Social Differentiation of Jamaica," *American Sociological Review*, XIX (April 1954), 115–25.

As the result of the draining off of the whites following the decline in revenues from tropical production, the white population of Jamaica which numbered about 15,000 in 1844 has scarcely changed during a hundred years. Nevertheless, the white population, which amounts to only 1 per cent of the population, still owns and controls the large estates, the shipping, and the finance on the island. The colored population which came into existence as a consequence of the mixing of whites and blacks gradually filled the lower positions which otherwise would have been filled by whites. Moreover, Chinese, East Indians, and Syrians who have come to the island have found a place in the racial division of labor.

The racial division of labor is indicated by the concentration of the various racial elements in different occupations. Of the blacks, who comprise four fifths of the population in Jamaica, almost one half are engaged in agriculture and nearly a fourth gain a living as laborers, while only 1 per cent of them are in clerical occupations and less than 1 per cent in professional services.[3] On the other hand, of the colored people, who comprise less than a fifth of the population, 10 per cent are in clerical occupations and 2.6 per cent in professional service. Nearly two thirds of the relatively small number of Chinese are engaged in trade and slightly more than a tenth are in clerical occupations. Of the East Indians, who comprise 2 per cent of the population, about two thirds gain a livelihood in agriculture while slightly less than two thirds of the Syrians are engaged in trade. The racial division of labor is related to the education and traditions of the various cultural groups.[4]

According to Lind, Hawaii has established and maintained, to a far greater degree than the majority of other

[3] See *Eighth Census of Jamaica and Its Dependencies, 1943:* Population, Housing and Agriculture (Kingston: The Government Printer, 1945), p. 179.

[4] See Broom, *op. cit.,* pp. 119–20, 125.

areas where Europeans have settled, "the capitalistic principle of freedom—freedom to compete for a place in the economic order, irrespective of race and origin." [5] The capitalistic economy which was introduced into the islands upset the existing occupational structure and set in motion a vertical mobility. This was necessary for efficiency, which depended upon increasing specialization in the labor force. Each successive immigrant racial group began at the bottom of the occupational pyramid, i.e. on the lower levels of plantation labor, and rose to higher levels as the expanding economy permitted. Each immigrant group—the peasant peoples of China, Japan, Korea, the Philippines, Puerto Rico, and certain European countries, notably Portugal and Spain—has begun on the plantation and, as it has moved up the occupational pyramid, has entered into competition outside the plantation. However, the plantation itself has provided some opportunity to move up the occupational ladder, and there is evidence that the various racial groups have improved their economic position over the decades. Nevertheless, the *haole* or white man in his position as overseer has never been threatened, and he has always occupied the higher managerial positions. In recent years the Japanese and, to a lesser extent, the Chinese, have made some progress in occupying positions of considerable responsibility. Outside the plantation, trade has usually provided the road to advancement, especially for the Orientals. The Hawaiians, who never had a trading tradition, generally found other roads to advancement, especially in law and as judges and teachers where political influence is important. Just before the opening of World War II, it appeared that the cycle of racial succession was drawing to a close and that the existing racial division of labor was becoming crystallized. However, World War II and changes in the world situation have set in motion

[5] Andrew W. Lind, *An Island Community* (Chicago: University of Chicago Press, 1938), pp. 245 ff.

changes in the islands which will probably increase the mobility of the various racial elements.

In Bahia, Brazil, according to Pierson, is found "a freely competitive order in which individuals compete for position largely on the basis of personal merit and favorable family circumstance. Individual competence tends to overbalance ethnic origin as a determinant of social status." [6] Bahia did have, however, a racial division of labor based more or less upon color. The whites in Bahia were concentrated in the higher levels of the occupational scale while the blacks were found in the lower occupations. The whites were predominant in such occupations as bank employees, priests, businessmen, professors, and lawyers; while the blacks were predominant in such occupations as stevedores, masons, domestics, and street laborers. The mulattoes or at least the lighter mulattoes were predominant in such occupations as barbers, band musicians, streetcar conductors, checkers of street conductors' records, street sweepers, taxi drivers and bus drivers. This division of labor according to race or color is, according to Pierson, the result of the fact that the ancestors of the Negroes began as slaves who owned no property. The superior occupational status of the mulatto has been due to the same causes as in the United States.[7] There is a fundamental difference, as Pierson points out, in that the mulatto in the United States has only been able to ascend the occupational ladder within the Negro community, whereas in Brazil the mulatto and the unmixed Negro have been able to rise within the total community.[8]

The principle that determined the racial division of labor which resulted in Negro slavery in the United States

[6] See Donald Pierson, *Negroes in Brazil* (Chicago: University of Chicago Press, 1942) , pp. 177 ff. Copyright 1942 by the University of Chicago.

[7] See Edward B. Reuter, *The Mulatto in the United States* (Boston: R. G. Badger, 1918) .

[8] Pierson, *op. cit.*, pp. 185–6.

was, as Reuter has indicated, "that of naked power." [9]
Even the division of labor which existed among the slaves
on the plantation, which was a relatively self-contained economic unit, was due essentially to the arbitrary action of
the white masters.[10] However, during the years before the
Civil War, a class of free Negroes, especially mulattoes,
came to occupy a position in the racial division of labor
which was due essentially to competition.[11] From the beginning of the enslavement of Negroes in the English colonies, a class of free Negroes existed owing to the fact that
the first Negroes introduced into the colonies had the same
status as the indentured white servants. Since under the
system of slavery the children inherited the status of their
mothers, the free Negro population was increased partly
by the mulatto children of free colored mothers and to a
lesser extent by mulatto children of white servant women
and by the offspring of Negro men and Indian women.
While some of the growth in the free Negro population
was due to natural increase, the major source of the increase was the slaves who were set free or who bought their
freedom. Many slaves were set free because of meritorious
services to the white community or because they were
mulattoes or because of their devotion to their white masters. But when one studies the distribution and growth of
the free Negro population before the Civil War, it is clear
that the growth of the free Negro population was due
chiefly to the decline of the plantation system of agriculture. In areas where the plantation system of agriculture
was proving unprofitable, slaves were liberated or they
were permitted to work on their own for a certain period
and very often accumulated enough money to buy their

[9] Reuter, "Competition and the Racial Division of Labor," in Edgar T. Thompson (ed.) , *op. cit.,* p. 56.

[10] Concerning the division of labor among the slaves on the plantation where mulatto slaves enjoyed certain advantages see E. Franklin
Frazier, *The Negro in the United States* (New York: The Macmillan Co.,
1949) , pp. 53 ff.

[11] See *ibid.,* Chap. IV.

freedom. On the other hand, where the plantation system of agriculture continued to be a profitable mode of economic exploitation, the free Negro population remained small and did not show an appreciable increase.

While in the North the free Negroes could not compete with immigrant European laborers, in many areas of the South they achieved a relatively high level of economic well-being, far above that of the landless poor whites. In Charleston, South Carolina, they acquired a monopoly in the skilled trades, and some among them acquired considerable wealth, including slaves. Likewise, in New Orleans, the free people of color, as they were known because they were largely mulattoes, were in skilled occupations and they accumulated property amounting to $15,-000,000 by 1860. Some of the free mulattoes of Louisiana owned plantations worked by black slaves.

After emancipation, when the great masses of the Negro population were thrown into competition with the nonslaveholding whites, the racial division of labor which developed was not due to the operation of impersonal competition but to the interference of social and political forces.[12] Likewise, in South Africa, the color bar in employment is the result of political forces which are recognized to be uneconomical under a system of competitive capitalism.

OCCUPATIONAL CEILING

In South Africa, "The most outstanding characteristic of the occupational distribution of the population is the close relation between occupation and race. The greatest occupational gulf is between Europeans and Africans. Coloured and Asiatics, in the districts in which they live, occupy an intermediate position. Professional, supervisory,

---

[12] Sterling D. Spero and Abram L. Harris, *The Black Worker* (New York: Columbia University Press, 1931), *passim.*

and skilled work is performed mainly by Europeans, to a lesser extent by Coloured and Asiatics, and to an almost negligible extent by Africans." [13] This racial division of labor is due to a color bar and is designed to prevent competition between white and non-European workers. Consequently, South African industry, as Buell has written, "is based upon a labor supply consisting of a large number of underpaid natives and a small number of artificially high-paid whites." [14] This wage structure is due, according to the *Economic and Wage Commission Report* of 1926, to the rapidly developing industrialization in which there was a scarcity of European skilled workers and an abundance of unskilled native workers.[15] But as the European population increased in urban areas, not all Europeans were capable of becoming skilled artisans, supervisors, or managers of industry. Moreover, among the native population there were those who showed themselves capable of doing skilled work while many whites during the expansion of industry were being drawn into unskilled occupations. The color bar represents an attempt of the dominant white group to stop the operation of the laws of competition in a society based upon economic competition which requires the economic use of human labor. The uneconomic use of human labor is part of the wage structure which arbitrarily places certain values upon European and native labor. Consequently, the shortage of native labor which often develops really means that there is an uneconomic use of native labor.[16]

The extent of the color bar in the mines is indicated by the fact that in 1920 out of fifty-one different occupa-

[13] Ellen Hellmann (ed.), *Handbook on Race Relations in South Africa* (New York: Oxford University Press, Inc., 1949), p. 109. Reprinted by permission of the publisher.

[14] Raymond L. Buell, *The Native Problem in Africa* (New York: The Macmillan Co., 1928), I, 58.

[15] See S. H. Frankel, *Capital Investment in Africa* (New York: Oxford University Press, Inc., 1938), p. 141.

[16] *Ibid.*, pp. 142–3.

tions, regulations prescribed the employment of natives in thirty-two occupations and custom prescribed their employment in the remaining nineteen occupations. About 11,000 European workers in the mines were protected from competition with native workers.[17] In the mining industry there is not only a clear-cut division of labor between European supervisor and miner and African laborer, but there is a great gap between the wages of Europeans and Africans.[18] African laborers, who are housed in compounds, with 16 to 20 men to a room, receive an average monthly wage about one tenth of that paid to European workers. It is the same in manufacturing though the disparity is not as great, probably because of the lower wages of white women. A similar differential exists in the payment of teachers; the European teachers being paid more than all non-European teachers with the same qualifications and the Africans being paid less than any of the other non-European teachers.

In the United States there has existed a color bar which places a ceiling upon the employment of colored workers—black, yellow, and red. The black workers include the Negro; the yellow, the Chinese, Japanese, and Filipinos; and the red, the Mexicans and Indians.[19] The restrictions placed upon the employment of Chinese and Japanese have been due in part to legal barriers affecting the employment of aliens, especially Orientals.[20] But attitudes of employers and of white workers toward Oriental workers have been similar to those toward Negroes.[21] Although the relatively small number of Filipinos were not classed as aliens, they suffered from the same discrimination as other Orientals.[22] The Mexican worker, who has

[17] Buel, *op. cit.*, I, 59.
[18] Hellmann, *op. cit.*, 128 ff.
[19] See Herman Feldman, *Racial Factors in American Industry* (New York: Harper & Brothers, 1931).
[20] *Ibid.*, p. 85.
[21] *Ibid.*, p. 88.
[22] *Ibid.*, pp. 97 ff.

been exploited as a seasonal worker and employed for the least desirable types of work, has never been considered as eligible for citizenship and has therefore often been caught between the grindstones of white and Negro labor.[23] The Indian has generally been discounted as an industrial worker because of his segregation in American society, his lack of education, and the popular beliefs concerning his ability to acquire civilization.[24]

The color bar in employment in the United States is concerned primarily with the Negro.[25] In the South the color bar is part of the effort to maintain a caste system based upon racial descent. Therefore, the color bar undertakes not only to prevent competition between white and Negro workers but to restrict Negro workers to occupations indicative of a low status; there is no opposition to the employment of Negroes as domestic servants and as common laborers. When Negroes are employed as skilled workers, they only work as a "helper" to a white worker who receives pay for skilled work. But Negroes cannot become foremen, which would place them in a position of authority over white men, nor can they become white-collar workers (except in Negro schools and businesses) because of the status involved in a white-collar occupation.

Although there has been a color bar in the North, it has never been as rigid as in the South. This may be seen in an examination of the occupational status of Negroes in the North as compared with the South. For example, in the largest Negro communities in southern cities in 1940, only 6 to 9 per cent of employed Negro men were in professional, business, and white-collar occupations.[26] The same was true of Negroes in the so-called border cities

    23 *Ibid.*, p. 122.
    24 *Ibid.*, pp. 124 ff.
    25 For a discussion of the various aspects of discrimination in the employment of Negroes and the rationalizations which are used to justify the discrimination see *ibid.*, Chap. II.
    26 See Frazier, *op. cit.*, pp. 285–97.

—Baltimore, the District of Columbia, Louisville, and St. Louis. On the other hand, in northern cities from 10 to 20 per cent of the Negro men were in professional, business, and clerical occupations. The extent of the difference between the North and South (including border states) is not disclosed by these figures in that the Negro white-collar workers in southern cities were employed in the segregated Negro community whereas many of the Negroes employed in the so-called white-collar occupations in the North were employed in "white" institutions or the institutions of the general community. Nevertheless, there has been a color bar to the employment of Negroes in the North.[27] Discrimination in employment has been especially marked during periods of economic depression when the competition between white and colored workers is intensified. Even during normal times Negro men and women are generally employed in domestic and personal service and are not employed in clerical and technical positions, especially those of a supervisory nature. Likewise, the Negro has been excluded from such white-collar occupations as salesmen and saleswomen in stores. Where the Negro secured a clerical position in the larger or white community, it was generally in some governmental agency and was due to the fact that in the northern city the Negro has the vote.

ORGANIZED LABOR AND COLOR

In South Africa the leaders of the labor movement gave their support to the color bar in employment on the grounds that the employers would lower the standard of living of white workers by using cheap native labor. Consequently, in considering the role of organized white labor in establishing and maintaining the color bar in employ-

[27] See St. Clair Drake and Horace R. Cayton, *Black Metropolis* (New York: Harcourt, Brace and Company, 1945) , Chap. IX.

ment, it is necessary to see its role in relation to white employers. In 1916, the South African Mine Workers Union demanded that such semiskilled work as drill-sharpening and track-laying, which in some mines had been performed by whites and in others by natives, should be reserved for white workers.[28] This demand was opposed by the Chamber of Mines representing the mineowners and in 1918 an agreement was reached according to which no positions held by Europeans should be given to natives and vice versa. The conflict between mine management and European miners continued and resulted in the Rand Strike in 1922.[29] The main issue of the strike was the decision of the Chamber of Mines to modify the color bar and employ non-Europeans in skilled work and increase the ratio of Africans employed to Europeans. After a struggle which lasted 76 days and caused the death of 230 persons, the white union was forced to call off the strike and the Chamber of Mines rehired workers on its own terms.

During the industrial unrest which followed the collapse of the boom during World War I, the native workers began to strike and to form unions of their own. In some cases the non-European workers had the sympathy and support of white unionists. Although because of race prejudice separate unions were generally formed, the white workers who were often employed in the same kind of work as non-Europeans recognized the necessity of cooperation. In 1946, of the 115 unions affiliated with the South African Trades and Labour Council, 50 were mixed unions with European, Coloured, and Indian members; 35 had an exclusively European membership; and 30 contained only non-Europeans, a small proportion of them being separate unions for Africans.[30] Only a few white trade unions like the mineworkers organization have a

---

[28] Buell, *op. cit.*, I, 59–60.   [30] *Ibid.*, p. 165.
[29] Hellmann, *op. cit.*, p. 160.

color bar in their constitution, but non-Europeans are excluded from the remainder by trade union monopoly, by employers, or by the law.

After the emancipation of the Negro in the United States, there was a violent resistance on the part of white workers to Negro competition in northern as well as in southern cities.[31] There were bloody fights between Negro and white workers in New York, Buffalo, and other cities in 1863 when Negro strikebreakers were brought in and later in Boston when southern Negro workers were employed to defeat the efforts of white workers to secure an eight-hour working day. Although the socialistic workingmen's societies were inclined to be sympathetic toward the Negro workers who served as tools of the employers, the trade unions which were controlled by skilled workers were less class-conscious and tended to exclude Negro workers on account of race. In Canton, Ohio, for example, the white workers went on strike because a Negro was employed as a foreman, and in Washington, D.C., the bricklayers unions would not permit their members to work alongside a Negro. This was indicative of the spirit among white unions which were developing along craft lines and which were creating an aristocracy of labor based partly upon racial exclusiveness.

There were, however, movements among white workers which included Negro workers.[32] The National Labor Union, which was sympathetic to independent political movements and opposed to the Republican Party, wanted to unite white and Negro labor. But many of the leaders of Negro workers, then beginning to form independent organizations, were influenced by Negro political leaders who were identified with the Republican Party because it had been responsible for the emancipation of the Negro.

[31] See Spero and Harris, *op. cit.*, pp. 17–18.
[32] See *ibid.*, pp. 23–52.

The widespread opposition of southern white workers to the political rights of Negroes helped to force Negro workers to ally themselves with the white employing classes. This trend for a time was stopped to some extent by the rise of the Noble Order of the Knights of Labor which undertook to bring about the cooperation of Negro and white workers, but this movement was defeated when faced by the rising power of the craft unions.

The triumph of craft unionism was marked by the rise of the American Federation of Labor which stood for craft autonomy and the exclusion of unskilled workers, white as well as black.[33] But for black workers, the dominance of the AFL meant the establishment of a color bar in many trades since white workers, through apprenticeship restrictions and other means, could prevent Negroes from becoming skilled workers. The racial policies of the constituent unions of the Federation varied considerably. Negroes were excluded from some unions by the constitution or the ritual; in other cases Negro workers were organized in separate locals which were under the jurisdiction of white unions. However, in the case of the mining unions, the Negro worker has held a strategic position and could not be eliminated.

The important change in the role of organized white labor in relation to the Negro worker occurred when industrial unionism became an important factor in the economic life of the United States. The Congress of Industrial Organizations, which came into existence as the result of mass production in the major industries, brought white and black workers into the same unions. The emergence of this organization occurred during an economic crisis which brought in its wake a political transformation, the New Deal. It was to be expected, therefore, that the CIO would be one of the chief supporters of the Fair Employment Practices Committee, which marked a change in the policy

[33] See *ibid.*, Chap. IV.

of the federal government in regard to discriminations against Negro workers.[34]

THE STATE AND THE COLOR BAR

As Reuter has truly stated, "In any going society the division of labor is in harmony with the distribution of power." [35] From the beginning of the color bar in South Africa, the whites have used their political power to prevent competition between white and colored workers. As early as 1890, the Transvaal required all persons who operated machinery to have a certificate, and in 1903 this requirement was extended to include the operation of locomotives in order to exclude the Chinese.[36] After the Union of South Africa was formed, a Mines and Works Act was passed in 1912 authorizing the Governor-General to make regulations concerning "the granting of certificates of competency to such persons employed upon machinery as he might determine." [37] Although the act made no reference to a color bar, the government issued regulations in harmony with policies existing in the Transvaal and the Free States. These regulations restricted the operation of and attendance on machinery to white men. In the Cape Province there was opposition to the establishment of the color bar. And, as we have seen, in 1916 the Chamber of Mines rejected the demand of the white unions that a color bar be maintained in semiskilled occupations. During World War I, the government relaxed its color bar in the interest of production.[38]

When a Transvaal court gave a decision against the color bar in 1923, the Nationalist Party, which represented

---

[34] See Louis Ruchames, *Race, Jobs, and Politics* (New York: Columbia University Press, 1953) , *passim.*

[35] Reuter, *op. cit.,* p. 52.

[36] Buell, *op. cit.,* I, 58.

[37] *Ibid.,* I, 58.

[38] *Ibid.,* I, 59–60.

the agricultural interest and therefore had no immediate interest in the white urban worker, nevertheless supported the Labor Party's demand for a color bar.[39] When the Nationalist Party won the election of 1924, it was dependent upon the Labor Party. In 1925, the government introduced the Mines and Works Amendment which restricted "certificates of competency to Europeans, Cape Coloured people, and Cape Malays." The passage of this law represented the establishment of the color bar. The color bar was further extended in the same year by a Wage Act, which was designed to prevent natives from competing with Europeans. Under the Hertzog government a Color Bar Act was passed in 1926, which practically declared that in the future natives might not aspire to skilled occupations in industry.[40] This act and the Hertzog measure in 1937, which provided that urban natives could be sent to reserves and refused passes to seek work in the cities, were the most important steps toward the institution of the apartheid racial policy.

Except in the case of alien colored peoples, the color bar in employment in the United States has been determined by employers and white workers and by customary practices. After the Civil War, when the Negroes were free to wander about the country and work at will, the legislatures of the southern states enacted the so-called Black Codes which were ostensibly designed to control vagrancy. In practice the Black Codes re-established the former master and slave relationship.[41] In South Carolina, persons of color were not permitted to enter any occupation except those of farmer or servant unless they secured a special license and paid an annual tax.[42] Since the Reconstruction

[39] *Ibid.*, pp. 61 ff.

[40] See Eugene P. Dvorin, *Racial Separation in South Africa* (Chicago: University of Chicago Press, 1952), pp. 26 ff.

[41] See Charles S. Mangum, *The Legal Status of the Negro* (Chapel Hill: University of North Carolina Press, 1940), pp. 153-5.

[42] Frazier, *op. cit.*, p. 127.

Period, legislation affecting the employment of Negroes in the South has been restricted to segregating the races, as for example in South Carolina, in the use of toilets, drinking utensils, entrances and exits, and pay windows.[43]

In fact, when either federal or state governments (in the North) have concerned themselves with discrimination in the employment of Negroes, they have undertaken to remove the color bar. The earliest attempt on the part of the federal government in this direction was during World War I.[44] A Negro was appointed Director of Negro Economics under the Secretary of Labor. Although there was need of utilizing Negro man power, "there is good reason to believe that the Department of Labor and the government created the Division of Negro Economics purely as a sop to Negro morale and never really intended to take decisive and effective action against discrimination." [45] It is not surprising, therefore, that the Negro director had no influence on discrimination in either government or private industry. The situation was entirely different during World War II. As a result of a more effective organization of the Negro's struggle against discrimination and as a result of the problems facing the United States, the federal government was forced to play a more effective role in modifying the color bar in employment.[46] Moreover, there were changes in the social organization of American life and in public opinion which aided the Negro in his struggle. After a threatened march on Washington of 100,000 Negroes in protest against discrimination in employment, the President issued his famous executive order prohibiting discrimination based upon race in the employment of workers in government and defense industry. A Committee on Fair Employment Practice was appointed by the President to receive and investigate cases of discrimination, redress valid grievances, and make recommenda-

43 Mangum, *op. cit.*, p. 175.
44 Ruchames, *op. cit.*, p. 6.
45 *Ibid.*, p. 7.
46 See *ibid.*, pp. 7–21.

tions to the President concerning the necessary means for implementing the order.

There was, of course, opposition to the FEPC, which marked a radical departure in government policy with reference to the race problem. Most of the opposition stemmed from the South since the Committee had been brought into existence as the result of pressure from Negroes and most of the cases were concerned with Negroes.[47] Although the Committee did not wipe out discrimination, it did succeed in increasing the employment of Negroes and other minorities. Moreover, the FEPC set in motion similar movements in various states and cities of the North which resulted in legislation against racial discrimination in employment.[48] It was much easier to secure state and municipal legislation than to secure federal legislation. Despite repeated efforts to secure national legislation, the Congress of the United States has consistently defeated proposals for the establishment of a permanent FEPC.[49]

The role of the state in South Africa in establishing a color bar in order to prevent competition between white and non-European peoples and the increasing use of political means to break down the color bar to employment in the United States both point to the importance of political power in race relations. An analysis of this phase of race relations will form the subject of the next section of this study.

[47] See *ibid.*, Chaps. V, VII.
[48] See *ibid.*, Chap. XI.

[49] See *ibid.*, Chap. XIII.

Political Organization

CHAPTER IX

Colonial Administration

INTRODUCTION

As was intimated at the end of part II, the economic organization of race and culture contacts is maintained by some system of political control. This first chapter in part III will outline the problems of European administration arising from the different types of political organizations among the colored peoples of the world. The character of European political control which has been established in any specific area has depended largely upon the stage of political development of the particular colored nation or tribe. In some cases European control has been restricted to ports or a small enclave of the territory of non-European peoples. A widespread type of political control, whether so designated, has been a system of indirect rule. Where multiracial communities have resulted from the settlement of Europeans, colored peoples have generally been wards of the white community or politically subordinated. Because of social developments among the colored peoples and changes in the economic and political organization of the modern world, there has been a struggle for independence in the colonial areas. As a consequence, nineteenth-century imperialism is fast disappearing, and the power conflicts of the modern world, in which colored nations are participating, are being aired if not resolved in the organization of the United Nations.

EXTENSION OF WHITE CONTROL
OVER COLORED RACES

The extension of control over the colored peoples of the world, as we have seen, grew out of the economic expansion of Europe. Administration of the conquered colored races was in the beginning in the hands of military leaders and, in the case of Catholic countries, missionaries. Later, civil representatives of the kings of Spain and Portugal were made responsible for the colonial territories of these countries. The chief responsibility of these administrators was to see that the wealth of the colonial possessions flowed to the mother country. When the Spanish Empire was destroyed by rival empires, trading companies chartered in Holland, France, and England were granted powers of administration.[1] The intensification of rivalries among the colonial powers subsequently prompted the European nations to assume direct responsibility for colonial administration. When, for example, England became the chief colonial power and leading industrial nation after the Napoleonic wars, the government took over from the East India Company the administration of India.

In fact, Britain played the main role in the expansion of European control over the colored world.[2] During three fourths of the nineteenth century, the British Empire established control over the peoples of India and annexed great territories in Asia and Africa. The extension of political control over non-European peoples followed the

[1] See Charles Sumner Lobingier, "Colonial Administration," in Edwin R. A. Seligman and Alvin Johnson (eds.) , *Encyclopaedia of the Social Sciences* (New York: The Macmillan Co., 1930) , III, 641–6.

[2] See Ramsay Muir, *The Expansion of Europe* (Boston: Houghton Mifflin Co., 1917) , Chap. VI.

growth of British trade, which dominated the world. After France had lost one empire she began to found another in North Africa within fifteen years after the fall of Napoleon. But France had already secured a foothold in Africa south of the Sahara, and in the Far East—in Indo-China, Tahiti, the Marquesas Islands, and New Caledonia. At the same time the Russian Empire, which had turned its back upon the West, was making conquests in Central Asia and thereby menaced the advance of the British Empire, which had taken over India.

During the last thirty years of the period in which European powers had begun to establish their suzerainty over the colored peoples, they were forced to give attention to struggles for national liberation in Europe. But beginning with the last quarter of the nineteenth century they entered upon imperialistic conquests which finally established the hegemony of the white race over the colored world. Germany, which under Bismarck's leadership first refrained from entering the struggle for empire, began building her empire by extending her protectorates in Africa, raising the German flag over hundreds of islands in the South Seas, and securing a port on the Chinese coast. Although Americans have smugly resented any assertion that the United States has pursued an imperialistic policy, the methods employed by the United States in Latin America were similar to those of the European nations within their spheres of influence.[3] The chief motive behind these imperialistic conquests was economic, or rather, the economic interests of a business class in the European nations.[4] The manufacturers of textile goods and steel products and the owners of coal mines had an interest in early imperialism just as the owners of the giant industries which require petroleum, rubber, cocoa, and fissionable ores have an in-

[3] See Parker T. Moon, *Imperialism and World Politics* (New York: The Macmillan Co., 1933) , Chap. XVI.
[4] See *ibid.*, Chap. IV.

terest in imperialism today. In order to justify their seizure of the lands of the colored peoples, the imperial powers had to find some moral apologetic. Thus there came into existence "the white man's burden," which simply meant that the "superior white race" had a duty toward the colored peoples. Among the French it was known as the *mission civilisatrice,* while President McKinley declared the following reason for annexing the Philippine Islands: "There was nothing left for us to do but to take them all and to educate the Filipinos and uplift and civilize and Christianize them as our fellow men for whom Christ had died." [5]

The forms of colonial administration that were set up by the various imperialistic nations were determined to some extent by their own systems of government and political ideologies. These forms were also determined by the stage of social development, especially the stage of political development, of the colored peoples. Although the Europeans might take advantage of the weakness of the Chinese Empire, and the internal dissensions within India, they could not refuse to deal with the Indian feudal lords who ruled the warring states or ignore the existing political organizations of China. Similarly, in establishing political control in Africa the white invaders could disregard the "stateless" African societies that lacked a centralized government, but in West Africa they had to recognize the existence of developed political organizations.

EXTRATERRITORIALITY

Extraterritoriality, or the granting of special privileges and immunities to foreigners, has existed since antiquity.[6]

[5] Quoted in *ibid.,* p. 73.
[6] See Philip Marshall Brown and Arthur N. Holcombe, "Extraterritoriality," in Edwin R. A. Seligman and Alvin Johnson (eds.), *Encyclopaedia of the Social Sciences* (New York: The Macmillan Co., 1931), VI, 36–8.

In the modern world it has represented one of the important phases of the power relations which were established between the European peoples and the older civilizations of Asia. As early as 1689 the Russians and Chinese signed a bilateral agreement which permitted the merchants of each nationality to "carry the laws of their country with them on visits to the other country." [7] The unequal treaties, which resulted from the weakness of China, began when the British after the Opium War forced the Chinese in 1842 to grant extraterritorial privileges to British subjects in China while the British did not grant the same rights to Chinese subjects in Great Britain. Two years later, the United States and France negotiated similar treaties and eventually China was forced to grant unequal treaties to eighteen countries.

There was a battle among the imperialistic powers for concessions in China. Japan, having defeated China in 1894, became one of the leading imperialistic powers in Asia. But Japan was restrained by Russia, France, and Germany who saw here a "Yellow Peril." It turned out that China's friends received more in economic advantages than her victorious enemy would have taken.[8] The Germans, who had been tardy in securing a part of China, suddenly found occasion to avenge the murder of two German missionaries by "leasing" 200,000 square miles of the shores of Kiaochow Bay for ninety-nine years. The struggle among the imperialistic powers for economic concessions in China was especially keen in regard to the construction of railways and mining enterprises. As the struggle developed, the imperialistic powers even looked forward to a partitioning of Chinese territory. The resulting threat of war between Russia and Britain was responsible for an alliance of England and Japan. When the Chinese resisted the encroachment of the foreign powers in the Boxer uprising, a coalition of European armies crushed the

[7] *Ibid.*, VI, 37. [8] Moon, *op. cit.*, p. 332.

rebellion. It was not until World War II and the events following the war that China regained control of her territory.

The unequal treaties provided the political basis for the economic penetration of China by placing the nationals of European countries outside Chinese law and by making the property of European nationals exempt from Chinese taxation.[9] In eighty Treaty Ports, twenty of which were located in foreign "settlements" and "concessions," Europeans could reside and trade without interference from the Chinese authorities. The most important of settlements, the International Settlement in Shanghai, was established in 1854 by the British and French. After the French withdrew and established their own municipality, the American settlement became a part of the International settlement. Although the land acquired by Europeans in the settlements was registered in the Chinese land office, the Europeans were granted a title of perpetual lease and together with the foreign consuls they controlled the settlement. In the case of the concession, the Chinese leased the land which was bought, sometimes by expropriation, by Europeans from Chinese owners. The largest of the foreign enclaves in China was the British colony which included 400 square miles near the most important center of Western influence, Hong Kong.

It was the United States that took the initiative in establishing extraterritoriality in Japan. As the result of the opening of Japan, Treaty Ports were established as in the case of China. By 1858 commercial treaties were signed between Japan and the chief European nations giving foreign consuls jurisdiction over their nationals and fixing customs duties.[10] Because of Japan's decision to adopt Western civilization as rapidly as possible, she was able to

[9] See George C. Allen and Audrey G. Donnithorne, *Western Enterprise in Far Eastern Economic Development: China and Japan* (New York: The Macmillan Co., 1954) , p. 14.

[10] See *ibid.*, p. 190. See also Moon, *op. cit.*, pp. 326–7.

negotiate with the Western powers and bring about an abrogation of the unequal treaties.

ASIAN AND AFRICAN FEUDAL SYSTEMS

The unequal treaties which created foreign enclaves on Chinese and Japanese soil represented a political accommodation of the European powers to the existing feudal societies. The only alternative to such treaties, which were based upon the superior military power of the Europeans, would have been a conquest of China and Japan. An attempted conquest of a huge country like China would have required the cooperation of the imperialistic powers who were competing with one another. The conquest of Japan would have been easier, but its cost would have been great in money and men. In the case of China, with an ineffective government, it was relatively easy to achieve some political accommodation by restricting European settlement and administration to certain Treaty Ports. A somewhat similar accommodation was established with the Japanese for a short period only, since the Japanese had a strong central government and adopted the Western ways of commerce and finance which enabled them to deal with the European on a basis approaching equality.

It was different, however, in the case of India where the British conquered practically the whole country and extended their administration over the conquered territory. Although the Indian states were not brought under British administration and remained independent, they were under the suzerainty of the Crown. It was, however, different in the areas where British administration gradually replaced the feudal organization under the Great Moghul who was a symbol of the overlordship of India. The institution of British administration was facilitated by the fact that the British were able to enlist the services of qualified Indians. Thus a direct form of administration was set up under the supervision of European officials. It was only later that the British administration encouraged the development of local institutions. In fact, the British administration was autocratic and the bureaucracy was almost entirely British except in the case of the unimportant lower positions.[11] It was only as the result of the growing Indian nationalism that reforms were introduced.

In what became the Federation of Malaya in 1948, the first problem of the British administration was to deal with the warring states and establish peace and order.[12] Under a system of Residents, the native chiefs were permitted to retain the forms of their local authority. For the loss of the substance of their hereditary authority, the Malay chiefs were allotted compensations. Through this means the British won their cooperation in the new order, which did not interfere with Malay religion and customs. The sultans, who had formerly delegated administration to their prime ministers, were required to entrust the administration to the Residents. The higher ranks of the technical departments, including engineering, medicine, education, surveying, and forestry, were all staffed by Europeans.

In 1861, after their conquest of Indo-China, the French instituted a system of direct rule.[13] White officials were substituted for the Annamite mandarins and the emperor, because of his refusal to cooperate with the French, was stripped of his powers and placed under Residents. Likewise, when it was discovered that the King of Cambodia was plotting against the French, he was forced to sign a treaty which placed French agents in every Cambodian province. The destruction of the traditional authority reached down to the local administration. In Annam local taxation was in the hands of French officials, and French

[11] Moon, *op. cit.*, p. 298.
[12] See Sir Richard Winstedt, *Malaya and Its History* (London: Hutchinson's University Library, n.d.) , pp. 82 ff.
[13] See Thomas E. Ennis, *French Policy and Developments in Indochina* (Chicago: University of Chicago Press, 1936) , pp. 53 ff.

officials supervised the deliberations of local councils created by the French in Cochin China. The local laws were changed when the Napoleonic Code was applied in Cochin China, and French legislation was imposed in Annam and Tonkin.

The attempt of the French to impose their political conceptions and political organization upon a people with deeply rooted political ideas and institutions similar to those of the Chinese was bound to fail. Even under the most favorable circumstances, the attempt to uproot a highly developed socio-political organization would have brought about social disorganization and resistance. The situation was made more difficult by the inadequacy of French personnel, the constant changes in French administrators, and by their lack of appreciation and understanding of the culture of the Indo-Chinese. This lack of appreciation was exhibited in the arrogance of the French officials who often had only contempt for the morals and manners of the Indo-Chinese. Despite the fact that French administration did much to modernize the country, introduce reforms, and aid in the education of the people, the people of Indo-China still regarded the French as "white masters." When the policy of direct rule and subjugation was supplanted by a policy of assimilation in 1879, the French hoped that opposition to white control would end. But as we shall see, the policy of assimilation did not bring such a happy solution.

From the beginning the Dutch introduced a system of direct rule in Java, although the Dutch East India Company found it necessary to deal with the native chiefs. After the fall of the company, the Dutch government continued a policy of economic exploitation of the island. Following the interim of British rule, the Dutch government introduced a system of "autocratic centralization." [14] The cen-

---

[14] Clive Day, *The Policy and Administration of the Dutch in Java* (New York: The Macmillan Co., 1904), p. 421.

tralized administration included a hierarchy of European officials from the Residents, with about a million people subject to them, to the various classes of controleurs, beneath whom were native regents and district heads whose duty it was to collect the taxes from the natives. This "centralized autocracy" was not able to stifle the growing resistance to Dutch rule. Some concessions were made to the growing demand for native participation in the government, and municipal and district councils were set up. But these concessions did not prevent the overthrow of Dutch rule during the crisis created by World War II.

When the Europeans began to establish their authority over Africa, they encountered peoples in various stages of political development. In the Western Sudan, the empires dating from the Middle Ages had left a heritage of feudal political organization among the existing states.[15] These empires, which had developed north of the forest lands along the coasts, had spread their influence among the coastal tribes. By the time the whites began trading with the peoples along the coast, these peoples had developed states which, when supplied with European weapons, were able to extend their political control over a wider area. The most important and most powerful of the states along the coast were Ashanti and Dahomey.[16] The growth of the Ashanti military power was due in part to the overseas commercial slave trade inaugurated by the Europeans. Dahomey achieved even greater military power and efficiency as one of the African states providing slaves for European slave traders.

Because of the strength of the Ashanti state, which

[15] See J. D. Fage, *An Introduction to the History of West Africa* (Cambridge: At the University Press, 1955) , Chap. II. See also W. E. F. Ward, *A History of the Gold Coast* (London: George Allen and Unwin, Lt., 1948) , Chap. VI.
[16] See Melville J. Herskovits, *Dahomey* (New York: J. J. Augustin, Inc., Publisher, 1938) . See also R. S. Rattray, *Ashanti* (Oxford: The Clarendon Press, 1923) .

had extended its power all along the Gold Coast, the British, Dutch, and Danes had to recognize the claim of the Ashantis to suzerainty. The British were drawn from time to time into the wars of Ashantis as the latter built up their empire.[17] Finally, the British took up the challenge of the Ashanti state to their growing interest in the Gold Coast and after a long struggle made the Ashanti state a protectorate in 1896. Although the Ashanti submitted to the British authority at the time, they rose in a bitter revolt in 1900 when the governor demanded that they surrender the Golden Stool which was the sacred symbol of the nation.[18] One of the results of this tactless move on the part of the governor was the stimulation of the study by the Europeans of native African political institutions, which had become necessary for an intelligent and humane administration of African peoples.

Dahomey, which stood in the way of French expansion in Africa, suffered a fate similar to that of Ashanti. There was a war between France and Dahomey in 1893 which ended in a French victory. After first deposing the king and placing their own nominee in his place, the French made Dahomey a colony in 1900.

Although Ashanti and Dahomey as well as other African states lost their independence, European administration had to take account of the fact that some African peoples had organized states. A recent survey of African political systems has revealed the important differences between African societies with governmental institutions and the "stateless" African societies.[19] The societies which have developed a state organization are characterized by a

[17] Concerning the relations of the British and Ashanti see Ward, *op. cit.*, Chaps. VII to XII.

[18] See Edwin W. Smith, *The Golden Stool* (New York: Doubleday, Doran and Co., Inc., 1928).

[19] M. Fortes and E. E. Evans-Pritchard (eds.), *African Political Systems* (London: Oxford University Press, 1950).

"centralized authority, administrative machinery, and juridical institutions—in short, a government—and in which cleavages of wealth, privilege, and status correspond to the distribution of power and authority." [20] One of these states, or nations as they are called sometimes, is the Zulu in South Africa, which was formed of members of hundreds of clans. Another is the Kede which is a section of the Islam kingdom, Nupe, in Northern Nigeria.[21] European administration of peoples with a state organization will be considered in the next chapter on indirect rule.

PRIMITIVE POLITICAL SYSTEMS

Europeans had less difficulty in dominating the so-called "stateless" people than in establishing their control over people with a developed feudal system or with a primitive political organization. In Australia, the Europeans encountered natives who were organized in local groups that were bound to their lands. Each of these local groups or tribes, which numbered about three hundred, hunted upon its own lands and seldom entered upon the territory of another tribe. The tribal lands were the basis of the religious life which held together the small local groups consisting of families. When the whites took the land from the natives, they destroyed the basis of native social life. And, as we have seen in chapter II, the Australian natives were practically exterminated by the ruthless policy of the white invaders.

An example of the administration of a "stateless" African society is provided in the case of the Gusii, a Bantu-speaking people in Kenya.[22] The Gusii are cultivators and pastoralists, the routine work of agriculture falling mainly

[20] *Ibid.*, p. 5.
[21] See S. F. Nadel, *A Black Byzantium* (London: Oxford University Press, 1942).
[22] Phillip Mayer, *Gusii Bridewealth Law and Custom* (The Rhodes-Livingstone Papers, No. 18 [London: Oxford University Press, 1950]), p. 1.

to women and stockkeeping being men's work. Traditional Gusii society was without a chief. The organization of their society was based upon bonds of lineage which formed a hierarchy, ranging "from the national unit itself down to the nuclear lineage consisting of one man with his legitimate sons." [23] The British made the lineage group which ranked above the clan and below the national unit the chief administrative unit. There were seven such administrative units, each of which constituted a tribe with a government-appointed chief. Each chief was assisted by a headman, appointed by the government, who had charge of one or more clans. At first the government conferred upon the chiefs the power of enforcing legal decisions. This was an innovation because in Gusii society the judicial system had consisted of arbitration at the kinship level by the family elders, while certain juridical specialists were arbitrators in a neighborhood group. Enforcement of judicial decisions was generally left to the successful litigant in a case. Later the British restricted the judicial powers of the chiefs and a system of native tribunals, providing appeal to European officers, was established, and more recently the native judicial specialists have been encouraged to assume their former functions.

The development of administration among the Gusii shows that even in dealing with the so-called "stateless" African societies European governments could not carry on administration "through an aggregate of individuals." [24] At first they chose as native administrative agents persons who were considered by Europeans to be the proper persons through whom they should administer. The persons chosen did not have the support of native peoples and very often they represented a violation of the traditional ideas and values of native peoples. The European bureaucratic system which came into existence as a part of

[23] *Ibid.*, p. 3.
[24] Fortes and Evans-Pritchard, *op. cit.*, pp. 15–16.

a centralized administration was, in fact, a system of direct rule. The system of direct rule has given way gradually to a modified system of indirect rule, which was originally set up to administer people who had developed governmental institutions.

CHAPTER X

Indirect Rule

INTRODUCTION

As a general principle, indirect rule has existed since ancient times wherever an imperial power has assumed control over peoples with a different culture. In the modern world it has grown out of the necessity of basing administration upon the traditional forms of political control which have existed among the colored colonial peoples. The British may justly claim that they were the first to develop the principle of indirect rule in the administration of territories in Nigeria with "a highly developed system of Muslim government, including a Fulah sultanate composed of numerous provinces, each administered by a feudal governor with his own council and executive, army, police, treasury, and judiciary." [1]

DIVIDE AND RULE

In a certain sense the technique of divide and rule which has been used by imperial powers may be considered a form of a system of indirect rule. It has been a

[1] C. K. Meek, *Law and Authority in a Nigerian Tribe* (London: Oxford University Press, 1937), p. 325. Reprinted by permission of the publisher.

crude form where domination on the part of the European peoples has been achieved simply by creating among the colored peoples warring factions and thereby weakening their resistance to European rule. The technique of divide and rule has been practiced in a more refined manner where Europeans have gained control over the colored peoples by gaining the adherence of the leaders or a section of the colored peoples. A crude form of the technique of divide and rule was utilized by the Europeans in their conquest of North America.[2] Wars between the various Indian tribes were encouraged in order to weaken them and the Indian was used as an auxiliary by the Europeans in their wars against the Indian. In Java the Dutch East India Company employed a somewhat more refined form of the technique of divide and rule which consisted of corrupting and bribing chiefs and sowing dissension among them.[3] In pursuing this policy, the Dutch also took advantage of the ceaseless quarrelling among the native states by always finding a person or party to defend.

A different form of the technique of divide and rule, which was inaugurated by the Belgians during the early years of European administration represented, in fact, a policy of direct rule.[4] The government ignored the traditional native political organization and instead of organizing tribes and peoples into chefferies, the government recognized families and clans as independent units. In some cases native states were divided up into numerous chefferies without recognizing the important chiefs or the traditional status differences among the native peoples. As the result of this policy, there were more than 6,000 chefferies in 1919, and the native population was drifting toward a

---

[2] William C. Macleod, *The American Indian Frontier* (New York: Alfred A. Knopf, Inc., 1928), Chaps. XIX, XXIII.

[3] Clive Day, *The Policy and Administration of the Dutch in Java* (New York: The Macmillan Co., 1904), pp. 48–9.

[4] Raymond L. Buell, *The Native Problem in Africa* (New York: The Macmillan Co., 1928), II, 480–3.

semianarchy. Some Belgians, including a Minister of Colonies, began to realize that this policy was causing many natives to grow up without any form of social discipline. As a consequence, after World War I there was a revival of the traditional tribal organization. The revival of the traditional tribal organization represented a shift from a policy of direct rule to one of indirect rule.

THE ROLE OF THE CHIEF

The principles of indirect rule in modern times were rationalized by Sir Frederick Lugard who, on the basis of these principles had achieved outstanding success as an administrator in Nigeria.[5] The principles of indirect rule were applied in Nigeria, especially in regard to the "advanced communities." [6] The primary objective of indirect rule was to make "each Emir or paramount chief, assisted by his judicial council, an effective ruler over his own people." The Emir or paramount chief presided over a "Native Administration" which was organized as a unit of local government. Each area over which the Emir or paramount chief exercised authority was divided into districts under the control of "Headmen," who collected the taxes in the name of the ruler, and deposited them into the "Native Treasury," "conducted by a native treasurer and staff under the supervision of the chief at his capital."

The district headman, who was usually a well-to-do man with local connections, was the chief executive officer of the area under his charge and he controlled the village headmen. The district headman assessed and was responsible for the taxes which were collected by the village headmen. The district headman was required to reside in his

[5] See Sir F. D. Lugard, *The Dual Mandate in British Tropical Africa* (4th ed.; London: William Blackwood and Sons, Ltd., 1929). See also Margery Perham, *Native Administration in Nigeria* (London: Oxford University Press, 1937).

[6] Lugard, *op. cit.*, pp. 200 ff.

district and was not allowed to assume any of the prerogatives of a chief, such as a retinue of his own or duplicate officials, and he had to report from time to time to the chief.

The British Resident, who acted as a sympathetic adviser and counsellor to native chiefs, was in charge of a province which contained several separate native administrations, whether they were Moslem Emirates or pagan communities. A British district officer was in charge of a division which might include one or more headmen's districts or more than one small Emirate or pagan tribe independent of other tribes. Although the Resident was not to interfere in such a manner as to lower the prestige of the native chief, the latter was required to follow the advice of the Resident. However, the native chief was permitted to issue his own instructions to his subordinate chiefs and district heads and was encouraged to work through his subordinates. The district officers supervised and assisted the district headmen, through whom they communicated instructions to the village headmen. Important orders emanated from the Emirs, whose messengers accompanied and acted as the mouthpiece of the district officers.

When Northern and Southern Nigeria were amalgamated in 1914, indirect rule was set up by Lugard in southwestern Nigeria similar to that in Northern Provinces of Nigeria.[7] It was based upon the political framework provided by the Yoruba. This required that steps be taken to restore the tribal machinery which had already disintegrated to a large extent. At first, artificial districts were marked out and chiefs were endowed with extensive powers that overrode the authority which the native councils and societies had possessed in the traditional organization. After adjustments were made to the requirements of the existing situation, a satisfactory native administration based upon indirect rule was set up.

Meek, *op. cit.*, pp. 328–9.

The system of indirect rule was not regarded as possible in southeastern Nigeria, since no political framework had been discovered on which a native administration could be built.[8] As a consequence the British introduced a system of direct rule. A native administration was "conducted through the artificial channel of Native Courts, the members of which, under the name of 'Warrant Chiefs,' " came to be regarded as corrupt henchmen of the government, "rather than as spokesmen and protectors of the people."[9] This led to much unrest among the people, which was not allayed when steps were taken to introduce indirect rule.[10] An attempt to introduce direct taxation in order to defray the costs of an adequate native administration resulted in riots, the most serious of which was the women's riot in 1929. The resistance of the natives was directed chiefly against the warrant chiefs, who were part of an administration that had no basis in native institutions. The government then realized that anthropological research was necessary in order to determine the nature of the native institutions.[11] Reforms were instituted on the basis of the inquiry into native institutions. The artificial district courts were gradually abolished and replaced by clan and village-group councils, which were a direct expression of the most important features of Ibo culture— the kinship grouping which is the fundamental unit of law and authority, and the village-group which is the highest unit of government.[12]

When the French entered Africa, they found a number of native states.[13] The French gained control of those states in most cases through the local chiefs, with whom they made treaties in which the French recognized the na-

[8] *Ibid.*, p. x.
[9] *Ibid.*, p. ix.
[10] *Ibid.*, pp. 329 ff.
[11] Meek's book on the Ibo was the result of the decision to have an anthropologist make this study.
[12] Meek, *op. cit.*, pp. 335 ff., 347 ff.
[13] Buell, *op. cit.*, I, 901 ff.

tive institutions. But later this policy was abandoned and a system of direct rule was established.[14] The reasons for these changes were supposedly administrative convenience and the desire to suppress certain abuses on the part of native chiefs whose power had been increased by the support of the French government. It is also probable that at the time the French thought that native institutions were not worth preserving and that the natives should become the heirs of French civilization. Nevertheless, the French had to depend on some form of native agents called chiefs for their administration.

The administrative machinery which was set up divided the various territories into *cercles* which were in turn divided into subdivisions.[15] There is a French *commandant* in charge of each *cercle* and a European administrator over each subdivision. The subdivisions are divided into provinces or tribes under a chief and these provinces are divided into cantons, each with a chief. The appointment of chiefs by the governor has depended upon the recommendation of the *commandant* of the *cercle*. Often the selection of chiefs has not been with a view to utilizing traditional institutions but rather with a view to obtaining persons who would fit into French administration. Hence a considerable degree of literacy and acquaintance with French administration are required. Toward this end a school for the sons of chiefs was established. As a result, through the method of direct rule the French administration has recruited a loyal body of educated native agents.

REVIVAL OF TRADITIONAL POLITICAL STRUCTURES

The utilization of the chief under a system of indirect rule has played an important part in the attempt to revive

[14] *Ibid.*, pp. 986 ff.
[15] Concerning the role of the Commandant of the Cercle see Robert Delavignette, *Service Africain* (Paris: Gallimard, 1946), Chap. I.

the traditional political structures among native peoples brought under European controls. The importance of the chief derives from the fact that though European governments can impose their authority on peoples with or without governmental institutions, they are unable "to establish moral ties with the subject people." [16] According to Fortes and Evans-Pritchard:

An African ruler is not to his people merely a person who can enforce his will on them. He is the axis of their political relations, the symbol of their unity and exclusiveness, and the embodiment of their essential values. He is more than a secular ruler; in *that* capacity the European government can to a great extent replace him. His credentials are mystical and are derived from antiquity. Where there are no chiefs, the balanced segments which compose the political structure are vouched for by tradition and myth and their interrelations are guided by values expressed in mystical symbols. Into these sacred precincts the European rulers can never enter. They have no mythical or ritual warranty for their authority.[17]

A system of indirect rule must undertake, therefore, to revive native institutions and native culture where these have disintegrated as the result of European contacts. In order to carry out such a policy, it has been necessary to make studies in order to learn the native political structures and to determine the real rulers. Since 1921, the European administrators in the Congo have been required to study the histories and customs of the tribes under their jurisdiction.[18] Although at first some of the studies did not influence the work of the busy administrators, they have increasingly provided the basis of native administration with the result that the administration of the natives has

---

[16] M. Fortes and E. E. Evans-Pritchard (eds.), *African Political Systems* (London: Oxford University Press, 1950), p. 16. This passage and the one that follows are reprinted by permission of Oxford University Press, Inc.

[17] *Loc. cit.*

[18] Buell, *op. cit.*, II, 483 ff.

improved. The British administrations have, as we have seen, carried out studies in order to provide a realistic basis for their policy of indirect rule. After the British took over Tanganyika, they maintained for several years the district organization set up by the Germans, but beginning in 1926, the British made studies of the traditional native organization and based their administration upon native institutions.

In an attempt to revive native institutions, a European administration is faced with difficult problems, especially in view of the changes which have occurred in African society as the result of European penetration. The difficulty of attempting to revive institutions is increased where urbanized natives are concerned. Barnes has made a study of the political history of the Ngoni in Northern Rhodesia, who were an armed nation on the march until their defeat by the British in 1898.[19] During the period of transition the Ngoni were administered through their indigenous chiefs and headmen. This method of administration was not based upon a professed policy of indirect rule, but was instituted because the administration wanted to preserve order as cheaply as possible and did not want to introduce changes that would interfere with the supply of labor to other areas. Incident to the transition of the Ngoni state from a continuously segmenting political system to a minor administrative unit in a modern state, an African civil service and a native authority bureaucracy came into existence. Both of these political structures are formally distinct from the old political system, though status in traditional terms such as chief or village headman is recognized in face-to-face relations. The white administrators who possess the real power are behind the African employees, who stand between them and the native masses. These African employees look forward to advancement, not in the tradi-

[19] J. A. Barnes, *Politics in a Changing Society* (Capetown: Oxford University Press, 1954).

tional order that still survives in the rural areas, but in the new urban society that is developing. As a consequence, "the Ngoni sovereign state has become more and more like a rural district council in a backward area." [20]

INDIRECT RULE AND POLITICAL DEVELOPMENT

"Most educated Africans, especially in West Africa and the Sudan," writes Miss Perham, "criticize or even strongly condemn 'Indirect Rule.' They say that 'Indirect Rule' gives power to uneducated chiefs and elders instead of to the educated; that it strengthens tribal feeling and so continues the disunity of the country. It is, they say, part of the old policy of 'divide and rule.' " [21] Meek has also referred to the suspicions of the educated Africans in regard to indirect rule, which "they mistakenly regard as a means of 'keeping Africans in their place' or of denying them the full benefits of the civilization" which Europeans enjoy.[22] A static policy of indirect rule would provide, he thinks, just grounds for these suspicions as, for example, in the southern provinces of Nigeria where there is a mass movement toward Christianity and Western education. As a result there has been a conflict between the younger generation who are Christians and literate and their pagan elders. It would be a mistake, as Meek has insisted, "to concentrate authority exclusively in the hands of the elders, most of whom are pagans, and to fail to give to the younger generation, who no longer respect the ancient sanctions, a reasonable share in the administration of local affairs." [23]

The conflict between the older and younger generations is an indication of the profound changes which are occurring in African societies as the result of the spread of

---

20 *Ibid.*, p. 72.

21 Margery Perham, *Africans and British Rule* (London: Oxford University Press, 1941) , p. 69. Reprinted by permission of the publisher.

22 Meek, *op. cit.*, p. xv.

23 *Loc. cit.*

European education, the increasing industrialization and urbanization, and the growing mobility of the native peoples. These new social and economic forces are dissolving the traditional kinship groupings and feudal organizations. Indirect rule which grants authority to traditional tribal chiefs or keeps alive an outmoded feudal organization may prevent the development of responsible self-government.[24] Some of the traditional African aristocracies are opposed to the democratic ideas now influencing the Africans who are forming the new societies. The British Labor Party has expressed its approval of indirect rule as a form of local government or method of integrating native institutions into the general government. But the Labor Party expressed its opposition to indirect rule if it was used as an excuse to maintain autocratic native rulers and to prevent the development of Africans so that they could "stand by themselves in the political and economic world which Europe is imposing on them." [25]

The political developments which have occurred in the Gold Coast and in Nigeria during and after World War II have shown that the policy of indirect rule is essentially a transitional stage in preparing native peoples for responsible citizenship in a modern state. As the result of economic and social changes in both the Gold Coast and Nigeria, it has been necessary to create modern organs of government. This has involved discarding the traditional tribal institutions since, as Busia has pointed out, "The evolution of local government under the policy of indirect rule was too slow and not sufficiently sensitive to changes in the social structure resulting from trade and commerce and education." [26] These changes were accelerated during

[24] See H. A. Wieschhoff, *Colonial Policies in Africa* (Philadelphia: University of Pennsylvania Press, 1944) , pp. 69 ff.

[25] Quoted in *ibid.*, p. 70.

[26] Kofi A. Busia, "The Gold Coast and Nigeria on the Road to Self-Government," in C. Grove Haines (ed.) , *Africa Today* (Baltimore: The Johns Hopkins Press, 1955) , p. 293.

World War II by the drawing of men into the armed forces and the employment of men and women in new occupations.

The main problem has been the development of secular political structures and a secular authority to supersede the traditional forms of authority.[27] This has been achieved in the central government of the Gold Coast by following the British parliamentary tradition.

The rules and procedures of the legislative assembly are derived from the practice of the House of Commons. Members of the assembly are chosen by an elective system. A cabinet and a prime minister, chosen on the basis of majority party membership in the assembly, are responsible for the operations of the government. A Gold Coast civil service coexists with the Colonial Service Officers, who are gradually being replaced by Africans.[28]

There is some formal recognition of chieftainship in the secular parliamentary government in territorial councils having only advisory powers. The councils of chiefs, one in each of the four areas of the Gold Coast, are a remnant from the days of indirect rule. A second secular system was imposed in 1951 under the Local Government Ordinance which established local councils with a two thirds elected membership and a one third traditional membership.[29] These councils are replacing the native system of authority which was set up under indirect rule. With the abolition of the secular authority which was bestowed upon chiefs and the dominance of a two thirds elected membership, the local councils have become involved in party politics at the local level.

The brief exposition of the main features of indirect rule in this chapter indicates that it is a general principle

[27] See David Apter, "Political Democracy in the Gold Coast," in Calvin W. Stillman (ed.), *Africa in the Modern World* (Chicago: University of Chicago Press, 1955), pp. 115–39. Copyright 1955 by the University of Chicago.

[28] *Ibid.*, p. 120.   [29] *Ibid.*, pp. 121–2.

which has been widely practiced where Europeans have
undertaken to administer colored peoples. The necessity
of some form of indirect rule has stemmed from the cultural differences between the white and colored races. The
policy of indirect rule has been contrasted with a policy
of assimilation which is regarded as synonymous with a
policy of direct rule. But, as Delavignette has pointed out,
the actual problem of administration is full of contradic-
tions and interchange between the two policies.[30] France,
the exponent of assimilation, has employed indirect rule
in dealing with Muslim states, while under the indirect
rule of England the natives have assimilated English culture and adopted English institutions. The new fact that
one must accept in administration is, as Delavignette emphasizes, that Africa, in its reaction to Europe, is developing its own peculiar type of regime as it is doing in other
spheres of human activity. Meek, writing in somewhat the
same manner concerning the adaptation of indirect rule to
a changing Africa, has pointed out that the policy of indirect rule may degenerate into a policy of stagnation and
segregation and that if it is to avoid this danger and become acceptable to native peoples it must be evolutionary
and constructive.[31] In view of the political development in
West Africa, indirect rule can only be regarded as a stage
in preparing natives for self-government in a modern state.

[30] See Delavignette, *op. cit.*, pp. 87–90.
[31] Meek, *op. cit.*, p. 327.

CHAPTER XI

Multiracial Communities

INTRODUCTION

The political organization of multiracial communities in which white and colored peoples dwell side by side or in different sections of the same administrative area has raised problems which are different from those where Europeans imposed their power upon the older civilizations of Asia or established their control among nonliterate peoples in tropical regions. In the case of the older feudal societies of Asia the imposition of white rule has been restricted to areas where it is required by economic relationships, while in the case of nonliterate tropical peoples, variations of the principle of indirect rule have been adequate to maintain white control. But where white settlement has created multiracial communities, it has been necessary to invent various patterns of political control in order to maintain the domination of whites. These various patterns of political organization have been related to the relative size of the white and colored populations, the stage of social development of the colored peoples, the extent of their amalgamation with whites and their assimilation of European

culture, and the character of the economic organization
of race relations.

WARDS OF THE WHITE COMMUNITY

Where multiracial communities [1] have grown up as
the result of white settlement in areas inhabited by colored
peoples or where colored peoples have been introduced
into white communities, the most elementary system of
political organization has been to treat the colored peoples
as wards of the white community. Generally, colored peoples who have been treated in this way were nonliterate or
so-called primitive peoples. Outstanding examples of this
are Kenya and South Africa.

In Kenya, the establishment of a political organization in which the conflicting interests of the white and
colored peoples could be reconciled has involved an Asian
population in addition to the European and African populations. The European population numbers about 40,000;
the Asian population, including Arabs as well as Indians,
is about four times as large. The Indian as well as the European represents an intrusion upon a territory occupied
by more than 3,000,000 Africans. The Indians played an
important role in the development of East Africa from
early days.[2] At one time they controlled the trade along
the coast, Indian troops were employed in the conquest of
East Africa, and the Uganda Railway was constructed almost entirely by Indian labor. Although most of the la-

[1] The designation "multiracial community" rather than "multiracial
society" is used because the author thinks that community in a technical
sociological sense designates the ecological aspects of human relations
which are based upon a division of labor and which give rise to an interchange of goods and services. If there is consensus where this interde-
pendence exists then these human relations constitute a "society." It follows, then, that white and colored peoples occupying the same territory
but having different cultural heritages which prevent the existence of a
consensus among them should not be regarded as forming a "multiracial
society."

[2] See Lord Malcolm Hailey, *An African Survey* (London: Oxford
University Press, 1938), p. 335.

borers returned to India, some remained to become cultivators, artisans, and traders. Their numbers were increased
from 1900 onward by a considerable immigration of artisans and traders from India. The presence of Europeans,
who numbered a little more than 3,000 in 1911 and increased rapidly after World War I, was due originally to
the desire of investors to have traffic for the railway. European colonists were attracted by large land grants on liberal terms. The highland areas of Kenya, which were well
suited for European settlement, soon came to be regarded
as a white man's country.

So far as the natives were concerned, the problem of
establishing political control by the whites arose from the
desire to protect "European ownership in the highlands
area, in which its capital is invested, and to maintain an
economy that will serve the standards of life of the class
which it represents." [3] In order to accomplish this aim,
the white officials subjected the native population to various types of differential legislation, including the native
reserves and labor-tenant regulations. Moreover, a system
of direct rule was introduced on the grounds that there
were no native institutions that could be used for administrative purposes. The policy of direct rule developed
through three stages: the employment of native headmen,
many of whom had no traditional authority, to maintain order; the institution of native courts to try minor
criminal offenses arising out of native law and custom;
and local governmental institutions represented by local
native councils. [4] While the evolution of the policy of direct rule reveals a growing recognition of the aspirations
and outlook of the native population, it has not solved
the conflicts existing between Europeans and natives
over the question of land and native representation in
government.

The European settlers have had to deal also with the

[3] *Ibid.*, p. 383.   [4] *Ibid.*, pp. 387 ff.

Indians, who were not a nonliterate or primitive people. More than half of the Indian population is engaged in commerce and a large part in industrial pursuits, while the remainder are government employees and domestic workers. The Indians resented from the beginning their exclusion from the highlands area which was reserved for white settlement. Then the Indians protested against communal representation in the legislative council, which was offered as a concession to their objections to being excluded from participation in that body. Probably owing partly to the demands of Europeans for self-government, the legislative council has gradually come to include Indians, who were elected, in its membership.

The problem of establishing an acceptable political government in Kenya has not been solved. This stems mainly from the determination on the part of the Europeans to maintain white supremacy.[5] The conflict between the Europeans and natives over land has resulted in the revolt and terrorist activities of the tribal-national association, the Mau Mau. The problem of the participation of natives in government has not been solved by a dual system of local government which recognizes a distinction between native and settled (principally European) areas.[6] Moreover, there are still rivalries and conflicts between the African, Asian, and European communities; hence the Africans and Asians who are safeguarded by a colonial administration thwart the efforts of Europeans to obtain self-rule.

The multiracial community in the Union of South Africa is much more complex than that in Kenya. In addition to more than 2,000,000 Europeans, over 8,000,000 Bantu peoples, and nearly 300,000 Indians, there are nearly 1,000,000 so-called "Cape Coloured." Moreover,

[5] See *Race and Politics in Kenya*, a correspondence between Elspeth Huxley and Margery Perham (London: Faber and Faber, Ltd., 1945).

[6] See John A. Noon, "Political Developments in East Africa," in Calvin W. Stillman (ed.), *Africa in the Modern World* (Chicago: University of Chicago Press, 1955), pp. 191 ff.

while Kenya is predominantly agricultural, the Union of South Africa is industrialized and more than half of the Europeans and nearly a fourth of the native Africans are in urban areas.

When the four colonies entered into the Union in 1910, there were brought together two completely different traditions. In the Cape Colony, whatever might have been the practice, the theory of government was based on the refusal to recognize race or color as a qualification or disqualification for political office. The franchise was open to all men who complied with certain qualifications and, theoretically speaking, any post in the Cape Colony might have been held by any voter. In the Transvaal and Orange Free State, on the other hand, there was an absolute exclusion from the franchise and from every public office of every man who was not a European. This exclusion was a matter, not of custom, but of written law. While this exclusion was not so absolute in Natal, the tendency was to approximate more closely to the Transvaal and Free State than to the Cape.[7]

Since the Union was formed, legislation, especially the Representation of Natives Act of 1936, has rejected the position of the Cape and has made race and color the basis of political participation and power. On the basis of the Representation of Natives Act and the Asiatic Land Tenure and Indian Representation Act of 1946, of the forty members of the Senate, ten (five elected and five nominated) would represent the non-Europeans,[8] but these senators were to be of European descent. Provisions for representation in the House of Assembly were more complicated. However, the underlying principles in regard to the representation of non-Europeans were that race and color should provide the basis of political participation, that the dominance of the Europeans should be maintained, but

[7] Edgar H. Brookes, "Government and Administration," in Ellen Hellmann (ed.), *Handbook on Race Relations in South Africa* (New York: Oxford University Press, Inc., 1949), p. 27. Reprinted by permission of the publisher.
[8] *Ibid.*, pp. 28 ff.

that non-Europeans should be represented in some manner. The Act of 1936 made provision for an advisory body, a Natives Representative Council consisting of the Secretary for Native Affairs, six Chief Native Commissioners of the Union, and sixteen Africans, four of whom were nominated and twelve elected. There were also provisions in municipalities and urban areas restricting the political activities of natives although Cape Coloured and Indians were not restricted to the same extent.

The rise to power of the Nationalist Party in 1948 has resulted in a new policy which will not only maintain the political subordination of non-Europeans but make them mere wards of the white community.[9] According to the apartheid policy there is to be complete physical, economic, political, and social separation of Europeans and non-Europeans. This is held to be necessary because non-European peoples are incapable of exercising political power and should be subject to the will of the white race. Moreover, the dominance of the white race is necessary in order to preserve the purity of the white race. The native reserves in which the Africans are segregated are to be industrialized and made ancillary to industry in European areas. The idea of industrializing the native reserves seems to have emerged in response to criticisms that apartheid implies the reversal of the economic and social development of South Africa. Since, however, the political aspects of apartheid are so opposed to the economic development of South Africa and to processes of urbanization, racial tensions have developed to the point that they may burst into violence.

POLITICAL SUBORDINATION

The pattern of political subordination of colored peoples in multiracial communities has grown up where

[9] See Eugene P. Dvorin, *Racial Separation in South Africa* (Chicago: University of Chicago Press, 1952).

colored peoples have assimilated enough of the culture and political ideals of Europeans and have acquired sufficient interests in the general community to seek power in the multiracial community. The techniques which have been invented by the white community to maintain its power represent in a sense a transitional stage in the political organization of race relations or an accommodation of the latent conflicts that have not been resolved. An outstanding case of the political subordination of a colored people in multiracial communities has been the manner in which Negroes have been prevented from voting and holding office in the southern states of the United States. The history of the relation of the Negro to the political life of the South is important because it reveals the interaction of economic, political, and social factors in determining the political organization of race relations.

Immediately following the Civil War and emancipation, the South attempted to restore the master-servant relationship between whites and Negroes. Consequently, there was no intention on the part of the white South to permit Negroes to participate in politics.[10] It was only after the triumphant North had divided the South into military districts and supported the Negro's right to vote as a citizen, which had been granted by the Fourteenth and Fifteenth Amendments to the Constitution of the United States, that Negroes began to participate in the political life of the southern states. Negro voters were organized in the Republican Party, which was primarily interested in representation in the national Congress in order to legalize the triumph of northern industrial capitalism. The agitation against the control of the northern industrial interests was carried on under the slogan of the "Restoration of White Supremacy." The military control of the North was withdrawn when there was substantial congressional sup-

---

[10] See E. Franklin Frazier, *The Negro in the United States* (New York: The Macmillan Co., 1949), pp. 124 ff.

port from the West for the program of expanding northern capitalism.[11]

The "Restoration of White Supremacy" in fact resulted in the political ascendancy of the so-called "Bourbons" who represented an alliance between the white planters and the emerging commercial and industrial interests in the South. The Negro was not completely disfranchised when the "Bourbons" gained power, since the planters especially sought at times to use Negro voters to defeat the aspirations of the poor whites who were clamoring for an improvement in their economic and social condition. Thus, the class conflict in the white community continued despite the "Restoration of White Supremacy." But every attempt to bring about cooperation on the part of the poor whites and the landless Negroes was labeled as treason against the white race. The demagogic leaders of the poor whites who rose to power during the last decade of the nineteenth century provided a solution of the class conflict which, while offering no menace to the white landowning class, made the Negro the scapegoat. Their program included (1) the diversion of the per capita appropriation of school funds from Negro to white schools; (2) the instituting of a legal system of racial segregation; and (3) the complete disfranchisement of the Negro.[12]

In order to justify this program before the nation, especially the North which had lost its idealism concerning Negro rights, the South through its political and other leaders attempted to convince the nation that the Negro was a morally degenerate subhuman species, incapable of being educated, and therefore unfit to exercise the franchise. Moreover, every form of subterfuge which did not openly violate the Amendments to the Constitution that guaranteed the rights of the Negro as a citizen was em-

[11] See Louis M. Hacker, *The Triumph of American Capitalism* (New York: Simon and Schuster, Inc., 1940), pp. 384–5.
[12] Frazier, *op. cit.*, pp. 155 ff.

ployed to prevent the Negro from voting.[13] Every form of violence and intimidation was used to keep Negroes from the polls. As a consequence, from 1890 onward, Negroes were completely eliminated from politics in the lower South and subordinated to the white community under the fiction that the Negro could not meet the legal requirements to vote.

The continuance of the policy of political subordination in the southern states has been made impossible for a number of reasons. First, there are the Negroes themselves who were not colonial or so-called primitive people. There were among them elements who, after more than 250 years of contacts with European civilization, would not accept the unscientific and fanatical statements about the Negro's inherent inferiority, to say nothing of those about his subhuman nature. All Negroes had acquired some conception of American political ideals and Christian moral ideals of human equality. Aided by Negroes in the North, they were able to carry their battle against political subordination to the Supreme Court of the United States. That they were able to do this suggests another factor of importance; namely, that the South was a part of a larger organization which was not based upon the type of white domination which the South was attempting to maintain. Then there were changes in the economic organization of American society that were affecting the relation of the Negro to American life. The mass migrations of Negroes from the South, which resulted partly from economic changes in the South as well as in the North, had given Negroes unforeseen political power. These changes had been set in motion by World War I and their tempo had been accelerated by World War II. Finally, there was a change in the relation of the United States to the rest of the world. The political subordination of the

[13] See C. Vann Woodward, *The Strange Career of Jim Crow* (New York: Oxford University Press, Inc., 1955), Chap. II.

Negro in the South became no longer a southern problem or even a domestic (American) problem. It was related to the new leadership which the United States was struggling to attain in a world where colored peoples were demanding the right of self-government and equality among the peoples of the world.

The struggle of the Negroes of the southern states to escape from political subordination was marked by a number of cases which were brought to the Supreme Court, chiefly through the agency of the National Association for the Advancement of Colored People. The grandfather clause was declared unconstitutional by the Supreme Court in 1915.[14] A struggle over many years was required to get the Supreme Court to outlaw the exclusion of Negro voters from the primary elections of the Democratic Party, which, realizing that as Negroes became educated it would be impossible to exclude them from voting on "educational" grounds, had attempted to maintain its right to exclude them on the grounds that the Party was a "private club." On the other hand, Negroes have not succeeded in having the poll tax laws of southern states outlawed. The attempts on the part of Negroes to exercise their right to vote have resulted in violence in some areas of the South. Although Negroes are participating on a larger scale in southern elections than at any time during the past sixty years, less than one fifth of the estimated 7,000,000 Negroes of voting age voted in the presidential election of 1952. The problem of the full participation of Negroes in the political life of the South is still in the conflict stage. One cannot foresee what crisis in American life may bring about a radical change in the situation.

[14] See Charles S. Mangum, *The Legal Status of the Negro* (Chapel Hill: University of North Carolina Press, 1940), pp. 391, 397–8. These were clauses in state laws providing that no person could vote whose grandfather had not been able to vote before a certain date, a date when no Negroes had been able to vote.

POLITICAL PARTICIPATION

Although Negroes who were free in the United States before the Civil War were not permitted to vote in most of the North and the West as well as the South, they were permitted to vote in all New England states with the exception of Connecticut.[15] Free Negroes were granted the right to vote in New York if they owned a specified amount of property, a qualification which was not required of whites. After the Civil War, the Fifteenth Amendment put an end to all state laws which limited the right to vote to white people. Negroes then began to vote without restrictions in the northern states. Unlike the situation in the lower South where Negroes constituted from a third to a half of the population of the different states, in the border states there was no strong opposition to the political participation of Negroes so far as voting was concerned. The border states had become differentiated from the lower South by the facts that the Negro population was smaller since the plantation system of agriculture did not develop on a large scale and that about a third of the Negro population was in urban areas.

In the North, where the vast majority of Negroes have always lived in cities, they were not important as a political factor until the mass migrations of Negroes from the South which began during World War I. The leaders of the political machines in the northern cities where large Negro communities came into existence sought to win the support of Negro voters. At first the Negroes, because of their traditional loyalty to the Republican Party, gave their support to the Republicans and they were able to elect a Negro to the Congress of the United States. But when the New Deal program was inaugurated to deal with the problems of unemployment during the Great

[15] *Ibid.*, pp. 371 ff.

Depression, the Negroes on the whole switched their support to the Democratic Party.

During the past quarter of a century Negroes have increasingly become a factor in politics, especially in northern cities. They have been absorbed in the political machines in the same manner as the various European immigrant groups. Although at times they have voted for issues which would benefit the Negro, there has not been a Negro vote as opposed to the white vote. Although Negro leaders have increasingly become important figures in the political machines, the Negro vote has never offered a challenge to the dominant economic or political power of the whites. In fact, in becoming a part of the political machines, Negroes have generally divided their support between the two major political parties. The increasing participation of Negroes in the political life of the North, which has resulted in their election to state legislatures and municipal councils and their election and appointment as judges, has been an outstanding feature of the changing status of Negroes in the American community.

Although Negroes have voted freely in the border states since emancipation, they have not been elected to public offices as in the North. The political machines in border states have generally managed to secure the support of Negroes by appointing a few Negro leaders to unimportant positions and in rare cases Negroes have been elected to municipal councils and state legislatures. In recent years the number of Negroes elected to state legislatures and municipal councils has increased, as has the number of Negroes appointed to minor offices as police magistrates. Even as regards such positions as policemen and firemen, only recently have Negroes held such positions except in the nation's capital. In a sense the political participation of Negroes in the border states has been intermediate between their political subordination in

the South and their growing importance in the political
life of northern cities.

The increasing importance of Negroes in the political
life of northern and border cities has been associated with
their increasing integration into the American community.
Their political power has not been in opposition to the
dominant white community. Nevertheless, the political
power of Negroes can be identified because of the segregation of Negroes in northern cities, which results partly
from economic and partly from social causes. Moreover,
the Negro is still identified in the American community
as a racial, if not a cultural, minority. Therefore, for an
example of political participation where racial identification has largely become unimportant, let us turn to Brazil.

In Brazil, from the beginning, there was never a division of political power along strictly racial lines. "In tropical America," as Freyre has stated, "there was formed a
society agrarian in structure, slave-holding in its technique
of economic exploitation, and hybrid in composition, with
an admixture of the Indian and later of the Negro." [16]
There was, of course, during the period of slavery a great
social distance between masters and slaves, corresponding
to differences in color, "the whites being really or officially the masters and the blacks really or officially the
slaves." [17] But the absence of white women resulted in
widespread race mixture, and the mestizo sons by Indian
and Negro women inherited parts of the large estates of
their white fathers. As a consequence, the master of many
a plantation was a mixed blood.

During the formative and colonial period, the political power in Brazil was concentrated in the hands of the
"great landowning and autonomous families, lords of the

[16] Gilberto Freyre, *The Masters and the Slaves* (New York: Alfred A.
Knopf, Inc., 1946) , p. 3.
[17] *Ibid.*, p. xiii.

plantation, with an altar and a chaplain in the house and Indians armed with bow and arrow or Negroes armed with muskets at their command; and from their seats in municipal council chambers these masters of the earth and of the slaves that tilled it always spoke up boldly to the representative of the crown."[18] This agrarian society was essentially patriarchal in character. But during the eighteenth century and the first half of the nineteenth century it underwent important changes as the result of urbanization and the emergence of the middle classes who gradually acquired political power. The tempo of change was accelerated in the nineteenth century as coffee became more important than sugar in the economic life of Brazil.

As Brazilian society underwent this change, during which the "rural patriarchate" declined, the "bachelor of arts" and the "mulatto," as Freyre has shown, rose to prominence.[19] The bachelor of arts and mulatto were often the same person, the son of a planter who had been sent to study in European universities. In the new urbanized middle-class Brazilian society, the bachelors of arts and the mulattoes became the lawyers, doctors, writers, army and naval officers, businessmen, and new political figures. Consequently, no problem of political power based strictly upon racial descent could arise in such a society. Nevertheless, in the process of social differentiation and division of labor, there has been, as we have seen, some relationship between color and occupation.[20] While there has been no color line in the matter of political participation in the city of Bahia, as Pierson's study shows, two thirds of the politicians were white, nearly a fifth were *Branco da Bahia* (white according to the loose definition of being white in Bahia), a little more than a tenth were mulattoes, and only

[18] *Ibid.*, p. 4.
[19] See Gilberto Freyre, *Sobrados e Mucambos* (São Paulo: Companhia Editora Nacional, 1936), Chap. VII.
[20] See p. 161 *above*.

1.7 per cent were black.[21] Partly because of the initial economic and social handicaps which Negroes, that is, black men, experienced in the evolution of Brazilian society, and partly because of their visibility, they have become identified as a proletarian group. This has been true despite the fact that individual black men have risen to prominence and power. Consequently, in Brazil as in other countries of South America where political lines have not been drawn along racial lines, class has come to play a more important role in politics than race.

The patterns of political organization which have developed in multiracial communities have been related, as we have seen, partly to economic factors and partly to social factors. The economic factor has been important where white and colored peoples have been in competition. Where Europeans have dwelt in the same community as colored peoples possessing a primitive or nonliterate culture, the colored peoples have been treated as wards of the white community. But where colored peoples have only represented a different type of literate culture, whites have attempted to maintain patterns of political subordination. This has involved conflicts that have not been resolved. The political problems of multiracial communities have only ceased to exist where there has been a free mixture of white and colored peoples, so that political problems growing out of class relations have supplanted those growing out of differences in race and culture.

[21] Donald Pierson, *Negroes in Brazil* (Chicago: University of Chicago Press, 1942) , p. 181.

CHAPTER XII

Regional Autonomy

INTRODUCTION

As Lord Bryce foresaw more than half a century ago, the relations of the colored and white races have become an important phase of international politics. The principle of self-determination, which grew out of World War I, could not be restricted to European peoples since non-European peoples had been influenced by the economic and social changes which were occurring in European civilization.

Two world wars and the economic changes which are transforming the world have destroyed the bases of nineteenth-century imperialism. In their struggle for self-determination some of the Asian peoples have freed themselves from European political domination while some African peoples are demanding self-determination. Nevertheless, because of the superiority of European technology and productivity, the white peoples have been able to maintain their economic dominance under new forms. The emergence of Russia as an industrial nation with a political and economic philosophy opposed to that of the West has brought into existence a system of regional power structures in which the colored peoples are playing an increasingly important role. The United Nations provides a stage on which the struggles of the regional power systems are publicly dramatized if not resolved.

SELF–DETERMINATION

Although the principle of self-determination had long been invoked by subject nationalities to justify the right to liberation, the expression which was given to the principle during the peace discussions following World War I was an outgrowth of the ideologies of democracy and nationalism which had developed together during the nineteenth century.[1] At the same time a great impulse was given to the principle of self-determination as the result of the Russian Revolution. One week after the revolution, the Council of Peoples Commissars issued the Declaration of the Rights of the Peoples of Russia, containing the following principles:

(1) equality and sovereignty for the peoples of Russia, (2) the Right of the People of Russia to self-determination, to the point of separation from the state and creation of a new independent government, (3) abolition of national and religious privileges, and disabilities, and (4) the free development of national minorities and ethnographic groups inhabiting the territory of Russia.[2]

When in 1925, in her struggle with the West, Russia became the champion of the colonial peoples, it was on the basis of these principles of national self-determination.[3] Although the principle of self-determination was invoked

[1] See Louis Wirth, "The Problem of Minority Groups," in Ralph Linton (ed.), *The Science of Man in the World Crisis* (New York: Columbia University Press, 1945), pp. 366 ff.

[2] Bernhard J. Stern, "Soviet Policy on National Minorities," *American Sociological Review*, IX, 231.

[3] See Hubert Deschamps, *La Fin des empires coloniaux* (Paris: Presses Universitaires de France, 1950), pp. 76 ff.

by the colored colonial peoples in their struggle to achieve independence, there were social and economic developments which had been undermining colonialism and preparing the way for self-assertion on their part.

According to Kennedy, there were three developments which with increasing momentum were weakening the institution of colonialism.[4] First, the practical advantages of colonialism, such as the cheapness and tractability of colonial labor, had declined because of the increasing political consciousness of natives and their demands for higher wages. Second, as the result of the diffusion of Western civilization, native peoples had become critical of their condition as compared with that of Europeans. Third, the rising tide of democracy in the West, which had acquired an international orientation, was tending to weaken colonialism.

Nevertheless, the revolt of Asia against Western dominance, which has become the most important factor in the new relations of the white and colored peoples of the world, was influenced largely by the Russian Revolution. In Russia there was established a University of Oriental Workers where an elite was trained to carry on agitation against colonialism in their respective countries. This elite was especially effective in China, Indo-China, and Indonesia where they were able to organize the masses of people who had long resented the European and regarded him as the chief cause of their poverty and humiliation. The Communist elite was able to accomplish this because they offered the Asians a vision of escape from their present condition by throwing off the European yoke and by establishing a society of their own on Communist principles.

When the Japanese armies defeated the armies of the British and French empires and conquered Indo-China, Malaya, and Indonesia, they opened the way for the revo-

[4] Raymond Kennedy, "The Colonial Crisis and the Future," in Ralph Linton (ed.), *op. cit.*, pp. 345–6.

lutionary leaders to organize the masses for revolt. As soon as it was rumored in Indo-China that the Japanese were about to surrender to the Allies, the underground organizations, which were preparing to revolt against the Japanese when the Allies landed, began to act.[5] But before the Allies were able to take over from the Japanese, the Indonesians launched their revolution and proclaimed a Republic. Despite the attempts of the Dutch with Western aid to regain power, they were driven out of Indonesia. There followed an internal struggle for power during which the Communists were defeated. After the Dutch were finally forced to surrender their sovereignty, the Republic of Indonesia was admitted to the United Nations. In Indo-China the revolt against French rule was complicated by French politics as well as by competing groups within Indo-China.[6] As a result the leader who was finally able to organize a mass basis for the revolt became allied with the Cominform. The struggle in Indo-China has not ended, but the Communist-dominated northern section may still gain control of the entire country.

Although the Soviet Union made appeals to Asians on the basis of self-determination, it has been charged that in dealing with the backward peoples of Asia the Soviet Union has adopted a colonial policy and imposed white rule upon colored people.[7] Although race prejudice has been absent, it is said that the European Russians who have settled in Asia have gone there as skilled industrial workers, as managers of the newly formed state enterprises, as officials of the bureaucratic machine, as teachers and professors, and as public prosecutors. But this has been inevitable in view of the Communist policy in regard to

[5] See George M. Kahin, *Nationalism and Revolution in Indonesia* (Ithaca: Cornell University Press, 1952).

[6] See Ellen J. Hammer, *The Struggle for Indochina* (Stanford: Stanford University Press, 1954).

[7] Walter J. Kolarz, "Race Relations in the Soviet Union," unpublished paper presented at the Conference on Race Relations in World Perspective (Honolulu: University of Hawaii, 1954).

self-determination and the relation of the advanced to the backward peoples. According to the Communist policy, minorities should have the right of cultural self-determination within the economic framework of communism.[8] Therefore, the Soviet Union has not only sent Russians into Asia but it has educated an elite among the backward peoples in order that they would be indoctrinated with Communist beliefs and would in turn become administrators among their people. It was through this means that social cohesion was created and the cultural minorities became a part of a monolithic state.

The achievement of self-determination on the part of the peoples of Africa has presented different problems from those which the Asians faced. The peoples of Asia who have an old historic tradition have been able to throw off European rule by force of arms, partly because of the stage of their social development and partly because they have found an ally in Russia. Nevertheless, in consolidating their political power, they must solve economic problems since they can not isolate themselves in the economic life of the modern world. Being accustomed to a low standard of living, the peoples of Asia are willing to undergo what in the Western world would be regarded as unbearable hardships, in order to free themselves from the humiliation and exploitation which they have suffered at the hands of Europeans. The peoples of Africa, however, are largely in a preliterate stage of culture and are without a historic tradition to unify them. Therefore, their struggle for self-determination depends largely upon the extent to which they have achieved literacy and experience in government and upon the extent to which the basis of unity has been laid under colonial adminstration. Because of the French policy of assimilation which makes Africans citi-

---

[8] See Joseph Stalin, *Marxism and the National Question* (New York: International Publishers Co., Inc., 1942), *passim.* See also Deschamps, *op. cit.*, pp. 83–4.

zens of France, the question of self-determination is ruled out theoretically. In the Belgian Congo where a native intellectual elite does not exist under the paternalistic native administration and where the natives are divided into numerous tribes, neither national nor political self-determination has become a problem. On the other hand, in British West Africa, especially in the Gold Coast and in Nigeria, the natives have gradually been prepared for self-government. Because of the rapid developments which have occurred in these two colonies since World War II, it is likely they will gain dominion status within the British Commonwealth of Nations within a year or so.

IMPERIALISM: NEW STYLE

In 1948, when Queen Wilhelmina of Holland announced the creation of the Union of Holland and Indonesia and declared that "Colonialism is dead," she was announcing the beginning of a new era in the relations of the white and colored peoples of the world. The fact that the union of Holland and Indonesia did not materialize only emphasized the fact that European imperialism in Asia was finding it impossible to devise a formula for survival.

Just seven years before this announcement, the signers of the Atlantic Charter declared that they respected "the right of all peoples to choose the form of government under which they will live" and that they wished "to see sovereign rights and self-government restored to those who have been deprived of them." This declaration was interpreted by colonial peoples as a proposal to give them the right of self-determination of their political affairs.[9] But they were soon to be disappointed when Churchill upon his return to England announced that while the declara-

[9] H. A. Wieschhoff, *Colonial Policies in Africa* (Philadelphia: University of Pennsylvania Press, 1944), p. 73.

tion did "not qualify in any way the various statements of policy which had been made from time to time about the development of constitutional government in India, Burma, or other parts of the British Empire," the declaration referred "primarily to the restoration of the sovereignty, self-government, and the national life of the States and nations of Europe" under Nazi control. Consequently, the Atlantic Charter dealt with a separate problem from that of the "progressive evolution of self-governing constitutions in the regions and peoples which owe allegiance to the British Crown." [10]

"In all parts of the colonial world," writes Wieschhoff, "as well as in many circles of Great Britain and the United States, Churchill's statement was interpreted as an exclusion of the colonial peoples from the high ideals of the Atlantic Charter. In Africa, N. Azikiwe, the editor of the *West African Pilot*, was particularly outspoken in his condemnation of such an attitude." [11] While this was an expected reaction to the Churchill interpretation of the Atlantic Charter, it was nevertheless true that there were qualifying sentences in Churchill's statement which implied that colonial peoples would be granted self-government when they were prepared for it. During the half century between the partition of Africa and the beginning of World War II, Britain along with the other colonizing powers had taken it "for granted that most of Africa should be, and would for long remain, under external control." [12] But as the result of World War II, the pattern of colonial control was changed in British, French, and Belgian territories.

The changes in British control have been characterized by (1) an increase in the representation of the natives

[10] Quoted in Wieschhoff, *loc. cit.*

[11] Wieschhoff, *loc. cit.*

[12] Kenneth Robinson, "Colonial Issues and Policies with Special Reference to Tropical Africa," *The Annals of the American Academy of Political and Social Science*, CCXCVIII (March 1955), 86–7.

in their Legislative Councils, (2) Cabinets composed of elected members of legislatures responsible for some department of government, (3) the replacement of native administrations, by local self-government, and (4) the speeding up of economic development.[13] In French tropical Africa, the rights of citizenship have been extended, the special legal system for natives as well as the system of forced labor have been abolished, and all the territories now send deputies to the French National Assembly, senators to the Council of the Republic, and councillors to the new Assembly of the French Union. "The local Assemblies established in all the territories are wholly elected, but except in Senegal and Togoland, the same system of two electoral rolls, one for French citizens and one for the African citizens, is used, though the majority of the members is, in every case, elected by the latter." [14] The changes in the political status of African natives have been less dramatic in Belgian territories where emphasis has been on industrial developments. Only as recently as 1952 has the basic law of the trust territory of Ruanda-Urundi been changed to permit the development of a system of representative local government councils.

The achievement of almost complete self-government in the Gold Coast is awakening political aspirations among all the peoples of Africa. At the same time self-government in the Gold Coast and in Nigeria is revealing the economic and political problems of the new independent nonindustrialized nations. As the colored peoples achieve political independence they are faced with the problem of developing an economic basis for their independence. This involves not only the securing of capital in the form of financial investments but also technical knowledge and managerial experience. At the present time the leaders in the Gold Coast and in Nigeria are attempting to accomplish this in such a way as to be as free as possible from the

[13] *Op. cit.,* p. 90.　　　　　[14] *Op. cit.,* p. 91.

dominance of white capital. Moreover, the Gold Coast and Nigeria will remain a part of the British Commonwealth of Nations. This is political realism in a world dominated by power systems from which small nations cannot escape.

REGIONAL POWER SYSTEMS

The present crisis in the relation of the white and colored peoples of the world has developed as a phase of the profound change in the power relations of the peoples of the modern world. This change in the power relations of the modern world has been developing since World War I. It was, however, as the result of World War II that the centers of power in the modern world shifted from western Europe to the Soviet Union and the United States. During World War II, the United States became the dominant industrial and financial as well as military power in the world. At the same time, the Soviet Union was able not only to gain control of eastern Europe but to secure the support of Asians by aiding them in their revolt against European domination. These two powers, the United States and the Soviet Union, are struggling to win the support of the peoples of the world who are not under their control. The peoples who are not under the control of these two power systems are mainly the colored peoples of the world who have either recently secured their independence, including most of the peoples of southeast Asia, or who have begun their struggle for independence or a greater amount of self-determination, including the peoples of Africa.

Although the shift in the centers of power from western Europe to the United States and the Soviet Union was due, from a long-term view, to the economic and social causes to which Kennedy attributed the weakening of colonialism, the immediate cause was the revolt of Asia against European domination. This revolt was facilitated

and encouraged by the conquests of the Japanese in southeast Asia during World War II. Although the Japanese occupation was resisted and the Japanese were disliked, they
nevertheless destroyed European prestige as well as European military power. Their role in the revolt of the Chinese was different since they had also become exploiters of
China. Nevertheless, the successful revolt of China against
domination by Europeans and Japanese came about also
as the result of World War II. The Chinese Revolution of
1911 had not brought political unity to the country nor
had it given the Chinese control of their economic life.
The revolution had resulted in civil wars and the surrender to some extent of extraterritoriality by the European
powers. In 1937 the Japanese, who had become a competi-
tor of European imperialists, invaded China. During
World War II, following soon after the Japanese occupation, the Chinese people fought the Japanese imperialists
and the Kuomintang, which had ceased to represent the
interests of the masses. The Communists became the leaders of the revolt of the masses, and when Japan was defeated they drove Chiang Kai-shek from the mainland.
After World War II, China became allied with the Russian
power system.

When India and Pakistan gained their independence
within the British Commonwealth of Nations, despite
their disagreements over Kashmir they were united in
their opposition to European dominance. Although Africa is not in open revolt against European domination, it
holds a strategic and perhaps decisive position in the struggle between the East and the West because it possesses important resources that are required by the industrialized
nations.

As the world stands today, the Soviet Union is supported by China and peoples in the other parts of Asia.
Although India maintains an independent position, she
supports the struggles of other colored peoples against ra-

cial discrimination and economic exploitation. The battle between the East and West has not been decided in southeast Asia, though the people of the region are opposed to the domination of colored people by white peoples. The United States, which has changed its policy toward the Negro, is attempting not only to hold the support of the Latin Americans, who are racially mixed, but also to secure the support of the people of southeast Asia and Africa.

The race problem in the modern world has become a part of the regional power systems which have supplanted Europe as a center of world power. The existence of these power systems and the importance of race are revealed in the United Nations. The importance of race appears in the statement of Mr. Nehru in a speech in New Delhi in 1952 concerning the attempt to raise the Tunisian issue in the General Assembly in 1951. He said, "If the whole of Asia and Africa combined cannot get a subject discussed because two or three great Powers object, then the time may come when the Asian and African countries will feel that they are happier in their own countries and not in the UN." [15] Similarly, the Pakistani delegate, on December 13, 1951, commenting on the same subject, remarked, "If the Assembly turn down this request [for a discussion of the situation in Tunisia and Morocco] the whole world, and certainly Asia and Africa, must draw their own conclusions." [16]

THE UNITED NATIONS

In addition to the provisions relating to the promotion of the economic welfare of colonial peoples, Article 73 of the charter of the United Nations states that the nations which have the responsibility of administering peo-

---

[15] *Times* (New York) , June 13, 1952.

[16] Quoted in Coral Bell, "The United Nations and the West," *International Affairs*, XXIX (October 1953) , 467. This passage and those that follow are reprinted by permission of *The Royal Institute of International Affairs*, London, England.

ples who are not self-governing should develop their subjects' capacity for self-government and should take account of their political aspirations. While the conflicts issuing from the struggle between East and West absorbed the attention of the General Assembly, there were only minor conflicts over the provisions of Article 73. Beginning in 1952, however, conflicts in the Assembly over the relations of European and non-European peoples dominated the discussions.[17] The attack against the West has been led by thirteen nations of the Arab-Asian bloc—Afghanistan, Burma, Egypt, India, Indonesia, Iran, Iraq, Lebanon, Pakistan, the Philippines, Saudi Arabia, Syria, and Yemen.

Though the attack, was originally directed against the status of "tutelage" or "clientship" rather than race discrimination, as such, the fact that the ex "tutor" States are European and the ex "client" States are non-European makes it inevitable that the trend should take on the appearance of a tension between Europe (or the European camp) and the rest of the world, not only in the geographic sense but, more disturbingly, in the racial sense also.[18]

It is for this reason that "The UN is, indeed, one of the principal mechanisms by which race relations are transformed into international relations." [19]

Much of the controversy in the General Assembly over the racial problem has been focused on Africa. France has been criticized concerning the situation in Tunisia and Morocco, and she has objected to the discussion of Tunisia and Morocco on the grounds that they are domestic issues and that the charter of the United Nations forbids interference with domestic problems. But the colored members of the United Nations are not willing to permit a dubious technical argument of this nature to interfere with their aim to destroy colonialism and the domination of colored peoples by Europeans. In 1947, the Egyptian delegate, in presenting his case against Britain in the Security Council,

[17] *Ibid.*, pp. 464–72.   [18] *Ibid.*, p. 466.   [19] *Ibid.*

declared, "We are here to challenge the basic assumptions of nineteenth-century colonialism." [20]

The racial problem which has become one of the main issues before the General Assembly includes the situation in Africa south of the Sahara. Outstanding among the racial problems of Africa is the one in the Union of South Africa where apartheid or racial segregation has become the official policy. When the General Assembly set up a commission to make a study of the apartheid policy, the South African delegation registered its protest and refused to participate in the discussion of the question because they insisted that it was a domestic problem.

In regard to the nonautonomous territories governed by European peoples, the General Assembly has been concerned with social and economic conditions as well as political developments. The struggle in the Assembly has centered about the responsibility of the administering powers to the United Nations, especially in regard to making reports to the Assembly, and the right of subject colored peoples to appeal to the United Nations. On these issues as on other matters affecting the status of colonial peoples, there has been a division largely along racial lines.

The racial question which has divided the General Assembly has special significance for the future of the British Commonwealth of Nations.[21] While the British are attempting to transform the Commonwealth of Nations from a white into a multiracial organization, there are conflicts between the white members of the Commonwealth and the newly elected colored members. Representatives of India and Pakistan attack the racial policies of South Africa, especially as they concern the Indians. South Africa not only resents the attack upon her racial policies but objects to the membership of colored nations in the Com-

[20] Quoted in *ibid.*

[21] See Vernon McKay, "The Rise of Africa in World Politics," in Calvin W. Stillman (ed.), *Africa in the Modern World* (Chicago: University of Chicago Press, 1955), pp. 301 ff.

monwealth. Moreover, South Africa is opposed to the British policy in regard to the political development of the Gold Coast and Nigeria, which eventually will become members of the Commonwealth. There is evidence that possibly one fourth of the Nationalist Party supporters in South Africa would like to set up a republic outside the Commonwealth.

The racial division which has developed in the United Nations is, of course, tied up with economic and political factors in the modern world. The so-called Latin American bloc, composed of nations which are racially mixed communities and have a colonial background, does not vote consistently with the Arab-Asian bloc. Nevertheless, they are on the anti-colonial side, and some among them vote consistently with the "left" on African questions. The position of the Latin American bloc is determined to a large extent by their economic dependence in relation to the industrialized nations.

Their point of view emerges clearly in the Argentine resolution at the Seventh Assembly that the prices of primary commodities should be kept in just relation to the prices of capital goods and manufactures, so as to permit greater domestic savings in underdeveloped countries, and in the Uruguayan proposal for a UN declaration to recognize the right of each country to nationalize and freely exploit its natural wealth as an essential of economic independence.[22]

Although the Arab-Asian bloc has become the spearhead of the attack on white dominance, its position too is influenced by economic and political considerations. While it is true that, having only recently emerged from European domination, they are still mindful of white domination, they are also keenly conscious of their low economic status. Although the countries of the Arab-Asian bloc have generally supported the West on matters dealing with

[22] Bell, *op. cit.*, p. 470.

peace and security, they have aligned themselves on other matters with those who are opposed to their former white masters. Although, according to Hourani, Russia "is still absent and unknown" to the Middle East, "to the poor, the perplexed, the humiliated, and the disinherited she holds out hopes that—in her ruthless way—she will cure what hurts them." [23] The changes in the political organization of race relations in the modern world are a reflection, then, of the shift in the centers of power from western Europe to the United States and Russia. The effects of this shift are seen in changes and tensions which are developing wherever whites govern colored peoples. The struggle between the new power systems which have emerged with the changes in race relations is dramatized in the present controversies in the United Nations.

[23] Albert Hourani, "The Decline of the West in the Middle East," *International Affairs*, Part II, XXIX, 170.

PART IV

Social Organization

CHAPTER XIII

The Plantation as a Social Institution

INTRODUCTION

This chapter and those which follow in this part of our study will be concerned with the problems of social organization which result from the contacts of white and colored peoples. As was stated in the Introduction to this book, the problems of social organization constitute the central problems of race and culture contacts, in the sense that they are concerned with the creation of a social order in which peoples with different racial and cultural backgrounds can develop a solidarity of interests and achieve a common identification which will transcend racial and cultural differences. The discussion so far of the ecological, the economic, and the political aspects of race and cultural contacts will provide, therefore, a basis for the analysis of the problems of social organization. This analysis will begin with the plantation and then consider in turn other forms of social organization in which peoples with different racial and cultural backgrounds have found an accommodation. In the analysis of the problems of social organization, special consideration will be given to caste, biracial organizations, nationalistic movements, and finally the relation of culture and personality.

FROM AN ECONOMIC TO A SOCIAL INSTITUTION

In chapter VI, we have seen how in the economic organization of race and culture contacts the plantation developed as an industrial institution. Here we are concerned with the evolution of the plantation from a purely industrial organization based upon slavery or some form of forced labor to an elementary form of social organization. Where the plantation existed as a purely industrial institution, natives were treated as instruments of production for profit. Under such conditions the relation between white planters and colored labor was symbiotic since little account was taken of the personality of the colored laborers. Nevertheless, even where colored laborers were regarded as mere utilities, some account was taken of the fact that they were individuals possessing a personality. Therefore, some form of authority was necessary and the plantation became not only an industrial institution, but a political institution.[1] Where the authority of the white planters developed beyond mere physical coercion and the lives of planters and workers became intertwined in a web of social relationships, the plantation became a social institution. As a social institution, the plantation has had its peculiar culture and a system of social control based upon traditions and customs.

The transformation of the plantation from an industrial to a social institution is seen in Brazil where "The Big House completed by the slave shed" represented an entire economic, social, and political system:

a system of production (a latifundiary monoculture); a system of labor (slavery); a system of transport (the ox-cart, the

[1] Edgar T. Thompson, "The Plantation: The Physical Basis of Traditional Race Relations," in Edgar T. Thompson (ed.), *Race Relations and the Race Problem* (Durham: Duke University Press, 1939), pp. 192 ff.

bangué [litter], the hammock, the horse) ; a system of religion (a family Catholicism, with the chaplain subordinated to the paterfamilias, with a cult of the dead, etc.) ; a system of sex and family life (polygamous familism) ; a system of bodily and household hygiene (the "tiger," the banana stalk, river bath, the tub bath, the sitting bath, the foot bath) ; and a system of politics (*compadrismo* [oligarchic nepotism and patronage]). The Big House was thus at one and the same time a fortress, a bank, a cemetery, a hospital, a school, and a house of charity giving shelter to the aged, the widow, and the orphan.[2]

This type of social organization had arisen when sugar raising supplanted the trade in brazilwood and hides and prevented the development of a diversified agriculture and herding in large areas surrounding the plantations. Although the Big House was associated with the sugar plantation and a patriarchal organization, it existed wherever there was slaveholding and latifundiary monoculture. It was created in the northern part of Brazil by sugar production and in the southern part by coffee production. During the first century of colonization the plantation tended to resemble a fortress, but at the end of the seventeenth century and beginning of the eighteenth century the plantations resembled more nearly "a Portuguese convent—a huge estate with the functions of a hospital and a house of charity." [3] The development of the Big House, which represented a patriarchal system of colonization, was an adaptation of Portuguese imperialism to a tropical environment.

The situation in Brazil favored the rapid transformation of the plantation from an industrial to a social institution. There was a scarcity of white women and the resulting race mixture tended to create ties between the white masters and the colored slaves. But the change in

[2] Gilberto Freyre, *The Masters and the Slaves* (New York: Alfred A. Knopf, Inc., 1946) , p. xxvii. Words in brackets are English translations.
[3] *Ibid.*, p. xxviii.

the character of the plantation was not due simply to these biological ties between the two races. Slavery in Brazil had its brutal aspects as did slavery in other countries; but, as Pierson has stated, "as an institution continuing over centuries it became more and more mild." [4] This happened because of the personal relations which developed between the races in their daily contacts. In Brazil there were many opportunities for these relations to develop, especially where the domestic servants were concerned. According to an observer, whose report is confirmed by others, the houses in Brazil were filled with servants who were constantly attending to the wishes of their masters.[5] Then as the institution of slavery developed, the slave acquired certain customary rights such as the right to cultivate his own plot of land two days a week, to transfer his property to his children, to take his master's name, and even in some cases to change masters.[6]

The same factors that transformed the plantation in Brazil from an industrial to a social institution brought about a similar transformation in the plantations in the United States. One must, of course, discount the historical value of the romantic literature on the patriarchal character of Negro slavery in the southern states.[7] Phillips was essentially correct when he stated that "All in all, the slave regime was a curious blend of force and concession, of arbitrary disposal by the master and self-direction by the

[4] Donald Pierson, *Negroes in Brazil* (Chicago: University of Chicago Press, 1942), p. 80. Copyright 1942 by the University of Chicago.

[5] *Ibid.*, p. 81.

[6] *Ibid.*, pp. 82 ff.

[7] See Francis P. Gaines, *The Southern Plantation* (New York: Columbia University Press, 1924), Chaps. VII, VIII, IX. The author here compares the actual facts with the romantic tradition which has grown up about the plantation. See also Frederick L. Olmsted, *A Journey in the Back Country in the Winter of 1853–54*, 2 Vols. (New York: G. P. Putnam's Sons, 1907). Concerning his doubts about the "patriarchal" character of slavery in Virginia, Olmsted writes: "I am here reminded that I may seem to have hitherto too much overlooked a certain view of Southern life, much delighted in by novelists and poets, and not usually neglected by travellers." *Ibid.*, II, 42.

slaves, of tyranny and benevolence, of antipathy and affection." [8]

The relative amount of "force and concession," of "arbitrary disposal by the master and self-direction by the slave," of "tyranny and benevolence," and of "antipathy and affection" that characterized a plantation depended upon a number of factors. One was the size of the plantation. Olmsted observed that "As a general rule, the larger the body of Negroes on a plantation or estate, the more completely are they treated as mere property, and in accordance with a policy calculated to insure the largest pecuniary returns." [9] Even where the wealthier planters were inclined to treat their slaves humanely, it was made difficult because of numbers, and as a consequence only those employed about the house benefitted from their benevolence. On the large industrialized plantations there was little chance for human relations to develop between the masters and the slaves, who were under the control of white overseers seeking to get the maximum amount of labor by treating them as work animals.

It was where the plantation became a settled way of life, as in Virginia and in sections of other states, that the plantation lost its purely industrial character and became a social institution. Under such circumstances the plantation developed a certain self-sufficiency which was made possible through a division of labor among the slave population.[10] This provided some opportunity for the expression of individuality on the part of the slaves. Some slaves, on the basis of their personal qualities, were chosen to be house servants. Then the mechanics who performed all the skilled work on the plantations were selected on the basis of their intelligence and peculiar talents. House servants,

[8] Ulrich B. Phillips, *Life and Labor in the Old South* (Boston: Little, Brown, and Co., 1929), p. 217.

[9] *Op. cit.*, I, 64.

[10] See E. Franklin Frazier, *The Negro in the United States* (New York: The Macmillan Co., 1949), Chap. III.

mechanics, and field hands all had a special status in the social organization of the plantation. On the basis of the division of labor, social distinctions developed among the slaves. Moreover, slaves were accorded differential treatment by the masters according to their role in the plantation organization.

As the plantation developed into a social institution, in both Brazil and in the United States, the relations between the races were regulated by an etiquette and social ritual. The social ritual and etiquette permitted the maximum degree of intimacy while preserving the maximum difference in social status.

THE PATERNALISTIC REGIME

The social ritual and etiquette of the plantation reveal the system of control's paternalistic character, which became one of its outstanding characteristics when it became a social institution. On the well-regulated plantations in Brazil, it was the practice for the slaves of both sexes and of all ages to request each morning and evening a blessing from their masters.[11] In fact, it was religion which tended to bind masters and slaves together as members of the same patriarchal family group. The law required that *Negros novos* upon their arrival in Brazil be baptized in the Christian religion on the penalty of being forfeited to the state. Slaves from Portuguese Angola were baptized before they left Africa, while in the case of slaves from other parts of Africa, masters were given a year in which to instruct them in preparation for baptism. Slaves, it was said, were not considered "members of society, but rather brute animals" until they could "lawfully go to mass, confess their sins, and receive the sacrament." [12] It was through participation in these religious ceremonies that slaves became fellow human beings to their masters.

[11] Pierson, *op. cit.*, p. 81.   [12] Cited in *ibid.*, p. 92.

Although religion did not play as important a role on the plantations in the southern states as on the plantations in Brazil, it was one of the factors that tended to create a sense of solidarity between masters and slaves. On most of the well-regulated plantations the religious instruction of the slaves was considered an indispensable part of plantation management. In the upper cotton region, the slaves generally attended the same church as the masters and occupied the gallery or some section of the church which was set aside for them. Moreover, very often the master, in what resembled to some extent the patriarchal household in Brazil, required the slaves to gather at family prayers and taught the catechism to them one or two nights a week. Usually, however, the task of giving moral instruction was left to the mistress of the household.[13]

The system of control characterizing the plantation which became a social institution was essentially paternalistic. However well the colored slave might be treated, he was still regarded as a child subject to the will of his white master. Moreover, wherever the plantation regime has existed, its influence has extended beyond the plantation. It has set the pattern of paternalism which has characterized the relationship of white to colored people in many parts of the world.[14] In their revolt against the West, Asians have expressed resentment against the paternalism of the whites. Africans, while admitting they have much to learn from the West, resent being treated as children.[15] Negroes in the United States have long resented the paternalism of the whites even when it represented the best of intentions.

[13] See Frazier, *op. cit.*, pp. 52–3, 339–43.

[14] According to Freyre, dictatorship with its paternalistic appearance in Brazil has been the result of the feudalistic regime which developed during the plantation regime. Freyre, *op. cit.*, pp. xiv–xv.

[15] Malengreau, in writing of the efforts of the government in the Belgian Congo to prevent the labor movement from becoming subversive, concludes: "But the movement did exist and the paternalistic attitude toward labor relations was growing obsolete." Malengreau, "Recent Developments in Belgian Africa," in C. Grove Haines (ed.), *Africa Today* (Baltimore: The Johns Hopkins Press, 1955), p. 341.

The southern states afford an example of how the paternalistic pattern of race relations which developed under a plantation regime has influenced subsequent race relations. Since emancipation, Negroes have been expected to observe the etiquette which developed between whites and Negroes on the plantations during pre-Civil War days.[16] Even in such secular transactions as buying land, the Negro is still supposed to be subject to a form of paternalistic control. The Negro "would-be-owner must be acceptable to the white community, have a white sponsor, be content with the purchase of acreage least desired by the whites, and pay for it in a very few years." [17] To be acceptable, a Negro must know his place and stay in it. Therefore, he must let the white man take the initiative in offering to sell the land to the prospective Negro buyer. The prospective Negro buyer may be a mulatto and a relative of the white man who offers the land for sale, or he may be some Negro who has found favor with a white man. In any case, the white man, who may be debt-ridden, sells the Negro the least desirable land and at the same time preserves his prestige and reputation of benevolence in the transaction.

The tradition of paternalism on the part of whites has often been matched by a tradition of dependence on the part of Negroes. Seventy years after the Emancipation Proclamation the plantation still cast its shadow over the relations of whites and Negroes in the plantation region of the South.[18]

[16] See Bertram W. Doyle, *The Etiquette of Race Relations in the South* (Chicago: University of Chicago Press, 1937) , Chap. X.

[17] Arthur F. Raper, *Preface to Peasantry* (Chapel Hill: University of North Carolina Press, 1936) , pp. 122 ff.

[18] See Charles S. Johnson, *The Shadow of the Plantation* (Chicago: University of Chicago Press, 1934) , pp. 27–8.

ACCULTURATION: LEARNING THE WAYS
OF THE WHITES

Where plantations have been established they have made possible the introduction of new tools and machinery among non-European peoples as well as new methods of work and new habits of dress. Thus, not only have plantations provided the means through which the so-called material aspects of European culture have been introduced among non-European people, but they have provided a channel by which non-Europeans have acquired new ideas concerning work and wages, new conceptions of health and sanitation, and new standards of living. Through missionary efforts and other means, colored workers on plantations have often acquired new religious practices and beliefs; under favorable conditions, non-Europeans have been introduced to European education. The extent of this process of acculturation [19] has depended upon the extent to which the plantation became a social institution as opposed to an economic or industrial institution.

Of course, white rulers have at times instituted policies that placed restrictions upon the acculturation process. It is said, for example, that "The Dutch administration of the East Indies offers a large-scale and highly organized attempt to erect barriers against acculturation of the native peoples." [20] This was characterized by Kennedy as an anti-acculturation policy, the aim of which was to foster native institutions, including the traditional forms of government and communalistic systems of landhold-

[19] For an analysis of the concept of acculturation and a review of studies of the process of acculturation see Melville J. Herskovits, *Acculturation* (New York: J. J. Augustin, Inc., Publisher, 1938).
[20] A. Irving Hallowell, "Sociopsychological Aspects of Acculturation," in Ralph Linton (ed.), *The Science of Man in the World Crisis* (New York: Columbia University Press, 1945), p. 187.

ing.[21] Yet, "In the areas of Java not affected by Western
estates the discontinuance of forced cultivation and the influence of such factors as individual liability for taxation
and the increasing pressure of the population on the available arable land gradually broke down the communal
landownership that the Company and Cultivation systems
had fostered." [22] From 1907 to 1932 communal ownership
of land declined from 31 per cent to 13 per cent with a
corresponding increase in individual ownership from 64
per cent to 83 per cent.[23]

This only tends to emphasize the fact that the impact
of European civilization upon the colored peoples of the
world has had unforeseen consequences, some of which
were opposed to the aims of Europeans in respect to native
people. Thus it was in the case of the plantation where it
acquired the character of a social institution and became
an important agency of acculturation. It was necessary
from the beginning that non-European workers learn some
European words in order to understand instructions concerning the tasks assigned them. On plantations that remained purely industrial institutions, the colored workers
were unlikely to acquire more than a superficial knowledge of the European language. But in the case of the Brazilian plantations where the Big House and the slave
quarters were part of the same social institution, it was inevitable that the slaves should learn the Portuguese language. In fact, the association between the Portuguese and
the Negro slaves was so close that the Negroes influenced
the language of their masters.[24] Nevertheless, it was

[21] *Ibid.*, pp. 187–8, quoting Raymond Kennedy, "Acculturation and
Administration in Indonesia," *American Anthropologist*, XLV (1943),
133–47.
[22] George M. Kahin, *Nationalism and Revolution in Indonesia*
(Ithaca: Cornell University Press, 1952) , p. 17.
[23] *Ibid.*
[24] Here we have an outstanding example of interpenetration of cultures which often happens when peoples with different cultures come into
contact. It should be noted, too, that many of the slaves brought to Brazil

through the association of master and slave in daily tasks in the Big House and in their religious life that Portuguese supplanted the African languages of the slaves.

The difference between the English spoken by the Negro field hands and that spoken by the household servants was noticeable on the plantations of the southern states.[25] The slaves who grew up with the children of their masters or associated with the masters spoke, on the whole, the same English as their masters. Frederick Douglass, the noted abolitionist orator who escaped from slavery, wrote: "I have been often asked during the earlier part of my life in the North how I happened to have so little of the slave accent in my speech. The mystery is in some measure explained by my association with Daniel Lloyd, the youngest son of Col. Edward Lloyd [Douglass's master]." [26]

The promotion of Negroes from the slave quarters to the more refined service of the Big House was of course, dependent upon their physical and moral qualities and was not done carelessly or at random. It was natural that the Negro or mulatto woman who was to suckle the master's son, rock him to sleep, prepare his food and his warm bath for him, take care of his clothing, tell him stories, and at times take the place of his own mother should have been chosen from among the best of female slaves; from among the cleanest, the best-looking, the strongest; from among the less ignorant ones, or "ladinas," as they called them in those days, to distinguish the Negroes who had already been Christianized and Brazilianized from ones who had only recently come over from Africa or who were more stubborn in clinging to their African ways.[27]

---

came from superior African groups and were literate in the Arabic language. See Freyre, *op. cit.*, pp. 314 ff.

[25] In fact, the language of the Negroes in the United States still reflects the influence of the relation of their ancestors to the masters on the plantation during pre-Civil War days.

[26] Frederick Douglass, *My Bondage and My Freedom* (New York: Miller, Orton and Mulligan, 1855), p. 33.

[27] Freyre, *op. cit.*, pp. 369–70.

In this statement one can see why the process of acculturation was not the same for all elements of the Negro
population. Moreover, it reveals the manner in which the
mixed blood was more likely to have intimate contacts
with Europeans, which would facilitate his acquisition of
European culture. The same process can be seen on the
plantations of the southern states, where Negro slaves were
selected for work in the master's house, although the mulatto was not likely to enjoy an advantage over the unmixed Negro to the same extent as in Latin American
countries.[28] However, in the United States it was generally
the son of a mulatto household servant who was appren-
ticed to learn some skilled trade. The process of acculturation was not restricted to learning the language of their
masters, certain work habits, and skill in the use of tools.
The close association between master and slave on the
plantation provided the means for the communication of
ideas and beliefs, of morals and manners, depending, of
course, upon the type of social control. This does not
mean that the plantation has been the only means by which
the colored peoples of the modern world have acquired
European culture, but it was an elementary form of social
organization which played the most important role in the
first stages of acculturation.

AMALGAMATION: ACQUIRING THE "BLOOD"
OF THE WHITES

Wherever contacts have occurred between the white
and colored peoples in the modern world, amalgamation
or the biological union of the races has resulted.[29] According to Keller, racial mixture has been one of the main fea-

---

[28] In Latin countries it was a definite policy to place the mulatto
slaves in the Big House.

[29] See E. B. Reuter, "Amalgamation," in Edwin R. A. Seligman and
Alvin Johnson (eds.), *Encyclopaedia of the Social Sciences* (New York:
The Macmillan Co., 1930), II, 16–17.

tures of the plantation type of colonization, especially the plantation colonies in Latin America.[30] As a consequence of the lack of white or European women when Brazil was first settled, the Portuguese, in opposition to the Jesuit policy, created a whole generation of mixed bloods. "Many *paulistas* or *bandeirantes*," writes Freyre, "never returned from the hinterland; they remained there multiplying themselves in mestizo children and founding towns in what were to be the provinces of Minas Gerais, Mato Grosso, Goiaz, and Bahia."[31] Then, when Negro slaves were introduced into Brazil, a mixed population on a larger scale was produced by the sexual association of Portuguese men and Negro women. So widespread has been the influence of the Indian and Negro that, according to Freyre,

Every Brazilian, even the light-skinned fair hair ones, carries about with him on his soul, when not on soul and body alike . . . the shadow, or at least the birthmark, of the aborigine or the Negro. Along the seaboard from Maranhao to Rio do Sul, it is chiefly the Negro. The influence of the African, either direct or vague and remote.[32]

In Spanish America where there was also a lack of European women, there was widespread racial mixture involving Indian and Negro women. It appears that "pride of birth and class distinctions which were so jealously guarded in semifeudal Spain were intensified in America where there were so many mixed bloods."[33] The distinctions between the whites and the various mixed types and degrees of racial mixture were recognized in law. "On the

[30] Albert G. Keller, *Colonization* (New York: Ginn and Company, 1908), p. 7.

[31] Gilberto Freyre, *Brazil: An Interpretation* (New York: Alfred A. Knopf, Inc., 1945), p. 44.

[32] Gilberto Freyre, *The Masters and the Slaves*, p. 278. For an excellent critical study of racial amalgamation in Brazil see Arthur Ramos, *Le Métissage au Brésil* (Paris: Hermann et Cie, 1952).

[33] C. H. Haring, *The Spanish Empire in America* (New York: Oxford University Press, Inc., 1947), p. 212.

one hand was discrimination in order to maintain purity of blood, *Limpeza de sangre,* a phrase writ large in the social and religious history of Spain. On the other hand, was the striving of the half-caste mixtures to enroll among the whites." [34] The extent to which racial mixture occurred is shown in the case of New Spain. In 1810, out of a total population of somewhat over 6,000,000, there were in addition to the 3,600,000 native Indians, more than 1,000,000 mixed bloods predominantly European, 624,461 mixed bloods showing African mixture, and 704,245 mixed bloods of Indian extraction. There were only 15,000 Europeans and 10,000 unmixed African Negroes. [35]

Racial mixture was widespread in the French West Indies. In Saint Dominique, it is said that a bachelor planter

. . . chose an overlapping succession of concubines from the ranks of his bondswomen; the latter were proud of the distinction and called one another "matelotte," an amusing variation of the old buccaneer term for a close comrade. A married planter, usually more circumspect, confined himself to a single illicit relationship on the plantation, and perhaps maintained a free colored mistress in town. [36]

As a consequence, a large class of mixed bloods came into existence who were divided into eight categories according to the "amount of white blood in their veins." [37] Despite the reputed Anglo-Saxon prejudice against racial mixture there was racial mixture on a large scale in Jamaica where there was a scarcity of white women. [38] Like-

---

[34] *Ibid.,* p. 212.

[35] See Gonzalo A. Beltrán, *La Poblacion Negra de Mexico, 1519–1810* (Mexico, D. F.: Ediciones Fuente Cultural, 1940) , Table, p. 237.

[36] W. Adolphe Roberts, *The French in the West Indies* (Indianapolis: The Bobbs-Merrill Company, Inc., 1942) , pp. 133–4.

[37] See *ibid.,* Table of Nomenclature, p. 134.

[38] See Fernando Henriques, *Family and Colour in Jamaica* (London: Eyre and Spottiswoode, 1953) , p. 35. See also Lowell J. Ragatz, *The Fall of the Planter Class in the British Caribbean, 1763–1833* (New York: The Century Co., 1928) , pp. 33–4.

wise, in the southern part of the United States racial mixture began soon after the Negroes were imported into the colonies. Since the intermarriage of Negroes and whites was prohibited by the laws of the colonies, race mixture was the result of a system of concubinage.[39] Although there has been an effort to place the responsibility for racial mixture upon the poor whites in the cities of the South, ample evidence exists to show that the planter class was responsible for a large proportion of mulattoes. In 1850 about 8 per cent of the slaves were mulattoes and nearly 40 per cent of the free Negroes in the slave states were mixed bloods.[40]

The racial mixture which produced the present Coloured people in the Union of South Africa began in the early days of the colony when Europeans formed regular or irregular unions with their slaves and the Hottentots.[41] At first, the slaves were brought from the west African slave markets, but later they were imported in large numbers from Mozambique and Madagascar. During the first twenty years of the settlement, 85 per cent of the children of the slaves were mulattoes. Although the sexual associations between the European settlers and slaves declined, racial mixture continued between soldiers and sailors in transit and slaves. Moreover, the mixture of Boers and Hottentots continued, sometimes within regular marriage unions. But during the eighteenth century a Boer who took a Hottentot became an outcast. Then, too, by the middle of the eighteenth century the Bastards, the name generally applied to European-Hottentot mixtures, were becoming a separate people.

In the Pacific area the contacts of Europeans with the

[39] See Edward R. Reuter, *The Mulatto in the United States* (Boston: Richard G. Badger, 1918) , pp. 128 ff.

[40] See *ibid.*, p. 116.

[41] J. S. Morais, *The Cape Coloured People, 1652–1927* (New York: Longmans, Green & Co., Inc., 1939) , pp. 9 ff.

various peoples have resulted in a Eurasian population.[42] This mixed population owes its existence first to the Portuguese who settled in India, but more especially to the British during the days of the East India Company. But the Dutch and French as well as the Portuguese and English have contributed to the growth of the Eurasian population. While probably the largest single group of Eurasians is in India, there are large groups in Burma, Ceylon, Malaya, Indonesia, and the French possessions in the Pacific.[43] In the Pacific region there are other areas in which racial mixtures have occurred. As we have seen, a relatively large part of the non-European population in Australia is comprised of mixed bloods, while in New Zealand many of the Maoris are of mixed descent.

Since the Revolution, the Russians, who have always mixed readily with Mongoloid peoples from their Chinese frontiers to Alaska, have been diluting Mongolian "blood" on an unprecedented scale, both within and without the Soviets. In the Manchurian Railway zone, for example, hordes of white Russians resident there have been compelled to accept the living standards of the Chinese, and it is estimated that the resulting relations have already produced more than 60,000 children of Sino-Russian origin.[44]

The manner in which racial mixture has occurred in Hawaii is of special interest because it represents a melting pot of European and several non-European races. According to Romanzo Adams, "In the story of the amalgamation of races in Hawaii the immigrant peoples, especially the white and the Chinese, appear to have played the more active part, while the role of the Hawaiian has been of a more passive character." [45] Racial mixture in Hawaii, even

[42] See Cedric Dover, *Half-Caste* (London: Martin Secker and Warburg, Ltd., 1937), pp. 113 ff.

[43] See *ibid.*, pp. 163 ff.

[44] *Ibid.*, p. 168.

[45] See Romanzo Adams, *Interracial Marriage in Hawaii* (New York: The Macmillan Co., 1937), p. 69.

from the earliest days of European contact, has occurred mainly within marriage.[46] During the early period, when there were very few European women, the European men married native women. Some of the few scores of white men in Hawaii before 1820 were given chiefly rank and married the native women of the same rank because they were chosen to serve the king. But the majority, who were deserters from sailing ships that touched the islands, were married to women of ordinary status and given an allotment of land.[47] As late as 1849 there were almost three times as many white men with Hawaiian wives as with wives of their own race.[48] The process of racial mixture was accelerated when laborers from a number of countries, after working a few years on the plantations, scattered over the islands and married native women. However, the mixture of whites and Asians has been carried on through an indirect process. "Caucasian-Hawaiians marry Asiatic-Hawaiians or pure Asiatics, and Asiatic-Hawaiians marry pure Caucasians; and the issue is a three-way mixture." [49]

Our brief summary of the areas in which amalgamation of European and non-European has taken place has only covered the more important regions in the world. It has not included areas, for example, in east Africa and west Africa and the Belgian Congo, where people of European-African mixture are to be found. Even in the Belgian Congo where the number of mulattoes is almost infinitesimal, there is nevertheless a problem of their relation to the native and the European population.

Our interest in the process of amalgamation and the mixed blood is twofold. On the one hand, in our analysis of the problems of social organization, our purpose will be to study the role of the mixed bloods as a buffer group in some areas, or as the spearhead of struggle on the part of colored people for equality in others. Our second inter-

46 *Ibid.*, pp. 20 ff.
47 *Ibid.*, pp. 69–70 ff.
48 *Ibid.*, p. 22.
49 *Ibid.*

est in the mixed blood will be concerned with him as a person or more specifically as a marginal man and the role which he plays in race relations. The terms which are widely applied to mixed bloods, "outcaste" and "half-caste," provide a clue to a widespread and fundamental pattern of race relations—caste—which we shall analyze in the following chapter.

CHAPTER XIV

Caste Systems

INTRODUCTION

From the standpoint of a conceptual analysis of race and culture contacts, caste may be said to represent both a stage beyond slavery in the development of race relations and also a generic form of social organization in which people with different racial backgrounds find an accommodation. This chapter will be concerned, therefore, with those situations in which Europeans have attempted to maintain a status structure in which they constitute a higher caste by prohibiting intermarriage and social intercourse with the lower colored caste. The organization of race relations on the principle of caste will be analyzed in relation to the occupational status of white and colored peoples, the cultural differences between them, and racial status and social control. The concluding section of this chapter will deal with the economic, political, and social forces which have undermined or are undermining the organization of race relations on the basis of caste, and which are making class an important factor in race relations.

RACE AND OCCUPATIONS

Historically it seems that "Conquest, race differences, religion, economic developments, all have contributed and in varying degrees to the growth of the several caste systems." [1] Caste systems or analogous institutions have existed in ancient Egypt, Burma, Africa, Fiji, and India. However, it is in India that the system of caste has reached its highest development and has permeated every aspect of civilization. A number of theories have been offered to explain the origin of caste in India. [2] Race and color, occupation, and religion have each been put forth as the basic factor in formation of caste. But it is likely that all three factors have contributed to the development of the caste system. Despite the lack of agreement concerning the origin of caste, there is almost complete agreement in respect to the chief features of the caste system.

According to Ghurye, there are six outstanding features of the Indian system of caste: [3] (1) segmental division of society, (2) a hierarchial order in which groups have a higher or lower status, (3) restrictions upon eating and social intercourse, (4) civil and religious disabilities and privileges of different groups according to their caste status, (5) lack of freedom in choosing an occupation, and (6) restrictions on marriage. In our analysis of attempts to maintain a caste organization of race relations in the modern world, we shall consider these different features. But at this point we are concerned chiefly with the lack of freedom in the choice of an occupation.

[1] A. L. Kroeber, "Caste," in Edwin R. A. Seligman and Alvin Johnson (eds.), *Encyclopaedia of the Social Sciences* (New York: The Macmillan Co., 1930), III, 255.

[2] See J. H. Hutton, *Caste in India: Its Nature, Function, and Origins* (Cambridge: At the University Press, 1946), Chap. XI. This is an excellent critical analysis and summary of available knowledge on caste in India.

[3] G. S. Ghurye, *Caste and Race in India* (New York: Alfred A. Knopf. Inc., 1932), pp. 2–22.

In India, the British imposed what amounted to a white ruling caste upon the indigenous organization. Even after the "Indianization" of the civil service was instituted, the upper ranks remained in the hands of the British who held the power. In fact, the Indianization of the civil service tended to strengthen British rule since the Indian civil servants "were the intermediaries between the British authorities and the people, and if they had to be obsequious to their superiors, they could be arrogant and exact obedience from their own inferiors and the people at large." [4] Likewise, in the tropical areas where Europeans have established white control, the Europeans constitute what might be considered a ruling caste. However, neither in the countries of Asia nor in the tropical areas of Asia and Africa has a caste organization of race relations been undertaken in industry. In multiracial communities a caste organization of industrial occupations has been attempted in order to prevent the competition of white and colored peoples.

In Africa, there has been an attempt to maintain a caste system in respect to occupations in the Rhodesias and in the Union of South Africa. After the white unions in Southern Rhodesia lost a strike against the employment of nonunion European workers, the representatives of the mines made the concession that the policy not to substitute colored workers for white workers would be maintained. The chairman of the mining representatives made the following statement:

We have no intention at the present time to employ either more or less natives than are at present employed. . . . There are mines which would not exist if they were not wholly and solely worked by the native. . . . As regards the bigger mines, I speak with due authority when I say that it is our wish and our hope that we may continue working always with white men in so far as it is possible. . . . I am speaking with all

[4] Jawaharlal Nehru, *The Discovery of India* (New York: The John Day Co., 1946) , p. 329.

seriousness on the question of the colour bar. . . . We have a vast race in the natives, and there is nothing to prevent them increasing their knowledge and utility and becoming more and more a great factor in labour. . . . Just look at what is taking place at the present time at the Wankie Colliery; a handful of whites, plus the intelligent native, are turning out two-thirds of the output which was turned out before the strike. . . . The native to-day reads our papers, he has his own little organizations—however faulty they may be—and you cannot expect the native to do otherwise than to say to himself: 'We have proved what we can do.' . . . Owing to these strikes they are given responsible positions which, to my mind, is aiding and abetting the greatest possible danger to this country, which is the possibility of the native superseding the white man in his work.[5]

In 1947 the British government sent a commission to examine the color bar in Northern Rhodesia. In the Dalgleish Report, which contained the findings of the commission, it was recommended that the color bar should be gradually lowered and that Negroes should be employed in occupations formerly reserved for whites.[6] These recommendations were not carried out, and as a result the white employers, who want to upgrade Negro workers, and the white unions are engaged in a battle over the status of black workers.

The attempt to maintain caste in the employment of colored workers in the Union of South Africa has attracted world-wide attention. The caste system which the whites, more especially the Boers, are attempting to maintain in the Union of South Africa has its roots in religious as well as racial attitudes which developed on the frontier during the eighteenth century.[7] Although during an earlier period racial distinctions existed, the drawing of a rigid line

[5] Quoted in Raymond L. Buell, *The Native Problem in Africa* (New York: The Macmillan Co., 1928), I, 231–2. Reprinted by permission of the Bureau of International Research.

[6] See H. Maclear Bate, *Report from the Rhodesias* (London: Andrew Melrose, 1953), pp. 175 ff.

[7] See I. D. MacCrone, *Race Attitudes in South Africa* (New York: Oxford University Press, Inc., 1937), Chaps. VI, VII.

between Christian and heathen, which came to mean white men and colored men, grew out of the determination on the part of the Boer frontiersman to dominate other men as well as his environment. When later the conflict developed between the Boer and Bantu, these attitudes had become crystallized.

The attempt to maintain a caste system in the occupational structure has resulted from the industrialization of South Africa. The movement of the Boers to cities threw them into competition with Africans and the colored people who had constituted the majority of unskilled labor.

The idea that skin-color and not skill should be the determining factor in the economic hierarchy and wage levels was developed quite naturally by the former pastoralists as a defense against the leveling tendencies of industrialization. When it became apparent, however, that not all poor whites were mindful of the superiority of their pigmentation, and that some, as the result of proximity and a low standard of living, were even "going Kaffir" the European authorities found it necessary to take administrative action on their behalf.[8]

The action which was taken was directed mainly against the Africans, but the Coloured people were affected too in the areas where they performed most of the unskilled work. The Coloured employees on the railways became increasingly subject to restrictions upon their upgrading, and in other branches of public administration they were restricted to unskilled labor.[9] When the Nationalist government took over in 1949 and issued an order against the employment of Africans on railways in order to provide jobs for whites, it might have been inferred that the Coloured people would not be affected. But actually they became subject to the caste barriers in employment. For example,

[8] Sheila Patterson, *Colour and Culture in South Africa* (London: Routledge and Kegan Paul Ltd., 1953) , p. 68. Reprinted by permission of the publisher.
[9] See *ibid.*, pp. 68 ff.

In the Post Office, after nearly eighteen months of segregated counters, seats, and telephone booths the salary scales had only just been settled by early 1951, and the first training scheme for about twelve Coloured clerks had not yet begun. On the railways, even less progress had been made, owing to the determined opposition of the white staff. Such opposition was probably the determining factor in the Post Office delay too.[10]

Although the Coloured worker in private industry enjoyed certain advantages over the African, the new policy has gradually affected his employment in private industry. The Coloured have been paid lower wages than whites and their chances for promotion are fewer. Moreover, it has become a fixed policy that Coloured employees cannot have European employees directly under them. The restrictions against the employment of the Coloured people in industry have been increased as the result of the apartheid program, which would maintain not only an occupational hierarchy but also a vertical separation of the races. The growing demand for non-European workers in South Africa is making impractical and undesirable both the vertical separation of white and non-European and the organization of industry on caste lines.

MacCrone has summed up the problem of attempting to maintain a caste system in an industrialized and urban community like the Union of South Africa. After pointing out that the differences between a genuine caste society and what exists in South Africa are greater than the resemblances, he writes:

A multi-racial society, such as we have in this country, is a society divided against itself; or, more precisely, it is a pseudo-society in which white and black co-exist together as distinct and separate societies in a state of chronic conflict and antagonism with each other. In a genuine caste society, on the other hand, the barriers based upon caste distinctions are accepted and upheld by both sides with the result that the caste system

[10] *Ibid.*, p. 70. Reprinted by permission of the publisher.

itself is never directly challenged. Although a great deal of rivalry and friction exists between the sub-castes within the caste system, the system as a whole has made it possible for these groups to continue to live together and to accommodate themselves to one another. In a multi-racial society, as we know it, the social system is in a state of extreme disaccommodation or disequilibrium since the existing dominating-dominated pattern of relations between white and black is not accepted by the dominated group and can only be maintained, in the last resort, by force.[11]

In the United States, the determination on the part of the southern whites to erect a legalized caste system grew out of the unresolved class conflict within the white community.[12] It was accomplished by reducing public education for Negroes, by disfranchising them politically, and by instituting a system of racial segregation or Jim Crow. All these measures tended to restrict Negroes to certain occupations. The operation of caste in respect to employment in industry has been most conspicuous in the almost complete exclusion of Negroes as workers in the textile industry. When this industry came to the South, partly as a civic welfare movement to provide employment for poor white people, the system of caste prevented the employment of Negroes as production workers.[13] The relatively few Negroes who were employed in the textile mills were utilized as menial workers. In fact, caste based upon race has been the most important feature of the occupational structure of the South.

The manner in which the principle of caste has functioned in the economic organization of the South has been studied intensively in one community by a group of an-

[11] I. D. MacCrone, "Race Attitudes: An Analysis and Interpretation," in Ellen Hellmann (ed.), *Handbook on Race Relations in South Africa* (New York: Oxford University Press, Inc., 1949), p. 685. Reprinted by permission of the publisher.

[12] See pp. 209–11 *above*.

[13] See Gunnar Myrdal, *An American Dilemma* (New York: Harper & Brothers, 1944), pp. 285–6.

thropologists.[14] A concluding observation of this study provides a close parallel to what MacCrone said of the effort to maintain caste in the Union of South Africa. When the poor whites who are almost as poor as the Negroes compete with the latter for the same jobs:

. . . it is most difficult to maintain caste lines with the rigidity and authority which the dogma of caste demands. In such a community, therefore, the white population must resort to terrorization continually in order to impress the colored group with the fact that economic equality or superordination on the part of the latter is not real equality or superordination—in other words, that caste exists all along the line, as the myth demands, and that actually any white man, no matter how poor or illiterate, is superordinate to any colored man and must be treated with the appropriate deference.[15]

RACE AND CULTURE

The development of race relations along caste lines has grown out of cultural as well as racial differences. In fact, the culture of a people has often been regarded as an expression of their racial characteristics.[16] MacCrone has pointed out in regard to race and culture contacts in the Union of South Africa that the consciousness of differences due to cultural differences has been enhanced by racial differences or the biological fact of skin color.[17] The "dominating-dominated" pattern of relationship which exists

[14] See Allison Davis, Burleigh B. Gardner, and Mary R. Gardner, *Deep South: A Social Anthropological Study of Caste and Class* (Chicago: University of Chicago Press, 1941) , Part II.

[15] *Ibid.*, Part II, p. 482. Reprinted by permission of the publisher, and copyright 1941 by the University of Chicago.

[16] Freyre writes: "It was my studies in anthropology under the direction of Professor Boas that first revealed to me the Negro and the mulatto for what they are—with the effects of environment or cultural experience separated from racial characteristics. I learned to regard as fundamental the difference between race and culture, to discriminate between the effects of purely genetic relationships and those resulting from social influences, the cultural heritage and the milieu." Gilberto Freyre, *The Masters and the Slaves* (New York: Alfred A. Knopf, Inc., 1946) , p. xxi.

[17] MacCrone, *loc. cit.*, p. 681.

between white and black in South Africa was an inevitable consequence of the conquest of one race or ethnic-cultural group by another race or ethnic-cultural group. At the same time the status system based upon racial and cultural differences is reinforced by religious sanctions.[18] The Dutch Reformed Church, which has been the chief means through which the Afrikaans language has been preserved, has exhorted its members for generations to hold fast to their cultural identity.[19] It has been the Dutch Reformed Church that has maintained the social cohesion of the Boers and kept them morally isolated from the outside world with its liberal and scientific ideas. Moreover, the preachers in the Dutch Reformed Church transformed their pulpits into political platforms. As a consequence the Boer finds within the Christian theology expounded by the Church a confirmation of his faith that "he is a member of a master-race, the Afrikanervolk." [20]

Race and, to a less extent, cultural differences were made the basis of the legalized system of caste which the whites undertook to set up in the southern states during the last decade of the nineteenth and first decade of the twentieth century. Although in the case of the American Negro cultural differences could not provide the basis of caste, nevertheless the culture of the rural Negro folk became the mark of an inferior race. The folk Negro's dialect, his religious beliefs and practices, and his unconven-

---

[18] After stating that contact between a member of a higher caste and a member of a lower caste makes for ritualistic impurity which must be expiated by a religious act, Weber wrote that "the status structure reaches such extreme consequences only where there are underlying differences which are held to be 'ethnic.' The 'caste' is, indeed, the normal form in which ethnic communities usually live side by side in a 'societalized' manner. These ethnic communities believe in blood relationship and exclude exogamous marriage and social intercourse. Such a caste situation is part of the phenomenon of 'pariah' peoples and is found all over the world." H. H. Gerth and C. Wright Mills (trans.), *Max Weber's Essays in Sociology* (New York: Oxford University Press, Inc., 1946), p. 189. Reprinted by permission of the publisher.

[19] See Eugene P. Dvorin, *Racial Separation in South Africa* (Chicago: University of Chicago Press, 1952), p. 39.

[20] *Ibid.*, p. 46.

tional and amorphous family relations, all of which had developed on American soil, were nonetheless regarded as barbarous African cultural survivals. Moreover, these cultural traits were supposed to be as much an expression of the Negro's racial heritage as his dark skin color and his woolly hair.

Although a religious sanction of a caste organization of race relations was not as marked in the southern states as in the Union of South Africa, it has nevertheless played a role in sanctioning the lower caste status of Negroes. The Bible was used to show that the Negro was the descendant of Ham, whom God had decreed should be the servant of the white man. But more often the imputed innate racial inferiority of the Negro was used to justify the necessity of a caste system in which all Negroes would be subordinate to all whites. It was argued that only through the establishment of a system of legalized caste could the "purity" of the white race be preserved. A race orthodoxy grew up in the South, which contained the following statements among the fifteen articles of the racial creed: [21] "Blood will tell," "The white race must dominate," "The Teutonic peoples stand for race purity," "The Negro is inferior and will remain so," and "Let the lowest white man count for more than the highest Negro." The final article of the racial creed states that all the antecedent "statements indicate the leadings of Providence."

RACIAL STATUS AND SOCIAL CONTROL

Whenever the relations of white and colored peoples have developed along caste lines, racial distinctions have become the basis of a system of social control. A caste organization of race relations is a form of accommodation in which the conflicting interests, aspirations, and wishes of

[21] See Thomas P. Bailey, *Race Orthodoxy in the South* (New York: The Neal Publishing Co., 1914) , p. 93.

whites and colored people are resolved, at least to the extent that cooperation is possible. In the area of personal relations, the accommodation generally takes the form of superordination and subordination.[22] The subordination of the lower caste is determined by heredity and is supported by traditions and sentiments which have a religious character. Although a caste may undertake to achieve, and may even succeed in achieving, a higher place in the hierarchy of castes, nevertheless the members of the caste accept their social status as a corporate or group status. The attempt to maintain a system of caste based upon race tends to immobilize the society by eliminating competition between white and colored people. And when colored people succeed in moving up the occupational ladder or increasing their incomes or acquiring a higher education, they cannot change their corporate status.

In South Africa, the principle of caste was proclaimed by the Boer republics when they declared that there should be no equality of whites and blacks in church or state. The inequality of whites and blacks could easily be maintained as long as the Boers remained in rural areas and whites monopolized the skilled positions in industry. Up to the time when the poor whites began to migrate to towns, "the deeply rooted tradition of economic life that the natural division of labour was between brain-power and muscular strength, between administrative skill and docility, between the few and the many" [23] remained in force. "During at least the last fifty years of the nineteenth century natives had held a virtual monopoly of unskilled and manual labour in every part of South Africa except the regions near Cape Town where their place was taken by the Cape Coloured folk." [24] When the poor whites came to

---

[22] See Robert E. Park and Ernest W. Burgess, *Introduction to the Science of Sociology* (Chicago: University of Chicago Press, 1924), p. 667.

[23] C. W. DeKiewiet, *A History of South Africa* (New York: Oxford University Press, Inc., 1946), p. 220.

[24] *Ibid.*

the cities and had to compete with the native African, the traditional division of labor along race lines was broken up.

In order to preserve the dominance of the whites it was necessary to prevent the economic competition between white and black men, because it was held that economic equality would create social equality between the races. "The threat was plain," writes DeKiewiet, "in the equally wretched habitations of poor whites and poor blacks in Johannesburg's slums." [25] The poor whites were a sort of frontier between the Europeans and the blacks, and if they were allowed to sink to the African's level, race mixture would occur. Therefore, it was necessary to protect the poor white in order to maintain the purity and solidarity of the white race. The color bar, the differential wage levels, and a system of segregation were all instituted as a part of a system of control which would preserve the racial purity and status of Europeans.

In the southern states of the United States the attempt to maintain caste in race relations is expressed in the oft-repeated assertion by white people that, "Negroes are all right in their place." When one attempts to discover what is meant by the Negro's place, one discovers that it does not refer to the physical relations between a white person and a Negro. Nor does it necessarily refer to the type of work that a Negro performs. It refers to the position which the Negro occupies in the social organization. Briefly, a Negro is in his "proper" place, no matter how close he is physically to a white person, as long as some symbol of his overt behavior, verbal or otherwise, indicates his subordinate social status. It is in this form of social control that one finds the similarities to a system of caste.

The very laws and customary regulations which maintain the segregation of Negroes also indicate that the question of racial status is paramount. In most places in the

[25] DeKiewiet, *op. cit.*, p. 221.

South, the most distinguished Negro, for example, cannot enter the front door of a hotel or a railway station, but a Negro butler or nurse may do so as long as it is known that he is a servant. An apparent contradiction in the attitude of whites toward race mixture disappears when the element of status is known. A white man may have children by a colored woman whom he supports as well as his white children. This behavior and its results are not considered mixing of the races or race mixture unless the white man would marry the Negro woman. Such marriages are forbidden by law. Thus race mixture is forbidden within the legal and moral order. When it occurs outside of the legal and moral order, it is a purely biological phenomenon and racial status is not involved. But, of course, any relation between a Negro man and a white woman is not only condemned but involves the most drastic penalty. It is apparent, then, that the so-called caste system of race relations is above all a system of social control which not only prevents economic competition between whites and Negroes but which also enables the white man to enjoy certain sexual and prestige advantages.[26]

The system of social control which the caste pattern of race relations undertakes to maintain is opposed to the economic and social changes now occurring in the South. Moreover, as the Negro acquires more education, enters new occupations, and improves his economic status, he is able to escape many of the quasi-caste controls. To take one aspect of race relations, transportation, Negroes through the ownership of automobiles have been able to avoid Jim Crow coaches on the railroads. Then, too, the white owners of gasoline stations, who represent large corporations and serve a mobile clientele, are not eager to add to their expenses by maintaining separate washrooms and toilets.

[26] See John Dollard, *Caste and Class in a Southern Town* (New Haven: Yale University Press, 1937), Chaps. V, VI, VII.

CASTE AND CLASS

Caste has flourished in relatively static societies which were predominantly agricultural. But even in India where caste reached its most complete development, the impact of industrialization, of urbanization, and of Western science has tended to undermine the caste organization of society.[27] The new systems of transportation—the highways and railroads—are bringing into closer contact on the buses and in the third-class railway compartments millions of people of all castes. Thus the physical conditions of association permit little opportunity for the observance of ceremonial purity. Likewise, in factories and in the slums of cities, the social distances and rituals required by a caste organization cannot be maintained. Moreover, industrialization is destroying or making obsolete old crafts which were organized on a caste basis, and occupational mobility and a money economy are tending to secularize social relations. The dissemination of new ideas through the media of mass communication, the development of secular scientific education, the rise of professional classes, the education of women, who are no longer bound by the ancient taboos and mores, all of these are destroying the economic, social, and ideological bases of the caste system.

A modern industrial urban society is opposed, therefore, to the sociological basis of a caste order of society. As Frankel has stated, the economic problem "in Africa is not one of dividing up the land between different races"; [28] the economic development of Africa depends upon the utilization of Africans and poor whites without racial restrictions in the European economy. The color bar which would exclude Africans from skilled occupations or restrict them

[27] See Mason Alcott, "The Caste System of India," *American Sociological Review*, IX (December 1944), 652.

[28] See S. H. Frankel, *Capital Investment in Africa* (New York: Oxford University Press, Inc., 1938), pp. 130 ff.

to certain types of occupations or establish a certain ratio of African and Coloured workers to white workers is inimical to the operation of an efficient industrial economy. Likewise, certain arbitrarily fixed wage scales based upon race tend to destroy incentive among the non-European workers who are needed by the industrial economy.

The development of an industrial urban society with a market economy gives rise to classes as opposed to status groups or castes.[29] It may be because of this fact that one school of social scientists in the United States has utilized the concepts of caste and class in the analysis of race relations, especially in the southern states.[30] According to the point of view of this school, race relations in the South constitute a caste system, and within each caste there is a class system. Therefore, in order to understand the operation of the caste system it is necessary to study the relations of the classes in one caste with the classes in the other caste. It is stated, for example, that whites and Negroes at the top of the two class systems cooperate in subordinating the lower class and that upper and upper middle-class whites protect the upper and middle-class Negroes from the lower white classes.[31]

A number of scholars have challenged the position of this school with reference to the utility and relevance of the caste concept in the study of race relations in the United States.[32] Although race relations in the South have

29 "With some over-simplification," wrote Weber, "one might thus say that 'classes' are stratified according to their relations to the production and acquisition of goods; whereas 'status groups' are stratified according to the principles of their *consumption* of goods as represented by special 'styles of life.'" Gerth and Mills (trans.), *op. cit.*, p. 193. Reprinted by permission of the publisher.

30 See W. Lloyd Warner, "American Caste and Class," *American Journal of Sociology*, XXXXII (September 1932), 234–7. See also W. Lloyd Warner and Allison Davis, "A Comparative Study of American Caste," in Edgar T. Thompson (ed.), *Race Relations and the Race Problem* (Durham: Duke University Press, 1939), pp. 219–45. See also Davis, Gardner, and Gardner, *op. cit.*

31 Warner and Davis, *op. cit.*, p. 241.

32 See Brewton Berry, *Race Relations* (New York: Houghton Mifflin Co., 1951), pp. 317–19. See also George E. Simpson and J. Milton Yinger,

a number of features which resemble a caste system, there are so many elements in the racial situation in the South which differentiate it from a genuine caste system that the employment of the concept of caste seems forced and pedantic. The most telling argument against the relevance and utility of the caste concept is that the system of race relations has to be enforced by laws and the threat of force. It is not based upon tradition nor does it have the sanction of religion. In fact, it is opposed to the teachings of Christianity and to the political ideology of the United States. Negroes are constantly invoking the laws of the United States to nullify racial distinctions and racial discriminations which place them in an inferior status. MacCrone found the caste concept irrelevant on somewhat similar grounds for the analysis of race relations in South Africa.[33]

Our review and analysis in this chapter of the attempts to maintain a caste organization of race relations in the modern world indicate that they are attempts to force into the mold of a static agricultural society the dynamic economic and social relations which characterize an industrial urban society. In the chapter which follows we shall consider another type of organization of race relations which has grown up in response to the economic, social, and ideological changes which have occurred as the result of industrialization and urbanization.

Racial and Cultural Minorities (New York: Harper & Brothers, 1953), pp. 327–30. See also Oliver C. Cox, *Caste, Class and Race* (New York: Doubleday & Company, Inc., 1948).

[33] See pp. 258–9 *above*, quotation from MacCrone, *loc. cit.* See also MacCrone, *loc. cit.*, p. 685.

CHAPTER XV

Biracial Organizations

INTRODUCTION

Unlike caste, the biracial organization of race relations does not imply, at least theoretically, that one race is inferior or subordinate to the other. It is said to be a means of keeping races distinct while at the same time enabling each race to develop completely its potentialities. Since the biracial organization of race relations is based upon certain theories about race as well as certain racial attitudes, this chapter will give attention first to racial ideologies as a basis of social organization. It will consider next the phenomenon of race prejudice or racial attitudes in relation to social organization. In the remaining sections of the chapter an analysis will be made of the various patterns of racial segregation, which is an essential feature of biracial organizations, and of racial segregation in relation to social status.

RACE AS A BASIS OF SOCIAL ORGANIZATION

Racial ideologies developed as a consequence of the contacts of European peoples with the peoples of Africa, America, and Asia. However, at the beginning of these contacts religion rather than race played an important role in defining the relationship of Europeans to non-Europeans. "Natives were outside the pale of humanity, but this was regarded as a consequence of the fact that they were not Christians, not of the fact that they belonged to the darker races." [1] When Europeans began to compete with the Arabs for the trade with Asia, the Christian merchants of Europe were inspired by a religious zeal to drive the infidel from the Indian Ocean and the Pacific Ocean. When slaves were first brought from Africa, the Europeans could justify their aggression by converting the heathen to Christianity. It was said that the zeal of Prince Henry the Navigator for religion:

led him to rejoice when a company of adventurers brought back cargoes of natives, because of the salvation of those souls that before were lost. He gave away those that fell to his share, for slavery was not in his design, though it was then and for centuries later considered lawful. [2]

But as the trade in black flesh brought wealth to Europe and as the Africans became Christians, the "racial" inferiority of Africans provided new justification of their enslavement. In fact, with the spread of European dominance in America, Asia, and Africa, the alleged superiority of the white race became the main justification of European control over the non-European world.

The European adventurers who engaged in the slave trade and established plantations with colored labor in Africa, America, and Asia were never influenced by the romantic notion of the "noble savage" which captivated the minds of Europeans who remained at home. [3] They were engaged in a struggle to subjugate colored people in order to make a fortune or, if they could not subjugate

---

[1] Ruth Benedict, *Race: Science and Politics* (New York: The Viking Press, Inc., 1943), p. 168.

[2] Quoted in I. D. MacCrone, *Race Attitudes in South Africa* (London: Andrew Melrose, 1953), p. 7.

[3] Benedict, *op. cit.*, p. 167.

them, to exterminate them. Although, as we have seen, the relations of Europeans to natives differed from area to area, nevertheless the spread of European economic and political control was justified on the ground that Europeans were dealing with inferior races. This was amply demonstrated in the case of the African. In the West Indies, in South Africa, and in the southern states, the idea of the racial inferiority of the African developed and became more deeply rooted as the exploitation of African labor and the subordination of the African became tied up with the economic interests of the whites.

However, the development of racial ideologies began with the Aryan myth when European philologists discovered the similarities between the Sanskrit, Greek, Latin, German, English, and Celtic languages.[4] It was, however, Count Gobineau who, in his famous four volume work, *Essai sur l'Inégalité des Races Humaines,* provided the ideological basis of the superiority of the white race, especially the Nordic branch.[5] Since he formulated his theory in the 1850's before the evolutionary hypothesis had been accepted, he assumed that the violence of climatic forms had brought about the differentiation of man into three races during 7,000 years between creation and the birth of Christ. The three races were the Negroid which was animal-like and derived from Africa; the yellow, stubborn and apathetic, which originated in America and spread across Asia to Europe; and the white, endowed with reason and excelling all others in physical beauty, which originated in the Hindu Kush region of Asia. Although Gobineau was not consistent about the characteristics of the Aryan branch of the white race, he claimed that Aryans were responsible for seven of the ten civilizations that had arisen among mankind. The cult of Gobineau found

[4] See Frank H. Hankins, *The Racial Basis of Civilization* (New York: Alfred A. Knopf, Inc., 1926), Chap. II.

[5] *Ibid.*, Chap. III.

a warm welcome in Germany.[6] According to Gobineau, though the Germans were being diluted by racial amalgamation, they were the last of the Aryans. A Gobineau Society was founded in Germany which propagated the doctrine of divinely ordained Germanic superiority. The works of scholars and literary men and artists, outstanding among whom was Wagner, supported the new racial patriotism. By the close of the nineteenth century, "the original mysticism of Gobineau had been raised to the exalted level of a holy and increasingly militant faith. In 1899 this was given a powerful expression in the writings of Houston-Stewart Chamberlain, another poet-musician-philosopher." [7]

Gobineau thought that there was some hope for mankind in the fact that Anglo-Saxons dominated Britain and America. However, the myth of Anglo-Saxon superiority was fostered in Britain by philologists, historians, publicists, and poets.[8] The historians were especially influential in disseminating the idea that the achievements of the English people were due to their Anglo-Saxon racial heritage. It was the mission of the Anglo-Saxon race, according to Carlyle, to take over the control of the backward regions of the world. With the election of Disraeli in 1874, the Conservatives preached the doctrine of the racial superiority of the Anglo-Saxons. One Conservative leader declared that the Anglo-Saxons would displace the colored races in the world. The most important literary figure who helped to establish the myth of Anglo-Saxon superiority was Rudyard Kipling, in whose poetry the Anglo-Saxon was exhorted to take up the "white man's burden" and bring the benefits of a higher civilization to the backward colored peoples of the earth. This mission of the Anglo-Saxon became the main justification for imperialism. At

---

[6] *Ibid.,* Chap. IV.

[7] *Ibid.,* p. 64.

[8] See Louis L. Snyder, *Race: A History of Modern Ethnic Theories* (New York: Longmans, Green and Co., Inc., 1939), pp. 212 ff.

the same time, however, Kipling in his famous line contending that East and West would never meet, gave classic expression to the idea of a racial barrier between the white and colored races, destruction of which would lead to the degradation of the white race.

During the nineteenth century, anthropologists were beginning to study in an objective and scientific manner the phenomenon of race.[9] But most people paid little attention to the new science except in so far as it tended to support their interests and their prejudices. They were more impressed by Herbert Spencer's statement of the classical theory of anthropology. In his attempt to apply the evolutionary explanation of the natural world to the social world, he placed the European at the top of the evolutionary scale, the Asians at an intermediate stage, and the Africans at the bottom. The defenders of slavery in the United States eagerly seized upon the myth of Anglo-Saxon superiority as a justification for Negro slavery. After the Civil War the myth was invoked constantly to justify the disfranchisement of Negroes, the system of legal segregation, and a narrow industrial education for Negro children.

These attempts to identify race and culture and to make a particular type of political or social organization the expression of race established the notion that white and colored people could not mingle freely in the same community or be a part of the same social organization. A corollary to this idea of racial determinism was the notion that an innate reaction generally known as race prejudice served to protect the superior white race against mingling freely with the inferior colored races.

[9] A controversy, obviously of political origin, split the anthropologists over the question of slavery when James Hunt read a paper on "The Negro's Place in Nature" in 1863. The thesis of the paper was that the Negro became "more humanized when in his natural subordination to the European" and that "European civilization is not suited to the negro's requirements of character." See Alfred C. Haddon, *History of Anthropology* (London: Watts and Co., 1910), p. 66 ff.

RACE PREJUDICE

In undertaking to answer the question of why race prejudice exists, Miss Benedict was led to conclude that "in order to understand race persecution, we do not need to investigate race; we need to investigate *persecution*." [10] Faris stated the paradox in another way when he wrote that "race prejudice is a phenomenon that is not essentially connected with race." [11] Then he went on to explain the apparent paradox:

Another way to say the same thing would be to assert that as races are dealt with and as races are disliked, there is little or no connection with the scientific concept of race. Not that this is without justification, for, in this crude world in which we live, it is of importance to determine not what races are, but what men call races when they manifest racial antipathy. And it is an extremely easy task to show in this connection that race prejudice is contingent upon a certain type of group consciousness which may have no defense in a scientific classification, but which does determine in large measure what men live by and what they do when they live. [12]

This statement places in clear focus the fact that the behavior and emotional attitudes which are generally defined as race prejudice are not related to the biological factors that physical anthropologists and geneticists have used as a basis for classifying the races of mankind. [13] Moreover, it reveals in a striking manner how little Vacher de

[10] Benedict, *op. cit.*, p. 230.

[11] Ellsworth Faris, *The Nature of Human Nature* (New York: McGraw-Hill Book Co., 1937) , p. 317.

[12] By permission from *The Nature of Human Nature*, by Ellsworth Faris, p. 317. Copyright, 1937. McGraw-Hill Book Company, Inc.

[13] For an analysis of the present status of anthropological theories concerning races see A. L. Kroeber, *Anthropology* (New York: Harcourt, Brace and Company, 1948) , Chaps. IV, V. See also M. F. Ashley Montagu, *Man's Most Dangerous Myth: The Fallacy of Race* (New York: Columbia University Press, 1945) .

Lapouge, a French pro-Aryan, understood the attitudes and behavior of men in regard to race when he wrote in the 1880's, "I am convinced that in the next century millions will cut each other's throats because of 1 or 2 degrees more or less of cephalic index." [14]

The attempts to explain race prejudice as an instinctive reaction have been abandoned because studies of children have revealed that race prejudice is acquired behavior. However, there is still lack of agreement concerning the nature of race prejudice. According to one widespread theory, race prejudice arises as the result of economic factors or when the exploiting race propagates race prejudice in its own interest.[15] There are psychological theories, according to which race prejudice is a reaction to frustration or some psychic need. There are also theories which emphasize the role of socio-cultural factors in the genesis of prejudice. In fact, in accounting for the existence of race prejudice in any specific situation, it is necessary to study both the economic and socio-cultural factors. On the other hand, the psychological approach to the problem of race prejudice is useful in discovering the differential responses of individuals to the milieu in which race prejudice exists.

Race prejudice is a social attitude with an emotional bias.[16] The object of race prejudice is not necessarily an individual with certain observable characteristics but an individual who is identified as a member of a racial group. It has often been said that race prejudice has resulted from some unpleasant experience with an individual of a different race. But it is more likely that the unpleasant experience has evoked a latent attitude which has been acquired

[14] Quoted in Benedict, *op. cit.*, p. 3.

[15] For theories concerning race prejudice see Brewton Berry, *Race Relations* (New York: Houghton Mifflin Co., 1951), pp. 104–16. See also Gordon W. Allport, *The Nature of Prejudice* (Cambridge: Addison-Wesley Publishing Company, Inc., 1954), Chap. 13.

[16] See Louis Wirth, "Race and Public Policy," *Scientific Monthly*, LVIII (1944), p. 303.

from one's own group. The latent attitude is directed against the "categoric picture" or, as Faris has pointed out, the concept of the individual as a member of a different race.[17] We know that a person who has race prejudice does not perceive any specific individual of a different race but rather sees each one in terms of the categoric picture. Hence all Chinese or Negroes look alike to white people. Since race prejudice is a social attitude, it comes into existence as the result of the relations which develop between different races. It is propagated through the channels of communication in a society and becomes a part of the social heritage. Race prejudice is generally supported by rationalizations which bear no relation to the real causes of race prejudice. The rationalizations represent an attempt on the part of prejudiced people to make their prejudices appear logical and just. This will become apparent during the course of our discussion of race prejudice in relation to a biracial organization.

MacCrone, who regards racial attitudes as essentially social attitudes, shows how racial prejudices grew out of a conflict situation in South Africa.[18] Out of this conflict have developed the dominance of the white group and the subordination of the Africans. The racial attitudes serve to "protect and preserve" the dominant position of the European with its "attendant social, political and economic privileges against any threat from the members of the dominated races." [19] Therefore, the European is extremely sensitive in regard to any behavior on the part of the non-European which offers a threat to his privileged position. This accounts for the fears and anxieties on the part of the European when he considers the large numbers of Afri-

    [17] Faris, *op. cit.*, p. 324.
    [18] I. D. MacCrone, "Race Attitudes: An Analysis and Interpretation," in Ellen Hellmann (ed.), *Handbook on Race Relations in South Africa* (New York: Oxford University Press, Inc., 1949) , pp. 675–6.
    [19] *Ibid.*, p. 687.

cans by whom he is surrounded. Moreover, it explains the various racial myths, stereotypes and rationalizations, and the whole psychopathology which characterize race and color prejudice.[20]

In the United States the prejudice of whites against Negroes has exhibited very much the same characteristics. In order to understand the manner in which it has developed and spread and been modified in recent years, it is necessary to study it in relation to certain economic, social, and political factors in American society. It should be indicated in the beginning that explanations which attribute race prejudice to slavery are completely misleading. In the United States, as in Brazil, slavery provided a modus vivendi for whites and blacks and therefore race prejudice tended to disappear, especially where the plantation acquired the character of a social institution. It was, to be sure, a paternalistic regime, but the Negro was regarded as a person and some degree of human solidarity developed between whites and blacks. The significance of this was pointed out by Thomas when he observed:

Of the relation of black to white in this country it is perhaps true that the antipathy of the southerner for the negro is rather caste-feeling than race-prejudice, while the feeling of the northerner is race-prejudice proper. In the North, where there has been no contact with the negro and no activity connections, there is no caste-feeling, but there exists a sort of skin-prejudice—a horror of the external aspect of the negro—and many northerners report that they have a feeling against eating from a dish handled by a negro. The association of master and slave in the South was, however, close, even if not intimate, and much of the feeling of physical repulsion for a black skin disappeared.[21]

20 *Ibid.,* p. 120. See also MacCrone, *Race Attitudes in South Africa,* Part III.

21 William I. Thomas, "The Psychology of Race-Prejudice," *American Journal of Sociology,* IX, 609–10. Published by the University of Chicago Press, and copyright 1904 by the University of Chicago.

This observation emphasizes an important fact concerning race prejudice in the South, namely, that it is not based upon physical repulsion. Some of the white people who objected to the mixing of the blood plasma of Negroes and whites during World War II would express their love of Negroes by saying that they had been nurtured by a "black mammy."

After the Civil War and emancipation when conflict developed over the status of the Negro in southern society, race prejudice developed on a wider scale than during slavery. But even then, race prejudice did not become as intense and widespread as it did later during the class struggle between the white landowning and new industrial and commercial classes on one hand, and the landless poor whites on the other. This struggle was resolved by the demagogic leaders of the poor whites who made the Negro the scapegoat. From 1890 to 1915, the Negro became the object of a systematic campaign of defamation in which he was represented as subhuman. During this period there was a marked increase in race prejudice among the masses of white people in the South. They became convinced that the only way that southern society could be saved from the moral and physical contamination of the Negro was by establishing a legalized system of segregation.

PATTERNS OF SEGREGATION

Even in a society like Brazil where there is a minimum of race prejudice and no laws requiring racial segregation, there is some segregation growing out of the Negroes' low economic status and the fact that they have not been drawn completely into the main stream of Brazilian culture. In Bahia, for example:

The residential pattern suggests a gradually evolving, freely competitive society in which Europeans settled on the ridges, and the Africans and their descendants, as propertyless slaves, as impoverished freemen, were relegated to less desirable territory. Although the Europeans have still today, to a considerable extent, maintained their original advantage, the blacks and darker mixed-bloods have gradually pushed themselves up the slopes from their less favored locations until now they have come, in some cases, to share a portion of the Europeans' favored position.[22]

The cultural segregation of Negroes has resulted partly from the survival of African culture in the *candomblé* which embodies customs and traditions associated with religious sentiments.[23] The members of these cults, which represent to some extent the fusion of Catholicism and African religion, are often members of the Catholic Church. As the cults disintegrate because of the economic and social changes in Brazil, this last stronghold of racial segregation is breaking down.

On the other hand, in the Union of South Africa, the most extreme form of biracial organization is being undertaken by the Nationalist Party. A form of biracial organization had, of course, existed before the Nationalist Party came to power. From 1920 onward all legislation concerning native Africans was designed to "more clearly define the separate provinces of white and black existence." [24] These laws were designed to place the native outside the political organization of South Africa and to make him subject to discretionary powers on the part of the government. The native chiefs were restored to some of the authority which had been taken from them in the nineteenth century and the once criticized customs, such as the *lobola* or bride price, were restored.[25] Whereas once the Europeans had complained about the menace of tribalism,

[22] Donald Pierson, *Negroes in Brazil* (Chicago: University of Chicago Press, 1942), pp. 21–2. Copyright 1942 by the University of Chicago.

[23] *Ibid.*, Chap. X.

[24] C. W. DeKiewiet, *A History of South Africa* (New York: Oxford University Press, Inc., 1946), p. 236.

[25] *Ibid.*, p. 237.

the tribe was now declared to be the only basis of native existence that would serve as a protection for the whites.

The determination to prevent the native from having the same place in urban life and industry as the European "carried with it the plain implication that the future of the native population was primarily on the land." [26] The rationalization that was used to support this policy was that if the natives were held to the soil and allowed to develop their own institutions, cooperation between whites and blacks would be encouraged and racial tensions would be reduced. According to the report of a competent commission:

It would be wise to develop the wealth producing capacity of these excellent areas and thus secure a larger amount to go round, rather than to allow a continuance of the present struggle between black and white for a larger share in the wealth being produced from the developed areas. With these areas developed to a reasonably productive level there should be enough to make possible friendly co-operation between the races. [27]

Then in 1936 the policy of segregation culminated in the passage of the Natives Land and Trust Act and the Representation of Natives Acts. The first of these was supposed to restore to the native the land which had been taken from him in order that he might have an economic basis for his segregated existence. The second act extended the disfranchisement of the natives in the Republics (Transvaal and Orange Free State) to Natal and took away the right of franchise which the African had once enjoyed in the Cape Province. The acts of 1936 were a failure from the standpoint of segregation. In response to the demands of industry, the natives continued to move into urban areas in search of money to pay their taxes as well as an opportunity to lead a fuller life. Moreover, "not even the 15,300,000 acres of 'released' land were enough

[26] *Ibid.,* p. 336.
[27] Quoted in *ibid.,* p. 237. Reprinted by permission of the publisher.

to permit the development of the native population as a self-sustaining peasantry." [28] The changes which had already transformed the native could not be undone by legislation.

The aim of the apartheid program, which the Nationalist Party is attempting to put into effect, is to bring about complete segregation of the races. The natives would be confined to their reserves and their tribal system would be "revitalized." [29] Only those natives required by industry would be allowed to remain in urban areas while the bulk of cheap native labor would be imported.[30] A system of native councils within the reserves and within urban areas would provide the limit of the political activities of the natives. In addition, this program would stop the duplication of European organizations and institutions among natives, a process similar to what has occurred in the Negro commuity in the United States.

It is in the United States, especially in the southern states, that a thoroughgoing system of racial segregation has developed, with the result that as far as possible all the forms of organized and institutional life which exist in the white community have been duplicated within the Negro community. A systematic study of the patterns of racial segregation has shown the most conspicuous forms of racial segregation to be:

(1) in residential areas, (2) in educational, recreational, and other public institutions, (3) in quasi-public institutions or privately operated institutions under public control, such as railroads, steamship lines, streetcar and bus systems, and hospitals, (4) in private business establishments, such as hotels and restaurants under customary or legal mandate to prevent racial contact on a level implying social equality or permitting social intimacy, (5) in other private commercial and profes-

[28] *Ibid.*, p. 243.
[29] Eugene P. Dvorin, *Racial Separation in South Africa* (Chicago: University of Chicago Press, 1952), Chap. IV.
[30] *Ibid.*, Chap. VII.

sional services, such as department stores, undertaking establishments and doctors' offices.[31]

The residential segregation of Negroes has resulted
from the interplay of economic, social, and political factors. In the North, except during periods when there was
a large influx of southern Negroes, economic and social
factors rather than race have been chiefly responsible for
the residential segregation of Negroes. The location of
Negroes in the ecological pattern of northern cities has
been due, on the whole, to the same economic and social
factors as those which have determined the location of
immigrant European groups. Contrary to popular notions,
the Negro was not segregated in the older cities of the
South. They were brought to these cities by their white
owners before the Civil War and it became customary for
Negroes and whites to live in the same residential areas.
It was in the border cities, where the location of Negroes
was determined neither by economic factors nor by historical conditions and custom, that the residential segregation of Negroes became a matter for legislation. It may
be said that the problem of residential segregation became
an acute racial problem when, during and following
World War I, Negroes began to move into cities in large
numbers.[32] When laws providing for the residential segregation of Negroes were declared unconstitutional, whites
resorted to covenants or agreements among themselves to
achieve the same end. These covenants were in turn declared unenforceable by the courts. This has tended to undermine the residential segregation of Negroes but racial
conflicts over housing have not disappeared. These conflicts are often due to political and economic considerations rather than to social factors involving the contacts of

[31] Charles S. Johnson, *Patterns of Negro Segregation* (New York:
Harper & Brothers, 1943), p. 7.
[32] For a comprehensive study of the residential segregation of the
Negro in the United States see Robert C. Weaver, *The Negro Ghetto* (New
York: Harcourt, Brace and Company, 1948).

Negroes and whites. One of the factors tending to undermine residential segregation is government-supported
housing with provisions against racial segregation.

In the other four areas of segregation listed by Johnson, as in the case of housing, the pattern of racial segregation is being broken down. Educational, recreational, and
other public institutions in the North and in the border
states are gradually removing racial barriers. In the South,
where there is still much vocal opposition to breaking
down the pattern of segregation, educational institutions
in some states are opening their doors to Negroes. Decisions of the Supreme Court have removed one phase after
another of the segregation pattern in transportation. While
there is no evidence that hotels and restaurants in the
South are more inclined than formerly to accept and serve
Negro patrons, in the North and to some extent even in
border states, on the other hand, racial barriers have been
removed in recent years. It is difficult to make generalizations concerning the segregation pattern in private commercial and professional establishments. In the North and
in border states the pattern of segregation has generally
been broken down in department stores, but in the case of
a professional service like undertaking, the pattern of
racial segregation holds as well in the North as in the
South. One could say almost the same in regard to barber-
shops although in rare cases in the North a Negro may be
served by some barbers who serve whites.

The most important result of the pattern of segregation has been growth in institutions in the Negro community which duplicate the institutions in the white
community.[33] There are Negro churches of the same de-
nominations as the white churches. The Negro church organizations are, with a few exceptions, independent of the

---

[33] Concerning the origin and growth of the major institutions in the
Negro community see E. Franklin Frazier, *The Negro in the United States*
(New York: The Macmillan Co., 1949), Chaps. XIV, XV, XVI, XVIII, XIX.

white organizations. There are separate mutual aid organizations chiefly among the rural folk, large fraternal organizations, and college Greek-letter fraternities. There are Negro newspapers and magazines, all designed to carry stories of happenings within the Negro community and to give the Negro's outlook and conception of the world at large. There are some Negro schools, especially church schools, which represent the efforts of Negroes; on the whole, however, the segregated private as well as the public schools and colleges represent the control of the white community over the Negro community. Finally, when one considers the futile attempts of Negroes to establish banks and other business enterprises within the Negro community, one realizes the limits of biracialism in an urban industrial community.

RACIAL SEGREGATION AND SOCIAL STATUS

In discussing the change in race relations in the southern states, Park observed that with the development of industrial and professional classes within the Negro group, a biracial organization was coming into existence in which the social distance which separated the races would be preserved but the attitudes would be different in that the races would no longer look up and down; they would look across at each other.[34] Anyone who is acquainted with race relations in the southern states would agree that there is some truth in this observation. As the Negro acquires education and as new industrial and professional classes emerge within the Negro group, the Negro is freed from a certain amount of dependence upon whites, he is able to avoid some of the cruder forms of racial discrimination, and he is not forced to observe to the same extent as formerly the etiquette of race relations.[35] The

[34] Robert E. Park, *Race and Culture* (Glencoe: The Free Press, 1950) , p. 243.
[35] An etiquette which implied his social subordination.

implications of Park's observation are that there has been a change in the social status of Negroes and that when a biracial organization has completely evolved there would be no suggestion of superiority and inferiority. In fact, these are the assumptions upon which every system of biracial organization, or parallel development as it is sometimes called, is based.

When one studies the actual method of operation of a biracial organization, it is apparent that equality does not and cannot exist between white and colored people. First of all, the biracial organization is imposed by whites. In South Africa, Prime Minister Malan told a delegation of natives in 1948:

I regard the Bantu not as strangers and not as a menace to the white people, but as our children for whose welfare we are responsible, and as an asset to the country. My Government has no intention of depriving you of your rights or oppressing you. Nothing will be taken from you without giving you something better in its place.

Your reserves will remain intact and when necessary will be enlarged. Your lands will be restored and your young men and women trained to improved methods of cultivation so that your reserves will be capable of supporting a larger population. What you want is a rehabilitation of your own national life, and not competition and intermixture and equality with the white man in his particular part of the country.[36]

In the United States, as in South Africa, it has been the white man who has been responsible for a biracial organization. Moreover, the white man has claimed, as has Malan, to have established a biracial organization in the interest in the Negro. But wherever a biracial organization exists, there are discriminations in favor of the whites.[37] In

[36] Quoted in Eugene P. Dvorin, *Racial Separation in South Africa* (Chicago: University of Chicago Press, 1952), p. 95. Copyright 1952 by the University of Chicago.

[37] Racial discriminations, which grow out of race prejudice, are objective conditions such as laws in regard to employment, intermarriage, and transportation or customary practices based upon racial distinctions.

South Africa, a biracial organization has meant and will mean poor land, poor housing, menial occupations, and low wages for non-Europeans. Likewise, in the United States a biracial organization has meant poor land, inadequate housing, unpaved streets, lack of sanitation, low wages, and unskilled occupations for Negroes. This has been the inevitable consequence of a biracial organization in an urban industrial civilization, which depends upon economic and social mobility for its existence. A biracial organization in such a society can only result in the elimination of competition between white and colored people since it is impossible to divide the economy into two insulated sectors. Moreover, white and colored workers cannot follow the same pursuits without associating in the same unions. White and colored professional men and women cannot confine their practice to one race and fail to associate with whites in the same clinics or hospitals or courts of laws or universities. White and colored businessmen and women must seek customers among both races, and white and colored people must have access to the same stores and other facilities of the community.

There is another aspect of a biracial organization which prevents it from offering any solution of the problem of race relations. Despite the theory that there is no implication of difference in social status in a biracial organization, the colored section of the organization is always stigmatized as unfit or ineligible for normal human association. Any attempts on the part of colored leaders to stimulate race pride can only be a type of compensation for the stigma of race or for implied inferior social status. When whites lend their support to such efforts they are practicing a form of patronizing that only emphasizes the stigma of race. In the United States, after over a half century of the supposed acceptance of the principle of a biracial organization, Negroes are more determined than ever to break down every form of the existing biracial organization. Their acceptance of a biracial system in the past was a form of accommodation to a situation that they could not change, but they were never unconscious of the social implications. Some of the Negro elite may have acquired a vested interest in the biracial organization but they had to deny it in public and assert the belief in a nonsegregated form of race relations.

The social implications of a biracial organization have been realized to some extent by those who formulate the foreign policy of the United States. This has resulted in a change in the official racial policy within the United States in recent years. The most significant expression of the new racial policy was the outlawing of segregation in public education. For it is realized that the most important factor in the relation of the white and colored races all over the world is the deep longing on the part of colored people for "freedom from contempt." [38]

[38] Hans J. Morgenthau, "United States Policy Towards Africa," in Calvin W. Stillman (ed.), *Africa in the Modern World* (Chicago: University of Chicago Press, 1955), p. 325. Copyright 1955 by the University of Chicago.

CHAPTER XVI

Nationalistic Movements

INTRODUCTION

In a previous chapter, some attention was given to the economic and more especially the political aspects of nationalistic movements which had developed as a reaction of colored peoples to white domination. The chief concern of this chapter will be with the cultural aspects of the various nationalistic movements and their relation to the problem of social organization. Consideration will be given, first, to the manner in which the folk and their traditional culture have been influenced by European civilization and the relation of these changes to the development of nationalism. The analysis will then be focused upon the role of the native *bourgeoisie* in spearheading the nationalistic movements. This will be followed by a study of political and cultural autonomy in relation to the factor of status in the relations of white and colored peoples. Finally, consideration will be given to the way the Soviet Union has dealt with the problem of nationalism through its policy of cultural autonomy and economic equality.

THE FOLK AND THE NATION

In his book dealing with the relation of race to nationality, especially in the development of English nationality, Oakesmith refers to one phase of the process as "the transformation of folk-land into book-land." [1] In a sense, this transformation from folk-land to book-land has been characteristic of nationalism wherever it has occurred. Its latest manifestation has been in the development of nationalism among the colored peoples of the world in their reaction to white domination. Although it may not appear at first glance to have the same importance among the older civilizations of Asia as among the preliterate peoples of Africa, this transformation has nevertheless played an important role in the development of nationalism among the old civilizations of Asia. The development of nationalism in India was directly related to the British conquest, and the influence of the British in creating a nationalistic spirit among the Indians was reflected in the political, economic, and social life of the country. [2] The British set up a single government which brought the entire country under the effective control of a central administration. The single governmental machinery facilitated the development of a unified economic life in the country. In addition to the political and economic unification of the country, the British made possible a system of communication among the people which enabled them to acquire a national consciousness.

The emergence of a national consciousness among the Indian people was mediated through an educated class who acquired their political and social philosophy from Europe. An Englishman had some part in the foundation in 1885 of the Indian National Congress, which became the chief agency for the development of Indian nationalism. Moreover, Indian leaders drew upon the principles of the French Revolution concerning Liberty,' Equality, and Fraternity. A society known as "Young India" and founded

[1] John Oakesmith, *Race and Nationality* (London: William Heineman, 1919), p. 138.
[2] William R. Smith, *Nationalism and Reform in India* (New Haven: Yale University Press, 1938), p. 269.

in India drew its inspiration from Mazzini in Italy, and Gandhi, who tended to resist Westernization, was influenced by the Russian thinker, Tolstoy. The influence of the West was not restricted to ideas. The conquest by the British tended to minimize differences among the Indians and to make them think of themselves as a single people. The consciousness of being a single people, different from their conquerors, was intensified by the fact that the British had a deep consciousness of race and nationality.

The Indians revealed their own consciousness of race by the way they were stirred by the news of the victory of the Japanese over the Russians, which represented to them the victory of Asians over Europeans who were their masters.[3] Indian nationalism like nationalism in the West meant more than political freedom; it meant freedom from the cultural domination of the British. Therefore, Indian nationalism looked to the past for inspiration and discovered that Indian spiritualism was destined to save the world from European materialism.[4]

Chinese nationalism developed as a reaction to a long history of foreign aggressions which destroyed the notion, earlier acquired by the Chinese in their relative isolation, that China was the center of civilization. When the Imperial authority, which embodied the idea of a unitary state, lost the loyalty of the officials of the landowning classes and of the scholars, practically every village became a self-governing unit. As a consequence, the country became an agglomeration of local units separated from each other by local loyalties and provincial dialects and customs. China's defeat by Japan in 1895 stirred a feeling of patriotism among the Chinese which resulted in the nationalistic movement with which Sun Yat-sen was associated. Even the overthrow of the Manchu dynasty did not

[3] Smith, *op. cit.*, p. 269.
[4] Hans Kohn, *Prophets and Peoples* (New York: The Macmillan Co., 1946), pp. 5–6.

lead to the unification of the country as the revolutionary leaders had hoped. Chinese nationalism was helped by the participation of China in World War I, at the end of which national self-determination became a principle of international relations. In an agreement with the Russian revolutionaries Sun Yat-sen attempted to arouse the Chinese to national consciousness. In the meantime another revolution was occurring in China which was not in the realm of politics but in the realm of language and literature.[5] This revolution created a new language which provided the basis of communication among the peoples of China and at the same time became the medium by which new ideas and ideals were received from the West. By means of a new living language the Chinese revolution was carried forward. The revolution became the means for consolidating the struggle against Japan, which had supplanted active opposition to the Western imperialists. In the struggle which developed between the Kuomintang and the Chinese Communists, the latter were able to carry their message to the peasants and succeeded in creating a Chinese nationalism which unified the country.[6]

The development of nationalism in Africa has been most conspicuous on the Gold Coast and in Nigeria. It had its roots partly in the native kingdoms which existed before the coming of the white man. In the Gold Coast the Ashanti confederacy, which carried on wars against the British, had a centralized form of government, while the Fanti, another branch of the Akan people, had established a federation on the basis of their traditional culture.[7] In

[5] Hans Kohn, *Geschichte der nationalen Bewegung im Orient* (Berlin: Kurt Vowinckel Verlag, 1928), pp. 127 ff. See especially John De Francis, *Nationalism and Language Reform in China* (Princeton: Princeton University Press, 1950).

[6] For an account of this struggle see Philip Jaffe, *New Frontiers in Asia* (New York: Alfred A. Knopf, Inc., 1945).

[7] See John R. E. Carr-Gregg, "Self-Rule in Africa," *International Conciliation* (New York: Carnegie Endowment for International Peace, 1951), pp. 319–82. For a systematic study of nationalism in Africa see

1897 the Aborigines Rights Protection Society was organized by chiefs and educated Africans to protect the rights of the aborigines of the Gold Coast and to secure reforms by constitutional means. The Aborigines Rights Protection Society was an *ad hoc* organization set up to oppose legislation designed to transfer lands then vested in chiefs-in-council into crown land. It could not, therefore, become the means for the expression of discontent among the growing body of educated Africans against colonial rule. Consequently, in 1920 the West African National Congress was organized under the leadership of a distinguished African lawyer and scholar, Joseph Casely Hayford, who was a firm supporter of the Aborigines Rights Protection Society. The West African Congress provided a medium by which the rising urban middle classes in West Africa could express their economic, political, and social aspirations.[8]

After the death of Hayford, the West African National Congress rapidly disintegrated. But that did not end the growing demands of the educated Africans for increased participation in the government of the Gold Coast. World War II, despite the concessions which were made by the British, tended to accelerate the movement for greater participation on the part of Africans in their government. The United Gold Coast Convention was established by a group of intellectuals who desired "that by all legitimate and constitutional means the direction and control of government should pass into the hands of the people and their chiefs in the shortest possible time." [9] But this new organization lacked a program of action until

Thomas Hodgkin, *Nationalism in Colonial Africa* (London: Frederick Muller, Ltd., 1956).

[8] George Padmore, *The Gold Coast Revolution* (London: Dennis Dobson Ltd., 1953), p. 47.

[9] *Ibid.*, p. 60. A preliminary account of the changing leadership in Africa may be found in P. Garique, "Changing Political Leadership in West Africa," *Africa*, XXIV (1954), pp. 220–32.

Kwame Nkrumah, a postgraduate student in London, was invited to return to the Gold Coast and become secretary of the organization. Because of the difference in outlook between the old leaders and himself, Nkrumah split with the United Gold Coast Convention and became the leader of the Convention People's Party.

This was inevitable since Nkrumah, who had a deep understanding and sympathy for the aspirations of the masses of Africans, wanted to make the nationalistic movement a mass movement. It is significant that the break was precipitated when he insisted upon establishing the Ghana (the traditional name of the old Sudanese empire) National College for students who had been expelled from St. Augustine's Roman Catholic College because they demonstrated in favor of the leaders of the United Gold Coast Convention who had been arrested. Moreover, when the U. G. C. C. removed Nkrumah from his position as secretary, it was the youth who helped to set up the Convention People's Party. Nkrumah was opposed, of course, by the educated Africans who had formerly constituted an elite, but because of his great organizational ability he won the masses of Africans. Even after he was imprisoned by the British authority and branded as a Communist, he retained the loyalty and support of the people. As a result he was released from prison and was empowered by the British to organize a responsible government along lines of the English constitution.

The problem of nationalism among the colored peoples who have revolted against white domination is not simply one of securing political power. The development of national consciousness is a long and difficult process depending on the traditions and stage of social development of peoples. In the older civilizations of Asia there were cultural barriers such as language and religion which had to be overcome. In the case of Africa, there are tribal and local attachments and loyalties which have to be dissolved.

In the Gold Coast, for example, there are the people of the Northern Territories, once military states, who formed a ruling aristocracy over the preliterate natives, and there are the Ashanti who cherish their native culture, which has not been affected by European civilization to the same extent as that of the people in the Gold Coast colony along the coast.[10] Likewise, in Nigeria there are cultural barriers between the Yorubas in the West and Ibos in the East to be overcome as well as cultural barriers existing between these two regions and the Hausa in the northern part of Nigeria.[11] These barriers are being broken down as the traditional economy is being undermined by industrialization and modern education is making possible a common social heritage.

The nationalistic movements in the Gold Coast and Nigeria have grown out of the acquisition of Western culture by Africans. The leaders of these movements are educated men and though they have the support of the masses, the masses want to acquire more of Western culture. In some parts of Africa where Africans have not had an opportunity for this type of development, their nationalistic revolt has become enmeshed in religious movements of a messianic character and they are inclined to reject Western culture along with European domination.[12]

THE ROLE OF THE NATIVE *BOURGEOISIE*

In a previous chapter we have seen the role of the native middle classes in the economic organization of race relations.[13] Here we are interested in the role of the middle classes in nationalistic movements so far as they represent

[10] See W. E. F. Ward, *A History of the Gold Coast* (London: George Allen and Unwin, Ltd., 1948) , pp. 342 ff.

[11] See Sir Alan Burns, *History of Nigeria* (London: George Allen and Unwin, Ltd., 1951) , Chaps. II, III, IV.

[12] See Georges Balandier, "*Messianismes et nationalismes en Afrique noire,*" *Cahiers internationaux de sociologie,* XIV (1953) , pp. 41–65.

[13] See pp. 148–51 *above.*

cultural movements. In India during the first period of
the nationalistic movement, it appears that the movement
was confined largely to middle class Hindus of the student
groups and of the professional classes.[14] Nehru has painted
a vivid description of the helplessness of the Indian middle
classes in the nationalistic struggle following World War I.
Unlike the peasantry who were accustomed to starvation
and to an unequal struggle against a hard environment but
who still retained a certain calm dignity, the partially developed and frustrated middle classes, especially the new
petty *bourgeoisie*

did not know where to look, for neither the old nor the new
offered them any hope.

There was no adjustment to social purpose, no satisfaction of
doing something worth while, even though suffering came in
its train. Custom-ridden, they were born old, yet they were
without the old culture. Modern thought attracted them, but
they lacked its inner content, the modern social and scientific
consciousness. Some tried to cling tenaciously to the dead forms
of the past, seeking relief from present misery in them. But
there could be no relief there, for, as Tagore has said, we must
not nourish in our being what is dead, for the dead is death
dealing. Others made themselves pale and ineffectual copies
of the West. So, like derelicts, frantically seeking some foothold of security for body and mind and finding none, they
floated aimlessly in the murky waters of Indian life.[15]

It was Gandhi, a lawyer educated in Western culture,
who was able to make articulate the aspirations of the Indian masses and to give direction to the nationalistic movement. Under his leadership, the Indian National Congress
became a democratic and mass organization. "Now the
peasants rolled in," wrote Nehru, "and in its new garb it

[14] Smith, *op. cit.*, p. 45.
[15] Jawaharlal Nehru, *The Discovery of India* (New York: The John
Day Co., 1946), p. 360. This passage and those that follow are reprinted by
permission of the publisher.

began to assume the look of a vast agrarian organization
with a strong sprinkling of the middle classes." [16] The
older leaders of the Congress were disturbed by the up-
surge of the masses and some of them fell away but some
of them were swept along with the feeling and sentiment
that swept the country. Gandhi sent innumerable messengers to the countryside with the new gospel of action,
which consisted of noncooperation with British imperialism. Although he was proud of his Hindu inheritance, he
attempted to make the movement universal, saying that
"Indian culture is neither Hindu, Islamic nor any other,
wholly. It is a fusion of all." [17] His efforts were designed
"to restore the spiritual unity of the people and to break
the barrier between the small westernized group at the
top and the masses. . . ." [18]

In Indonesia, the middle class "was predominantly
non-Indonesian, being largely Chinese and Eurasian, and
was likewise wedded to the political and economic *status
quo* and with few exceptions hostile to the nationalistic
movement." [19] As the result of three centuries of Dutch
rule, there was practically no entrepreneurial element
among the Indonesian middle class,[20] which consisted almost entirely of Western-educated natives who were salaried employees, most of them civil servants. It was mainly
the intellectual element among the Indonesians who
aroused national consciousness among the agrarian masses.
Those who had been educated in the Netherlands had
been impressed by the difference between the democratic
government there and the autocratic government of Indonesia. Moreover, they were influenced by the Dutch so-

---

[16] *Ibid.,* p. 363.
[17] Quoted in *ibid.,* p. 366.
[18] *Ibid.*
[19] George M. Kahin, *Nationalism and Revolution in Indonesia*
(Ithaca: Cornell University Press, 1952) , p. 59.
[20] *Ibid.,* p. 29.

cialists who had favored independence of Indonesia after the Communist Party had come out for complete independence of Indonesia. For many of them Leninist Marxism "seemed to posit a satisfactory solution to the antithesis presented by western political concepts of liberty and equality and western colonialism." [21]

As we have seen, the first steps toward a nationalistic movement in the Gold Coast were taken by a group of middle-class educated Africans. These middle-class intellectuals spent their time in philosophizing about the building of a Gold Coast nation rather than in engaging in action which would unite the masses in a nationalistic movement.[22] When Nkrumah undertook a program involving action on the part of the masses, these middle-class leaders repudiated him, and even after he had been accepted by the British government, they continued to oppose him because they were opposed to arousing the masses, who represented a threat to their economic interests as well as to the cultural values which they cherished. Nkrumah also had to face the opposition of some of the chiefs who were opposed to any program that threatened their authority. Some of the opposition to the leadership and program of Nkrumah is based upon loyalties to the traditional institutions and traditional culture. The cultural differences and divergent interests within the former colonial territories have become important when the pressure of white control was lifted. Nkrumah's success as a leader is a demonstration of his understanding of the processes of social change and his appreciation of the relative influence of various classes and elements in the new Gold Coast society which is coming into being.

[21] *Ibid.*, pp. 50–1.
[22] For example, their leader expounded a credo which was called "the Seven Postulates of Gold Coast Races Nationalist Movement." See Padmore, *op. cit.*, p. 57.

POLITICAL AUTONOMY AND STATUS

The aim of all nationalistic movements is to acquire the status of a nation-state. In the case of the nationalistic movements which have emerged as a reaction to white domination, the question of status has been of major importance because at the heart of the problem of the relation of white and colored people in the modern world is the longing for "freedom from contempt." This is due to the racial ideology which came into existence to justify modern imperialism, that is, the domination of the colored races by the white race. As a missionary who has worked among the Africans has observed, European civilization is not simply a different organization with a different system of values. It is the proof of the superiority of white men over black men and no teaching of race pride or encouragement of native arts on the part of white men can remove the implication of black inferiority.[23]

The feeling of inferiority is shared by all the colored peoples of the world. This is especially true of the colored peoples who have left their country and have had contacts with the European peoples. Writing of the Western-educated man in India, the Useems state that "The outstanding social weakness of the West [the United Kingdom and the United States] that most of the foreign-returned mentioned is racial discrimination. . . . Racial prejudice is a hypersensitive spot with Indians, whether they are objects of discrimination or only spectators of discrimination imposed on other colored peoples." [24] The implications of a foreign education to many Indians were expressed in the statement:

[23] Pierre Charles, S.J., "*Le Traumatisme noire*," *Zaire*, VII (May 1953) , 451–68.
[24] John Useem and Ruth H. Useem, *The Western-Educated Man in India* (New York: The Dryden Press, Inc., 1955) , p. 145.

I was never much of a nationalist before; I became more of one there [England]. I, along with others, decided that it was up to the educated people to do more for India—it gave us a sense of self-respect.[25]

In England, West Indian and African students become disillusioned as to the genuineness of English democracy and freedom when they encounter racial discrimination and the attitude of superiority on the part of the Englishman. According to Little, "The Africans translate their emotion into demands for the speedy elevation of the political status of their country; in part, as fulfilment of their patriotic aspirations; in part, on the reasoned assumption that equal political status abroad will enhance their own individual social status in this country." [26]

In the United States, Negroes have had little opportunity to seek an escape from the feeling of inferiority in nationalistic movements, and for this reason, they are often regarded by the colored peoples of the world as a people without a homeland and without national identification. Marcus Garvey, who became the leader of the only important nationalistic movement among American Negroes, is regarded with respect by Negroes outside the United States.[27] Garvey, a West Indian Negro who had risen above the black masses in Jamaica, had become a marginal man, so to speak, especially as the result of his travels. His success in arousing Negroes to nationalistic aspirations was no accident. The nucleus of his movement was first formed by West Indian Negroes who had migrated to the United States. But the majority of his followers were American Negroes who had migrated to northern cities hoping to find a Promised Land. In their

25 Quoted in *ibid.*, p. 61.
26 K. L. Little, *Negroes in Britain* (London: Kegan Paul, Trench, Trubner and Co., Ltd., 1947) , p. 265.
27 See E. Franklin Frazier, *The Negro in the United States* (New York: The Macmillan Co., 1949) , p. 528.

frustration and disillusionment resulting from racial discrimination and contempt, they turned to a movement which offered them a national home of their own in Africa. The message that Garvey constantly drove home to his followers was that a Negro would never be anybody in a "white man's country and that Negroes could only gain respect of white men by having national independence." Because of their struggle for status and recognition in the white man's world, the Negro middle classes refused to associate themselves with the black masses who followed Garvey. Moreover, the black middle classes sought a compensation in wealth for their rejection by the white man, and refused, on the whole, to be identified with the Negro artistic and literary renaissance in the 1920's which was centered in Harlem in New York City.[28] As Negroes improve their economic and social status in the United States they continue to slough off their folk heritage, which developed in the South, and they become increasingly bewildered and frustrated in the white man's world.

CULTURAL AUTONOMY AND ECONOMIC EQUALITY

As a result of the Russian Revolution, the problem of nationalism and self-determination was redefined. We have already given some attention to the political implications of self-determination resulting from the Russian Revolution.[29] Our interest here is in the Russian policy of self-determination in relation to the cultural aspects of nationalism and in the effects of this policy upon the social organization of people with different racial and cultural backgrounds. Consequently, we are interested in the expan-

[28] See E. Franklin Frazier, *Bourgeoisie noire* (Paris: Librairie Plon, 1955), pp. 108 ff.
[29] See pp. 219–22 *above*.

sion of Russia in Asia and the contacts of Russians with Asian peoples. The Russian expansion into Asia began about the same time as the Portuguese were opening the sea route to the Indies.[30] By the end of the sixteenth century the Russian expansion east of the Urals began to assume large proportions. The Cossacks and frontiersmen became leaders of a movement which later included peasants, who began "to till the plains of Siberia." During the first half of the seventeenth century the Cossacks reached the northeast shore of Asia and by the close of the century there were Russian colonies in Kamchatka. At the same time the Russians were expanding into Central Asia where they came into conflict with the Chinese. Although the Russian expansion was halted, agreements were reached whereby the Russians were permitted to carry on trade with the Chinese.

During the expansion of Europe, Russia never became identified with the colonial powers in the sense that she represented white dominion over colored peoples. While the Russian Empire under the czars extended its control over non-European peoples, this expansion often took the form of a conflict between the Eastern Church and the Mohammedan emirates. In the Caucasus and in northeastern Asia, the Russians came into contact with so-called primitive or nonliterate peoples who had developed no sentiment of national solidarity.[31] Moreover, in their dealings with Asian peoples the Russians never exhibited the same consciousness of race as the English and Americans, and to some extent, even the French. The czars utilized a policy of divide and rule in setting one cultural minority or nationality against another. In an empire which included in addition to many Caucasian peoples a number of

[30] See Kenneth S. Latourette, *A Short History of the Far East* (New York: The Macmillan Co., 1947), pp. 270–1.

[31] See Avrahm Yarmolinsky, *The Jews and Other Minor Nationalities Under the Soviets* (New York: Vanguard Press, 1928), Chap. XIII.

Asian peoples, "The half-religious, half-nationalistic creed
of Pan-Slavism adhered to by the ruling classes dictated a
policy of forcible 'Russification' of such minorities as
seemed assimilable, and a policy of discrimination, segregation and persecution against such groups as the Jews,
who could obviously never be made good and loyal Russians." [32]

As we have seen, within a week after the Russian
Revolution broke out, there was a complete reversal of
this policy in a Declaration of the Rights of Peoples of
Russia. According to the new policy, all the national minorities and ethnic groups in Russia had the right to self-
determination and free development. The policy of the
Soviet Union was based upon Stalin's leadership in developing the Communist Party's program of racial and national equality.[33] In his discussion of Marxism and the national question which appeared in 1913, Stalin stated:

What is it that particularly agitates a national minority?
A minority is discontented not because there is no national
union but because it does not enjoy the right to use its native
language. Permit it to use its native language and the discontent will pass of itself.
A minority is discontented not because there is no artificial
union but because it does not possess its own schools. Give it
its own schools and all grounds for discontent will disappear.
A minority is discontented not because there is no national
union, but because it does not enjoy liberty of conscience,
liberty of movement, etc. Give it these liberties and it will
cease to be discontented.
Thus national equality in all forms (language, schools, and so
forth) is an essential element in the solution of the national
problem. A state law based on complete democracy in the
country is required, prohibiting all national privileges without

[32] Frederick L. Schuman, *International Politics* (New York: Mc-
Graw-Hill Book Co., Inc., 1933), p. 310.
[33] See Frederick L. Schuman, *Soviet Politics* (New York: International Publishers Co., Inc., 1942), p. 65.

exception and all kinds of disabilities and restrictions on the rights of national minorities.[34]

Each ethnic group was guaranteed cultural autonomy and local self-government within the economic and political framework of the Soviet Union. This did not mean that the backward nations and peoples were to be organized in national cultural unions. Taking the Transcaucasian Tatars as an example, Stalin wrote: "It is not difficult to understand that to organize them into a national cultural union would be to place them under the control of the mullahs, to deliver them to the mercies of the reactionary mullahs, to create a new stronghold of spiritual enslavement of the Tatar masses to their worst enemy." [35] Therefore, the only solution of the national problem in the Caucasus was to draw the backward peoples into "the common stream of a higher culture." [36]

Here is an implication of a process of assimilation, although the primitive or nonliterate peoples of Russia were encouraged to develop a literature of their own as a part of a program of developing literacy among them. The Soviet minority policy has varied according to the stage of social development of the people. The more advanced peoples were permitted to retain their culture although an elite among them was trained as political leaders. With the industrialization of Russia and the increasing mobility of the various peoples of Russia, it is inevitable that assimilation should occur. At present we do not have the materials to know to what extent the individuals of the various nationalities are beginning to think of themselves as Russians rather than as Tatars, etc., and to what extent they experience a conflict of loyalties. However, if one were

[34] Joseph Stalin, *Marxism and the National Question* (New York: International Publishers Co., Inc., 1942), p. 65. Reprinted by permission of the publishers.

[35] *Ibid.*, p. 55.

[36] *Ibid.*, p. 55. See also Joshua Kunitz, *Dawn Over Samarkand* (New York: International Publishers Co., Inc., 1935).

to seek an answer to the question of whether the Russian policy has solved the problem of nationalism, one can only say that in World War II the various nations and peoples were loyal to the Soviet Union and fought enthusiastically in its defense.

An analysis of the relation of culture and personality naturally follows the question of nationalism. This will be considered in the next chapter.

CHAPTER XVII

Culture and Personality

INTRODUCTION

In an analysis of the problems of social organization which have arisen as the result of race and culture contacts in the modern world, one must inevitably come to a consideration of the influence of Western civilization upon the personalities of non-European peoples. Among the agents of Western civilization whose contacts with non-Europeans have effected changes in the personalities of native peoples, the Christian missionary has occupied a strategic position. A personality type which has emerged partly as a result of the activities of missionaries, has been the marginal man. Where non-Europeans have been assimilated in European societies, it has been the marginal man who has played an important role in the process. His role has varied according to the nature of the racial frontier. Whatever may have been the role of the marginal man, it is evident that on the frontiers of race and culture contacts new peoples and new cultures are coming into existence.

THE ROLE OF THE MISSIONARY

In a study of the changes which have occurred in the personalities of peoples influenced by European civilization, the influence of the missionary has been of prime importance. For of all the representatives of Western civilization who have been in contact with non-European or colored peoples, the missionary has been the one who has dealt with them as personalities, and, in fact, has undertaken to change their personalities. Of course, there are missionaries who disclaim that they are representatives of Western civilization. For example, Smith has claimed that Christianity "is not a British or American institution; that Christ transcends all nationalistic divisions." [1] At the same time he admits that the "Christian faith has vast sociological implications" but he holds that people make the mistake "of confounding Christianity with western civilization." [2] According to Smith, because of the creative and transforming power of Christianity, missionaries should encourage Africans, Chinese, and Indians to express the essential Christianity in their own forms of thought and in what is best in their tradition.

The position of Smith represents a new attitude on the part of missionaries toward the customs and beliefs of non-European or colored peoples. This new doctrine of the missionaries was given expression at the International Conference on Christian Missions at La Zoute in 1926, where there was "a change in emphasis by all missions from outright condemnation to general sympathy toward African custom." [3] Although missions were recommended to condemn "evil customs," they were not to condemn customs compatible with Christianity, and were enjoined to purify and use African customs which have a valuable substance, though some features of them are evil.

The new attitude of missions toward native customs and beliefs does not alter the fact that it was inevitable that the missionary was an agent of Western civilization.

[1] Edwin W. Smith, *Knowing the African* (London: Lutterworth Press, 1946) , p. 18.

[2] *Ibid.*, pp. 18–19.

[3] See Arthur Phillips, *Survey of African Marriage and Family Life* (London: Oxford University Press, 1953) , pp. 371–2.

In the early stages of missionary endeavor, before anthropologists began their studies of the nature of culture, missionaries had little understanding of the customs of non-European peoples and had little or no sympathy for behavior which was contrary to the ways of Christians. In fact, the main reason for their presence among non-European peoples was to bring them the "true" religion and a "better" way of life. When the missionary movement began in the sixteenth century, the priests who accompanied the Spanish and Portuguese conquerors were primarily interested in adding members to their own church which had been weakened by the Protestant Reformation.[4] Nor did the Protestants, when they began their evangelization on a world-wide scale in the eighteenth century, concern themselves with more than the inner life and future state of their converts among the heathen. The idea of bringing a better way of life to non-Europeans only developed with the expansion of European domination and European ideas. At first the missions tended to insulate their efforts to save the souls of men against the scientific and social developments which were occurring in Western civilization. Therefore, it was not until the latter part of the nineteenth century that missionaries began to work for the economic, social, and intellectual development of those whom they were seeking to evangelize.

Even when the Christian missionary sought only to evangelize the colored peoples of the world, he was nevertheless transforming their way of life. When the missionary succeeded in converting the heathen to the true religion, he gave the convert a new conception of himself and of the world, and of his relations to other men. Westerman has pointed out that:

. . . conversion is a personal matter, an affair between man and God. A man may draw his family with him, but for them

[4] See Edward C. Moore, *The Spread of Christianity in the Modern World* (Chicago: University of Chicago Press, 1919), pp. 12 ff.

as for him it is a personal step. When a person living in pagan surroundings adopts Christianity he often loses the protection or even membership of his group and has to stand by himself.[5]

Conversion undoubtedly tended to encourage individualism among people who, like the Africans, have been dominated by the idea of community. But individualism, as it exists in the Western world, is a product of economic and social forces inherent in Western civilization.

The idea of saving the soul of the heathen and preparing him for a future state inevitably resulted in interference with native customs. In their passion to evangelize the heathen, missionaries were naturally opposed to any form of ancestor worship. But in attempting to uproot the practice of ancestor worship they little realized that they were destroying the basis of social cohesion. Likewise, missionaries were from the beginning opposed to polygamy because it represented in their eyes uncontrolled sexual passion and sin. They were not aware of the consequences of their policy since polygamy was tied up with the economic organization of the people with whom they worked.

When missionaries turned their attention to the improvement of the native's lot on earth, their role as agents of Western civilization was obvious. In the field of education the missionary naturally used the ideals and methods which he had acquired in his own country. The content of the education was determined by European ideas of the mental capacity of colored people and by European conceptions of the function of education among natives. In any case the missionary was bound to give native peoples the rational scientific conceptions which had developed in the West. This was especially apparent in the area of health and sanitation.[6] Western ideas concerning health

[5] Diedrich Westerman, *Africa and Christianity* (New York: Oxford University Press, Inc., 1937), p. 102.

[6] Concerning missionary activity and Western medicine in China see Edward C. Moore, *West and East* (London: Duckworth and Co., 1920), pp. 159 ff.

were bound to conflict with the superstitious beliefs and ideas of non-European peoples concerning diseases and sanitation. In fact, in recent years, the missionaries have justified their activities among non-Europeans on the grounds that they have introduced Western civilization among the colored peoples of the world.[7]

In considering the role of the missionary in race and culture contacts, one should not overlook the tremendous influence of the northern missionaries among the former slaves in the United States. Following the Civil War and Emancipation, the South was invaded by the much maligned New England school marms whose passion for humanity and belief in the potentialities of the Negro inspired them to devote their lives to the regeneration of the emancipated blacks.[8] These teachers were supported by northern missionary societies and churches which provided money to educate Negroes and to assist them in assuming the responsibilities of citizenship. As the result of the teachers' broad educational program and close sympathetic contacts with the Negroes, they were able to create a generation of educated Negroes who had completely assimilated the best culture of New England. The schools and colleges which the New Englanders created for Negroes in a hostile environment have continued to the present day as the most important institutions through which Negroes acquire the main elements of European civilization.[9]

Yet, despite the achievements which missions may rightly claim, it was recognized even before World War II that the Christian missionary as the agent of Western civilization must adjust his activities to the awakening, for which he is partly responsible, among the colored peoples

[7] See Jean-Marie Sedes, *Histoire des missions françaises* (Paris: Presses Universitaires de France, 1950). See also *Christian Action in Africa,* report of the Church Conference on African Affairs (New York: Foreign Missions Conference of North America, 1942).

[8] See Horace M. Bond, *The Education of the Negro in the American Social Order* (New York: Prentice-Hall, Inc., 1934), pp. 127 ff.

[9] *Ibid.,* pp. 358 ff.

of the world.[10] In their revolt against white domination, the colored peoples have often regarded the Christian missionary as a partner in white exploitation and domination. The Chinese have expelled Christian missionaries while in other countries of Asia Christian missionaries are tolerated only as long as they do not oppose the political aspirations of the people. Even in Africa, the missionaries must not appear to be agents of the ruling whites if they are to have any influence among the natives.

While the role of the missionary is being redefined by economic, political, and social changes, their influence upon the culture and personalities of native peoples is still visible. Although they have a better understanding and appreciation of native cultures and are more skillful in their methods, they are agents of social change and of change in the personalities of the people with whom they work. Miss Kingsley, writing at the close of the last century, described the missionary-made man as follows:

The missionary-made man is the curse of the Coast, and you find him in European clothes and without, all the way down from Sierra Leone to Loanda. The pagans despise him, the whites hate him, still he thinks enough of himself to keep him comfortable. His conceit is marvellous, nothing equals it except perhaps that of the individual rife among us which the *Saturday Review* once aptly described as "the suburban agnostic"; and the missionary man is very much like the suburban agnostic in his religious method. After a period of mission-school life he returns to his country-fashion, and deals with the fetish connected with it very much in the same way as the suburban agnostic deals with his religion, i.e., he removes from it all the inconvenient portions. "Shouldn't wonder if there might be something in the idea of the immortality of the soul, and a future Heaven, you know—but as for Hell, my dear sir, that's rank superstition, no one believes in it now, and as for Sabbath-keeping and food-restrictions—what utter rubbish for enlight-

10 See Kenneth S. Latourette, *Missions Tomorrow* (New York: Harper & Brothers, 1936), pp. 109 ff.

ened people!" So the backsliding African deals with his country-fashion ideas: he eliminates from them the idea of immediate retribution, etc., and keeps the polygamy and the dances, and all the lazy, hazy-minded native ways.[11]

Miss Kingsley's description of the missionary-made man provides a vivid and classic picture of a poorly educated and unsophisticated marginal man.

CULTURE CONFLICT AND THE MARGINAL MAN

The marginal man, wrote Park, is "an incidental product of a process of acculturation, such as inevitably ensues when peoples of different cultures and different races come together to carry on a common life. He is . . . an effect of imperialism, economic, political and cultural." [12] The marginal man is a cultural hybrid in the sense that he lives in "two societies and in two, not merely different but antagonistic, cultures." [13] As a result, there is a cultural conflict within the "divided self" of the marginal man who often lives in a permanent state of crisis. The marginal man is usually:

. . . a mixed-blood, like the mulatto in the United States or the Eurasian in Asia, but that is apparently because the man of mixed-blood is one who lives in two worlds, in both of which he is more or less a stranger. The Christian convert in Asia or in Africa exhibits many if not most of the characteristics of the marginal man—the same spiritual instability, intensified self-consciousness, restlessness, and *malaise*.[14]

[11] Mary H. Kingsley, *Travels in West Africa* (London: Macmillan and Co., Ltd., 1897) , pp. 660–1.

[12] Robert E. Park in "Introduction" to Everett V. Stonequist, *The Marginal Man* (New York: Charles Scribner's Sons, 1937) , p. xviii. The concept of the marginal man was first developed by Robert E. Park in his article, "Human Migration and the Marginal Man," *American Journal of Sociology*, XXXIII (May 1928) , 881–93.

[13] Robert E. Park, *Race and Culture* (Glencoe: The Free Press, 1950) , p. 373.

[14] *Ibid.*, p. 356.

In his study of the marginal man, Stonequist devotes a section first to the racial hybrid.[15] The Eurasian, who was placed between societies neither of which accepted him, exhibited feelings of inferiority and subservience which produced in turn a heightened self-consciousness, sensitiveness, and psychological overcompensation. He tended to hate the Indian, but at the same time he showed resentment against the English upon whom he was dependent.

Although the Cape Coloured occupies a somewhat different position in South Africa from that of the Eurasian in India, he exhibits characteristics of the marginal man. In the United States, the mulatto has the characteristics of the marginal man, but because of the racial creed which identifies him from birth with the Negro group, these characteristics are not as obvious as in mulattoes in other countries. On the other hand, in Jamaica the mulatto is more conscious of his mixed ancestry and as a result exhibits considerable prejudice toward the Negro, while at the same time he resents the whites who refuse to accept him. The Indo-Europeans in Java once tended to become identified with the Dutch, but as the result of the increasing competition with the whites and the rise of nationalism, they developed the characteristics of marginal people. Even in Hawaii, where racial consciousness is at a minimum, there is some feeling of marginality on the part of Caucasian-Hawaiian mixtures. They seem to have very much the same attitude as the mixed bloods of Brazil where assimilation has been easy. Although Stonequist's study did not include the French West Indies, it appears that despite the French policy of assimilation, the mixed bloods from these islands act and feel very much like marginal men.[16]

In dealing with the cultural hybrid who has emerged as the result of the spread of European culture rather than

[15] Stonequist, *op. cit.*, Chap. II.
[16] See Frantz Fanon, *Peau noir masques blancs* (Paris: Editions du Seuil, 1952), *passim.*

as the result of racial mixture, Stonequist includes cases of Asians and Africans who show the characteristics of marginal men.[17] In India, for example, the conflict of culture within individuals has been created largely by Western education. One Indian writing about the effects of the conflicts of Western ideas and Indian traditions stated that this conflict had created a race of neurasthenics. In the case of Africans, Stonequist gives special attention to the effects of the teaching of missionaries, who have created a group who no longer identify with the native African and are not accepted by the European. Lord Lugard arrived at the same conclusion:

The educated African imitates European dress and customs closely, however ill adapted to his conditions of life, and may be heard to speak of going "home" to England. He has, as a rule, little in common with the indigenous tribes of Africa, and seldom leaves his native town except to travel by sea or railway. The Europeanised African is indeed separated from the rest of the people by a gulf which no racial affinity can bridge. He must be treated—and seems to desire to be treated—as though he were of a different race. Some even appear to resent being called negroes, the universal race-term in America.[18]

Buell has noted the same effect resulting from the French policy of assimilation in Africa.[19] A French scholar and traveler expressed the fear that instruction in the French language was creating a group of *déclassés* who, alienated from the natives and not assimilated by the French administration, would become the leaders of discontent and revolt.[20]

The above observation by a French traveler is of spe-

[17] Stonequist, *op. cit.*, Chap. III.
[18] Sir F. D. Lugard, *The Dual Mandate in British Tropical Africa* (4th ed.; London: William Blackwood and Sons, Ltd., 1929), pp. 80–1. Reprinted by permission of the publisher.
[19] Raymond L. Buell, *The Native Problem in Africa* (New York: The Macmillan Co., 1928), II, 9.
[20] Jacques Weulersse, *Noirs et blancs* (Paris: Armand Colin, 1931), p. 16.

cial significance for our study because it indicates that the
manner in which the marginal man resolves his inner conflict is related to the process of social organization in race
relations. Because of his intense self-consciousness, which
results from his rejection by the dominant white group,
the marginal man becomes extremely race conscious. The
marginal man then identifies himself with the colored subordinate or oppressed group and assumes a leadership role
in their struggle for freedom.[21] In Indonesia, however,
where the Eurasians formed a buffer group between the
Dutch and the Indonesians, it was not the Eurasians who
became the leaders of the nationalistic movement, but
those Indonesians who had received a Western education.[22]
Although private enterprise discriminated against the Eurasian in favor of the Dutch, as a rule the government discriminated against the Western-educated Indonesians in favor of the Dutch and Eurasian. As the Western-educated
Indonesians became politically conscious, they resented the
many discriminations to which they were subjected. Moreover, as the Western-educated Indonesians increased their
competition in the professions, the Dutch opposed the
opening of law and medical schools in which the Indonesians could receive training. Finally, the Dutch began to
speak out against the Western education of the Indonesians, regarding it as politically dangerous. The Western-
educated Indonesians were thus driven to seek a solution to
their problems in a nationalistic movement which ended
in political independence for Indonesia.

Likewise, in Africa the cultural hybrid has become the
leader in the nationalistic movement. Kwame Nkrumah,
who became the leader of the struggle of the people of the
Gold Coast to achieve self-government within the British
Commonwealth, was educated in the United States and in

[21] See Stonequist, *op. cit.*, pp. 159 ff.
[22] George M. Kahin, *Nationalism and Revolultion in Indonesia*
(Ithaca: Cornell University Press, 1952), pp. 52 ff.

England.[23] During this time he became associated with the Pan-African Congress, which during several sessions since World War I had dealt with the question of the freedom of Africans.[24] In Nigeria the nationalistic movement has developed largely about the personality of Azikiwe, who is the symbol of the aspirations of the Ibos and in some respects of the country as a whole.[25] Before becoming a political leader in Nigeria, Azikiwe had been educated in the United States where he learned that the educated black man was not accepted by whites in this country any more than he was under colonial administrations in Africa.

In the United States, the educated Negroes who exhibit the characteristics of the marginal man have not been able to seek a solution to their personal problems in a nationalistic movement. They have no traditional culture to fall back on when they are rejected by the white world. The leading Negro intellectual in the United States, W. E. B. Du Bois, in whose *The Souls of Black Folk* appears a classic document of the marginal man, became the leader in the Negro's struggle for equality in American life.[26] However, most of the educated Negroes, who are confined more or less to the black ghetto, live in a world of make-believe in which they can play as if they were a part of American life.[27]

SOCIAL ASSIMILATION

When the marginal man becomes the leader of a nationalistic movement, he turns his back on the dominant

[23] George Padmore, *The Gold Coast Revolution* (London: Dennis Dobson, Ltd., 1953), p. 61.

[24] See W. E. B. Du Bois, *The World and Africa* (New York: The Viking Press, Inc., 1947), pp. 7 ff., 226 ff.

[25] See C. Grove Haines (ed.), *Africa Today* (Baltimore: The Johns Hopkins Press, 1955) pp. 176, 234, 237.

[26] W. E. B. Du Bois, *The Souls of Black Folk* (Chicago: A. C. McClung and Co., 1920).

[27] See E. Franklin Frazier, *Bourgeoisie noire* (Paris: Librairie Plon, 1955), Part II.

group and becomes assimilated in the subordinate group. Whereas he once was a divided person with ambivalent feelings toward the subordinate group with which he is biologically identified, he becomes a new person completely identified psychologically with his group. Therefore, assimilation involves something more than acculturation or the acquisition of the language, moral and religious ideas, and patterns of behavior of the dominant group. Assimilation includes a subjective element—identification with the members of the society. When this occurs, physical or racial characteristics cease to be marks of identification, and people who are assimilated not only share in the traditions of the society but identify themselves with these traditions. As Delaisi has pointed out, the brunet school children of France recite without any consciousness of their black eyes and brown curls that their ancestors were the tall, blue-eyed, blond Gauls.[28] In Brazil people of Negro ancestry generally think of themselves as Brazilian and Latins. On the other hand, in the United States, practically all persons with a Negro ancestor, however remote, think of themselves as Negroes first and only secondly as Americans. Therefore, one can say that colored people in Brazil are not only acculturated but are assimilated Brazilians whereas the Negroes of the United States are acculturated but not assimilated.

The assimilation of people of Negro ancestry in Brazil has been facilitated by the mixture of the races and the absence of barriers to intermarriage. In this sense amalgamation may be regarded as a forerunner to assimilation. It is through intermarriage that there is an interpenetration of cultural heritages and people become identified with each other regardless of color differences. The mayor of a Brazilian city once remarked to this writer that it would be impossible to have a color line in Brazil like that

[28] Francis Delaisi, *Political Myths and Economic Realities* (New York: The Viking Press, Inc., 1927), pp. 167–8.

in the United States because it would split Brazilian families. In the United States the chief bars to the assimilation of the Negro have been laws against intermarriage or public disapproval of it. Although a large proportion of the Negro population is mixed with whites and Indians,[29] there are laws in 28 states prohibiting the marriage of Negroes and white people and in the remaining states there is public disapproval of intermarriage. Although during the past decade a newspaper account of the marriage of a Negro and a white person has not provoked vociferous protests, as it formerly did, against the menace of the Negro, intermarriage is still frowned upon. In fact, the most vocal objections to the outlawing of segregated public schools in the South are based upon the claim that it will lead to the "mongrelization" of the white race.

It has been a part of the etiquette of race relations for Negroes to deny that they wanted to marry white people and to affirm that they were opposed to intermarriage. Even blue-eyed Negroes indistinguishable from Europeans were thought to be opposed to intermarriage. Moreover, they were supposed to be proud of being Negroes and to desire to maintain the purity of the Negro race. Of course, these people were marginal men and could only regard the fact that they had a remote Negro ancestor as a taint of "inferior blood." With darker Negroes the taint that set them apart from the rest of the population was visible.

In either case, the Negro could not be an assimilated American. Whatever means he might use to escape from the stigma of being a Negro, he has borne in his personality the mark of oppression and of his hurt self-esteem.[30] Hundreds of Negroes, especially mulattoes, who because of physical appearance can pass for white, have escaped

---

[29] See Melville J. Herskovits, *The American Negro* (New York: Alfred A. Knopf, Inc., 1928).

[30] See Abram Kardiner and Lionel Ovesey, *The Mark of Oppression* (New York: W. W. Norton & Company, Inc., 1951).

and continue to escape into the ranks of whites.[31] They intermarry with whites or with Negroes who can pass for white, and their children are reared without ever knowing that they had the "taint" of Negro blood. It is only through this means that colored people may become assimilated where intermarriage is forbidden by law or disapproved by public opinion.

Adams, in his discussion of assimilation and amalgamation, shows the difference between the relationships of Chinese and whites in Hawaii where there are no barriers to intermarriage, and in California where there is a barrier to the intimate association of white and colored peoples. He concludes that "In short, if intermarriage is legally permitted and socially approved as between two or more peoples they are sure to become one people, one in social inheritance and one in ancestry and race." [32] Hawaii is one of the frontiers of race relations where a new people with a new culture is coming into existence.

NEW PEOPLES AND NEW CULTURES

When race relations in the modern world are viewed from the standpoint of culture and personality, the most important development appears to be the creation of new peoples and new cultures. The manner in which new peoples and new cultures are emerging differs on the three racial frontiers which were defined at the beginning of this study. The development of new peoples with new cultures among the older civilizations of Asia is not the same as the creation of new peoples and new cultures in the tropical regions of Africa, or in the multiracial communi-

[31] See John H. Burma, "The Measurement of Negro's 'Passing'," *American Journal of Sociology*, LII (July 1946), 18–22. For the most reliable estimates on the number of Negroes who pass for white each year see E. W. Eckard, "How Many Negroes 'Pass,'" *American Journal of Sociology*, LII (May 1947), 498–500.

[32] Romanzo Adams, *Interracial Marriage in Hawaii* (New York: The Macmillan Co., 1937), pp. 317 ff.

ties. Nevertheless, as the result of the impact of European civilization upon the colored peoples of the world, new peoples with new cultures are coming into existence on all three racial frontiers.

In Asia, where the basic cultural pattern has not been uprooted to the same extent as among the nonliterate peoples of Africa, the impact of Western civilization is nevertheless transforming the social life of the people. Although China has expelled the Christian missionaries, who were regarded as the agents of Western imperialism and Western culture, China has adopted Marxist ideology, which is a Western creation. More important still, China is adopting Western technology as rapidly as possible in order to achieve national solidarity and to establish herself among the powers of the world. Nevertheless, China has rejected some of the most important conceptions and values upon which Western society is based. The adoption of Western technology is bound to affect the traditional basis of Chinese society. Already it is evident that the family system, which was the basis of the political as well as the social structure, is being modified by the change in the status of women and by the introduction of collectivization in agriculture. To what extent can the five social relationships upon which Chinese society was based continue to be the basis of their social life? [33]

In China and the other older civilizations of Asia, there are indications that new societies and new cultures are coming into being. These societies are taking over the technology of the West, and as a result changes are occurring in their traditional culture. But there is a resistance

[33] The five social relationships were, as Mencius said: "Father and son should love each other. Sovereign and subject should be just to each other. Husband and wife should distinguish their respective spheres. Elder and younger brothers should have a sense of precedence. Between friends there should be good faith." Fung Yu-lan, "The Philosophy at the Basis of Traditional Chinese Society," in F. S. C. Northrop (ed.), *Ideological Differences and World Order* (New Haven: Yale University Press, 1949), p. 25.

not only in China but in other parts of Asia to the non-material aspects of Western culture. In fact, a scholar in India has emphasized the conflict of cultures within his country which has resulted from the impact of European civilization and has called attention to the need for social machinery and institutions to resolve the conflict.[34] The conflict of cultures in India is described as follows:

India, with her rural, agricultural, handicraft culture, with a moneyless economy and village communism, with its social and political democracy through harmonious relations among the various groups, with an integrated view of life and education, with emphasis on indefinable, qualitative values, on a subjective, broad-based nationalism and on man and the machinery of the government, with a life of religious experience and spiritual freedom for the individual through general human welfare, with emphasis on power through repose, is confronted by a culture that stands for science, machine and mass production, for an urbanized, industrialized order, for analytical view of life with its emphasis on neuroses and complexes, for quantitative values and monetary economy, for struggle for existence and survival of the fittest, for accumulation of wealth and economic imperialism, for assertive, arrogant nationalism, for religion of scientific humanism and rationalism. India has sought the Vision of the Whole, not of the parts; she has been interested in Life, not merely in the means of livelihood. She has combined philosophic calm and contemplation with dynamic action; she has stood for beauty and dignity, combined with utility. But today, the culture of science and machine has taken a firm grip of India and is slowly seeping into her soul.[35]

It seems unlikely that "the culture of science and machine" will seep into the soul of the people of Asia when one considers the nature of nationalism in Asia. Although all the countries of Asia may not adopt Communism as

[34] See Kewal Motwani, *India: A Conflict of Cultures* (Nagpur: Nagpur University, 1947).

[35] *Ibid.*, p. 26. Reprinted by permission of Nagpur University and Thacker and Co., Ltd.

China has, it appears that the economic and social philosophy of the West will not become the economic and social philosophy of Asia. The peoples of Asia are not only seeking a solution to their present problems within their traditional philosophies but they are also endeavoring to create new values and ideas in respect to the economic and social relations of people.

Since World War II much has been written on the awakening of black Africa.[36] The changes in Africa south of the equator are not occurring at the same rate among all peoples and the responses of the native peoples to European contacts have varied. Nevertheless, the old tribal existence with its collectivism and religious attachment to the earth is being uprooted. As a result the African is becoming a new person. In this connection, the observation of Malinowski provides an insight to what is actually occurring when he writes that the ethnographer can not "accomplish the task of sorting out a westernized African into his component parts without destroying the one thing in him that matters — his personality," and that "the educated African is a new type of human being, endowed with abilities and energies, with advantages and handicaps, with problems and visions, which neither his European neighbor nor his 'blanket' brother are heirs to." [37]

Although the Negroes in West Africa have taken over English political institutions and are utilizing Western technology, the African leaders do not think of themselves as black Englishmen nor do they believe that they are creating a black English nation. They are increasingly aware that the nations that are coming into being will represent a fusion of African culture and Western civilization. Even

---

[36] See, for example, Emmanuel Mounier, *L'Éveil de l'Afrique noire* (Paris: Éditions du Seuil, 1948).

[37] Bronislaw Malinowski, *The Dynamics of Cultural Change* (New Haven: Yale University Press, 1949), p. 25. One may accept this statement while not agreeing with his opposition to the study of the historical processes in cultural changes.

the Africans who have been educated in French schools in Africa or in France in accordance with a policy of assimilation are aware that new peoples and new cultures are emerging in Africa. A number of African leaders who are the product of the finest French culture object to what they call "false assimilation" which would make all Africans into black Frenchmen.[38] They insist that Africans have cultural traditions which should not be destroyed and that there are elements in these traditions which should be incorporated into the new cultures now developing in Africa. Evidence of this orientation toward their African heritage may be found in the works of African painters and poets and men and women in other fields of literature who are seeking inspiration in the African heritage.[39]

It is on the frontiers of race relations where multi-racial communities have grown up that the emergence of new peoples and new cultures is most apparent. The outstanding case is Hawaii, where through intermarriage the various racial elements are being fused into a new race with a culture that includes Oriental and Western elements. The same process is apparent in other parts of the world. In the Americas, with a total population of nearly 300,000,000, there are about 16,000,000 Indians, 34,000,-000 mestizos, 26,000,000 Negroes, and 15,000,000 mulattoes.[40] In all of the countries of the Americas the fusion of Europeans, Indians, and Negroes is occurring. Even in the United States, where the mixing of whites and Negroes slowed down after emancipation, the urbanization of the Negro and his rise in economic and social status are accelerating racial mixture. The absorption of the Negro will scarcely change the physical character of the population

[38] See Henri Labouret, *Colonisation, colonialisme, décolonisation* (Paris: Larose, 1952), p. 89.

[39] See Leopold Sedar Senghor, *Anthologie de la nouvelle poésie nègre et malgache* (Paris: Presses Universitaires de France, 1948). See also the publications of Présence Africaine, Paris.

[40] See Frank Tannenbaum, *Slave and Citizen: The Negro in the Americas* (New York: Alfred A. Knopf, Inc., 1947), Table following p. 14.

but the cultural influence of the Negro, especially in music, has left its imprint on the new American culture that is evolving.

In some of the countries of the Americas, as, for example, in Mexico, Chile, and Peru, the Indian has left his imprint upon the physical constitution of the population, and as the Indian rises in economic and social status his influence upon the physical constitution of the people as well as upon their culture will increase. In the West Indies the Negro will determine the physical character of the population, although in Trinidad the Hindu will make a considerable contribution. The physical fusion of peoples in the West Indies as in other parts of the Americas is associated with a social and cultural evolution that is creating a *new* culture. For some of the features of the new cultures one may turn to Brazil where the fusion of three races has gone far and where the outlines of a new culture, which is a fusion of Europe, America, and Africa, are visible.

Conclusion

CHAPTER XVIII

Federated Cultures
and Cosmopolitanism

In this final chapter the analyses of the major aspects of race and culture contacts are considered in relationship to the economic and political organization of the modern world. This involves a treatment of the ecological, economic, political, and social aspects of the problem in the three types of racial frontiers which correspond roughly with the regional power systems in the world today. These power systems have come into existence largely as the result of the change in the relations of the white and colored peoples—a fact which is made clear in the controversies and debates in the United Nations. The three racial frontiers which have developed in the modern world represent an aspect of the ecological organization of race relations on a world-wide scale.

The economic expansion of Europe resulted in the displacement by the white race of the Indians in a large part of North America. At the same time it established the dominance of the white race in South America and other parts of the New World. Except in the United States and Canada, the establishment of white domination was associated with the creation of a large mixed population. In the West Indies, in Central America, and in a large part of South America, economic and political developments indicate that the native Indian and Negro populations as well as the mixed bloods will increasingly acquire economic and political power and thereby destroy the pattern of white domination.

In the case of the older civilizations of Asia, there was never any prospect of the native peoples being displaced by the white race. Race relations remained on an ecological basis where economic relations were limited to contacts in port cities and where plantations were established with native labor. Demographic factors first became important when the Asian peoples sought expansion in the empty lands which were held for white settlement.

Therefore the ecological aspects of race relations in Asia and the Pacific become intertwined with the economic, political, and social factors. The ecological basis of race relations assumes a different character when the poverty-stricken masses of Asia seek a higher standard of living in the empty lands of Australia or New Zealand and are able to back up these demands with political power.

The racial frontier in tropical Africa has been changed as the result of industrialization and the social development of native peoples. Here as in the case of the older civilizations of Asia, the white man has not and probably will not displace the black man. Therefore, the demographic factor is not important from the standpoint of the biological struggle of the races. The demographic factor becomes important only in relation to the economic development of these areas, the demand of the natives for higher standards of living, and their place in the political organization of the world.

The ecological organization of race relations becomes extremely important on those racial frontiers where multiracial communities have come into existence as the result of the expansion of Europe, because this organization of race relations provides the basis for the economic, political, and social relations which develop between white and colored peoples. Whether Africans are permitted to hold their lands for cultivation and pasturage or are pushed off their lands to make way for white farmers and mining will determine the economic relation of white and colored peoples. Whether native colored peoples are drawn into the labor force of European enterprises and compete with white workers or are confined to reserves will likewise determine the economic organization of race relations. Whether colored peoples become a part of the urban areas which grow up as the result of industrialization or are kept on farms or in reserves will influence the political and social relations of the races. While the important fact concerning the ecological organization of race relations is that on this level race relations are symbiotic, nevertheless the ecological organization provides the foundation for the development of race relations at the economic, political, and social levels.

The economic aspect of race and culture contacts in the modern world has become important on all three racial frontiers. When Europeans began to trade and to develop economic relations with the old civilizations of Asia, they possessed no technological superiority over the latter. But as the result of inventions and the industrial revolution, the Europeans began to look upon these countries as sources of raw materials and as fields for investments. European economic methods of exploitation as well as European technology have changed the economies of these countries. But as the result of political events, economic ties with some of these countries have been destroyed. The economic problem in the relationship of Europeans and the peoples of Asia grows out of the fact that the highly industrialized European nations are dealing with the technologically backward peoples of Asia, who are attempting to overcome their economic handicaps which are due to their technological backwardness. How far can these nations become industrialized? It does not appear that in the near future they can attain the technological development of the Europeans. With the exception of the larger centers of industry and trade, it does not appear that urbanization will become as important as in Europe and America. Moreover, in view of political ideologies, it does not seem likely that capitalism will develop in Asia as in Europe and America. Therefore, it appears that economic relations between Europe and the peoples of Asia will have to develop new forms, with Asia having largely a rural economy and the West being predominantly urban and industrial.

The economic relations of the Europeans to the colored peoples in the tropics will be of a different character. What is happening in the case of the Gold Coast and Nigeria provides some indication of what may be expected of African countries that are able to secure control over their own economic life. Increased political power can bring about increased production so that Africans can have a larger share of the wealth. But they must still depend upon Europeans for capital and the technical skills and managerial knowledge and experience. When the peoples of the Gold Coast and Nigeria secure their political independence, they can speed up the process by which Africans can secure these skills and knowledge. On the other hand, in French Africa and in the Belgian Congo, where the Europeans must depend upon Africans for both skilled and unskilled labor, the Europeans can continue to control the extent to which Africans acquire the higher technical knowledge and managerial experience. With the development of university education in the Belgian Congo there will be a growing demand by Africans to enter the higher positions in the economic life. Unlike the peoples of Asia at present, the peoples of Africa will continue to be subjected to the economic dominance of Europe until they can exert sufficient political pressure in conjunction with economic competence to control their economic destinies.

It is in the multiracial communities that the economic relations of white and colored peoples are complicated by political and social factors, including personal relations. Racial problems in the area of economic relations do not arise as long as there is a racial division of labor based upon an impersonal competitive process. Racial problems arise when political and social pressures are used to restrict colored peoples to certain occupations or to prevent competition between members of different racial groups. These pressures are utilized where an industrial order, which presupposes the mobility and competition of workers irrespective of racial or cultural background, has come into existence. The United States and the Union of South Africa, which is entering a period of industrialization, are the two areas in which competition between white and colored peoples has been restricted. But today in the United States both political and social measures are being utilized to break down the caste restrictions upon the mobility and competition of colored workers, whereas in South Africa political and social means are being utilized to prevent the competition of white and colored workers.

The political organization of race relations, which is really a question of power relations between white and colored peoples, reveals the essential difference between the three racial frontiers. The political dominance which the Europeans established over the older civilizations of Asia was always of an uncertain and partial character. Except in the case of India and Indonesia, the political dominance of the white man was not based upon conquest but upon a precarious system of indirect rule and occupation of strategic coastal areas. Although the European nations possessed technological superiority over the peoples of Asia, they could never unify their power to bring about the complete subjugation of the Asian people. Not only the competition among the European powers but also the stage of civilization of the Asian peoples made their subjugation impossible. As Asians acquired the tools and arms of the European nations they were able to resist the domination of Europe. A shift in the power relations of Europe which made Russia and the United States the two centers of world power was brought about by the destruction of colonialism in Asia.

In the tropical areas of the world, whites have established their political control to conform to the social and political systems of the indigenous peoples. This has generally required some system of indirect rule whether or not it was consciously designated as such. Although the English consciously employed a system of indirect rule, the French despite their policy of assimilation have had to take account of the indigenous systems of social control. Because of the political development of native peoples in the Gold Coast and Nigeria, where economic and social changes had destroyed or undermined the traditional system of control, the system of indirect rule had to give way to political forms similar to those developed in Europe. In these areas, the changes in the social as well as in the political organizations are giving birth to nationalism similar to what occurred in Asia. Even in the areas which have not advanced as far as West Africa, it has been necessary for Europeans to develop new forms of political organization to provide means for the people to make known their wishes and aspirations.

The political aspects of race relations become acute in the multiracial communities where whites attempt to treat colored peoples as mere wards of the whites or to keep them in a state of political subordination. Whites have generally attempted to treat colored peoples as their wards where the colored peoples are in a preliterate stage of culture. Sometimes the colored peoples have been restricted to reserves. In such cases some system of indirect rule, although not formally designated as such, has been instituted. But where colored peoples have a historic tradition and a civilization, as have the Indians in East Africa and in the Union of South Africa, an attempt has been made to maintain their political subordination by some system of communal representation. In the Union of South Africa, where there is a population of mixed bloods with a European culture, a policy has been instituted to bring about their political subordination by the segregation of their votes.

The history of the efforts to maintain the political subordination of Negroes in the southern region of the United States is especially significant because it tends to clarify the problem of the political aspects of race relations in multiracial communities. For a few years after emancipation, the political participation of Negroes on the same basis as whites was maintained by the Union army. However, the Negroes were not completely disfranchised when white supremacy was re-established and the northern armies were removed from the South for the reason that it was in the interest of the planter class to use Negro voters against the poor white voters. The disfranchisement of the Negro was the result of the unresolved class conflict within the white community. This fact tends to emphasize the relation of the political participation of subordinate colored peoples to their economic and political status. The increased political participation of Negroes is related to changes in the economic and social life in the South, to changes in the political organization of American society which affect the South, and to changes in the relationship of the United States to the world community.

In the racially mixed countries of Central and South America, the lines of political power have not coincided with a racial division of the population. Although the

Spaniards and Portuguese made the Indians subject to their political authority and imported Negro slaves, racial mixture precluded the drawing of political lines along racial lines. As a consequence, although the majority of the Indian population remains in a subordinate political position, there is no contest for political power on the basis of racial groups. Political cleavages are based upon class though the masses of the submerged classes are predominantly of Indian extraction.

When the political relations of white and colored peoples are viewed in world perspective, they are seen to be a phase of the developing social organization of the world. Not only has the economic expansion of Europe brought into existence a world community; it has created regional power systems which coincide with the racial frontiers. Moreover, there is a developing system of social relationships resulting from the breakdown of the social isolation of peoples. By isolation we refer especially to barriers which have prevented white and colored peoples from having a realistic knowledge of each other and from associating with each other. These barriers have consisted in the past in difficulties of transportation and the lack of the means of communication. The barriers of transportation are being broken down today by the airplane which brings Europeans and non-Europeans into contact within hours or less than a day's travel. The radio and cinema are enabling millions of white and colored people to hear and see each other in a way that was before impossible; they need depend no longer upon the tales of a few travelers. This does not mean, of course, that prejudice will be broken down immediately since the manner in which mass media are utilized will make all the difference in the world. Whatever racial ideology is propagated among white or colored people, it will be difficult to base it upon mere stereotypes. Through pamphlets and various means of mass communication, UNESCO has undertaken as one of its responsibilities the destruction of racial stereotypes and false ideas concerning colored peoples.

The increasing mobility of both white and colored peoples will not only provide a first-hand knowledge of each for the other but will encourage a certain cosmopolitanism. That means that there will be a growing number of marginal people who will break away from their cultural roots. These marginal people will help to create not only an international community but an international society. In becoming free from their local attachments and provincial outlook, they will lose at the same time their racial prejudices, which were a product of their isolation. Many of these marginal people will form interracial marriages because they are more likely to find suitable marriage partners in the cosmopolitan circles than within their native countries.

This does not mean that the three major racial groups will become fused in a new racial stock, or that, in the words of Tagore, the "colourless vagueness of cosmopolitanism" will cover the earth. There is no reason to doubt that, even though the means of rapid transportation will increase and more people will become mobile, the masses of the three racial groups will remain spatially isolated on the whole. Because of economic factors and the increasing facility of travel, enclaves of Negroes may be found in Great Britain, or Negro soldiers may leave colored children in Germany and France. But the masses of black people will remain concentrated on the African continent, the masses of white people will occupy Europe and North America, while Asia will remain the home of the yellow people.

There is evidence that the material culture which was responsible for the white domination of the colored peoples of the world will spread among the peoples of Asia and Africa. In the Union of South Africa and in the Belgian Congo, industrialization is proceeding at a rapid pace.

Russia, England, and the United States are all offering to set up atomic energy installations in Southeast Asia, and at the same time China is industrializing as rapidly as possible. The only limit to the expansion of the machine in Asia and Africa will be the factor of relative costs in terms of the output of energy by men and machines. The adoption of the material culture of Europe will result in a change in the so-called nonmaterial culture—habits, ideas, and beliefs—of the peoples of Asia and Africa.

In the current phase of race and culture contacts, the vital question is this: To what extent will a uniform culture be created in the world as the result of the industrialization of the areas inhabited by the colored peoples? It is already apparent that the impact of technology on Asia has not destroyed or affected fundamentally the basic traditions, values, and beliefs of the people. In fact, there is a tendency in Asia to reject the nonmaterial aspects of European culture. Even in Africa where there is no ancient historic tradition, it is evident that France cannot turn Africans into black Frenchmen. The English and Belgians have always recognized that even the culture of preliterate people cannot be completely uprooted, however much it is changed by new industrial techniques and education. The situation of Negroes in the United States, who lost their traditional culture, is unique, whereas in Latin America the traditional culture of the Indian population still survives. In Brazil, where racial mixture has occurred on a large scale, the culture of the Negro has left its mark upon the country.

Here we come to the question of nationalism in its social and cultural aspects. Despite the internationalism of the Communist program, it recognizes the national culture as providing the content of a Communist economic organization. In Communist China as well as in the other new countries of Asia a new nationalism is being cultivated. The formation of new societies is being accomplished by the development of nationalism in Asia and Africa. The development of nationalism is evident in the Gold Coast and in Nigeria. Even in the Union of South Africa a spirit of nationalism is developing as a reaction to the policy of apartheid. In Kenya and other parts of Africa, nationalism is developing within religious movements with messianic aims.

How then will these nationalistic movements fit into the new patterns of race and culture contacts which have emerged in response to the shift in the centers of world power and the development of regional power systems? The answer to this question seems to be found in a world based upon federated cultures. As we have stated, there are limits to the development of a cosmopolitanism in which white and colored peoples become fused in a single race. Nationalism in its social and cultural aspects is a phase of the relations of the white and colored peoples of the world that cannot be eliminated. Race prejudice may decrease as scientific knowledge is more widely disseminated. Even more important, it may decrease when the white peoples of the world no longer have an interest in cultivating a racial ideology of the inferiority of the colored peoples. Race consciousness may decrease in time among both the white and colored peoples of the world as conflicts between them subside.

At the present time, however, the colored peoples of the world are developing a solidarity of interest which is based in part upon race consciousness. This was dramatized at the Asian-African Conference in Bandung, Indonesia. In his opening speech on April 18, 1955, President Soekarno stated almost at the beginning:

As I survey this hall and the distinguished guests gathered here, my heart is filled with emotion. This is the first intercontinental conference of coloured peoples in the history of mankind! [1]

[1] George M. Kahin, *The Asian-African Conference* (Ithaca: Cornell University Press, 1956), p. 40.

Although the conference was concerned chiefly with imperialism and colonialism, there was, nevertheless, the feeling among the participants that they were united by the common identification of race. This sentiment was expressed by President Soekarno when he declared that the members of the Conference were "united by a common detestation of racialism." [2] This same feeling of racial solidarity was echoed in the Final Communiqué which stated that the conference deplored policies and practices of racial segregation and discrimination against Africans and Asians in Africa and in other parts of the world. [3]

In the foreseeable future the great masses of the various cultural groups in the world will continue to be identified with some national or racial group. Indeed, for the great masses of people a national or racial tradition will provide the basis of their solidarity as well as the basis of their personal identification. As imperialism and colonialism based upon color disappear, racial and cultural differentiation without implications of superiority and inferiority will become the basic pattern of a world order.

What then will become of the racial frontiers? They will become the areas in which new cultures will ever be born and new peoples will continue the evolution of mankind.

[2] *Ibid.*, p. 43.   [3] *Ibid.*, p. 81.

Index of Subjects

Index of Names